CHALLENGING
STORIES

D1737564

CHALLENGING STORIES

Canadian Literature for Social Justice in the Classroom

Edited by Anne Burke
Ingrid Johnston
and Angela Ward

CANADIAN
SCHOLARS

Toronto | Vancouver

Challenging Stories: Canadian Literature for Social Justice in the Classroom
Edited by Anne Burke, Ingrid Johnston, and Angela Ward

First published in 2017 by
Canadian Scholars
425 Adelaide Street West, Suite 200
Toronto, Ontario
M5V 3C1

www.canadianscholars.ca

Library and Archives Canada Cataloguing in Publication
    Challenging stories : Canadian literature for social justice
in the classroom / edited by Anne Burke, Ingrid Johnston, and
Angela Ward.
Includes bibliographical references and index.
Issued in print and electronic formats.
ISBN 978-1-55130-973-6 (softcover).--ISBN 978-1-55130-975-0 (EPUB).--
ISBN 978-1-55130-974-3 (PDF)

    1. Education--Social aspects--Canada. 2. Teaching--Social aspects--
Canada. 3. Social justice--Study and teaching. 4. Canadian literature--
Study and teaching. 5. Critical pedagogy. I. Ward, Angela, 1944-, editor
II. Johnston, Ingrid, 1946-, editor III. Burke, Anne M. (Anne Michelle),
1966-, editor

LC191.8.C2C43 2017   370.11'5   C2017-902093-5
                                              C2017-902094-3

Cover design: Em Dash
Interior design: Peggy & Co. Design Inc.

17   18   19   20   21   5   4   3   2   1

Printed and bound in Canada by Webcom

MIX
Paper from
responsible sources
FSC® C004071

Dedicated to our friend Mary Clare Courtland

Mary Clare established a reputation as a leading Canadian scholar in language arts and children's literature, co-editing many widely cited articles. She engaged actively with colleagues across the country on a number of successful research projects, collaboration being the form of scholarship she enjoyed most.

Mary Clare will be remembered for her smile, her mischievous intentions, and her spot-on comments about language arts and literacy teaching. Mary Clare epitomized a love of life and a love of literacy. She cared deeply about her students, her teaching, her writing, and her research. We were privileged to work with Mary Clare as a colleague and friend over eight years on our two research projects. We wish to dedicate this book to her memory.

We would like to thank the Social Sciences and Humanities Research Council of Canada (SSHRC) for their generous funding that made this study possible and all the teachers and students who participated in the research.

Contents

Foreword

Dr. Joyce Bainbridge

hallenging Stories: Canadian Literature for Social Justice in the Classroom essentially addresses one major pedagogical problem: How do we teach students (and our broader society) an awareness and sensitivity to other people's experiences, especially through the horrific chapters in history that Yoder and Strong-Wilson (in this book) maintain "confound and defy our understanding?" I often hear people speaking about world events say, "How can human beings treat each other that way? How can they do that?" It is likely impossible for most of us to understand the human suffering generated by historical events such as the Holocaust, internment camps, and residential schools, or by contemporary struggles such as human migration, racism, homophobia, the plight of children living in refugee camps and conflict zones, or the many other social and political issues of our time. It can be distressing to read about these issues, and it's hard to "get our heads around them." The writers in this volume describe the concept of "difficult knowledge" and explore how teachers and students might process and respond to that knowledge in school.

Following on the heels of a previous book entitled *Reading Diversity through Canadian Picture Books* (2013), *Challenging Stories* explores philosophical and pedagogical issues raised in the pursuit of social justice education in K to 12 schooling. The scholars contributing chapters to this book undertook significant research in classrooms, working with teacher participants and engaging with a range of Canadian children's and young adult books that address social justice issues. The research reported in the book drew from theories of education that regard teachers as agents of social change, individuals who attend to issues of ethnicity, race, religion, class, culture, gender, sexual orientation, language, and exceptionalities.

The teachers in the study participated because they were interested in developing pedagogies and using literature that introduced social justice issues to their students. They were committed to learning *alongside* their students—to reading new books and learning about topics on which they had little background knowledge themselves. They read widely about the topics the books dealt with—First Nations history, human rights, and the Holocaust, for example—and they learned much from their explorations of the children's and young adult books they selected. They aimed to choose literature that "gives voice to the voiceless"—a task that is extremely challenging for most classroom teachers. They understood the power of a good text to promote discussion, and they acknowledged the danger of alienating students and parents if they got either book selection or pedagogy "wrong." They saw literature as both a mirror and a window, and understood that looking in the mirror would be a particularly challenging undertaking. They also recognized the need to provide a supportive environment so these conversations and inner struggles could take place.

Through accessing selected children's literature, such as *Hana's Suitcase* (Levine, 2002) or *Fatty Legs* (Jordan-Fenton & Pokiak-Fenton, 2010), teachers and students have the opportunity to recognize social justice issues, name them, and come to significant realizations about themselves, other people, and the world around them. Having once recognized social injustices, we need to be able to address them. What actions can we take; what is demanded of us? This volume shows that engaging with literature in school is not only a way to teach critical literacy but also allows for the development of empathy and social awareness. It can open up our own culture for exploration and allows us to engage in conversations about our often unexplored values and beliefs. It is not an easy task for teachers. The approach has been called a "pedagogy of discomfort." It is difficult for most of us to move out of our comfort zones. We can feel defensive, vulnerable, offended, and hurt. As we saw in *Reading Diversity*, there can be significant push back and a refusal to engage—by students, teachers, administrators, and parents.

The educators involved in this research project developed thoughtful relationships with colleagues, students, and parents, and they made careful decisions about how they allocated their time, the resources they selected, and the teaching strategies they employed. As demonstrated here, they were not complacent about Canada's policy of multiculturalism and diversity. They continued to explore new pedagogies as they came to know their students and acknowledged the significant shifts that are occurring in Canadian society and around the world.

The discussion questions posed at the end of each chapter in this volume should be beneficial to prospective readers (e.g., pre-service and in-service teachers) as they explore children's and young adult literature, and become aware of the kinds of books that are currently available to school and classroom libraries, and which can be incorporated directly into classroom teaching. The discussion questions may help readers engage with the challenges of teaching in contemporary classrooms, as well as in exploring their own personal biases and how they deal with them in the context of teaching for social justice.

As a member of the research team for *Reading Diversity*, I deeply appreciate the insights provided throughout the chapters of *Challenging Stories* and the issues and problems the teachers and researchers pose for educators to further ponder and address. We must continue to pay attention to the increasing diversity of our school population, the nature of that diversity, and to the great challenges world events impose on us in Canada. They are challenges that will remain with Canadian society and with Canadian educators far into the future.

Introduction

Anne Burke, Ingrid Johnston, and Angela Ward,
with contributions from the authors

This book invites you, the reader, into the professional worlds of teachers across Canada as they collaborated in lively discussions about teaching for social justice and explored recent Canadian children's literature to introduce to their students. The writers, as scholars and teachers, shared a commitment to social justice and a passionate desire to support practical ways of engaging students in Canadian literature. The book highlights the rich and dynamic landscape of Canadian authors, illustrators, and texts, and the development of culturally sensitive curricula and empowering pedagogies that address contemporary and historical issues both local and global. Simultaneously, the book underscores the importance of critical literacy and critical media literacy, strategies to support literacy development, and differentiated instruction to enable all students to succeed as literacy learners and responsible citizens.

The chapters in this book were written by participants in a longitudinal qualitative research study conducted by a national team of literacy scholars and practising teachers from eight sites across Canada. The research investigated how groups of literacy teachers, working collaboratively, selected texts and developed and implemented curriculum to promote their own and their students' understandings of social justice. The book is also informed by a previous longitudinal study on pre-service teachers' understandings of the ideological representations of Canadian identity perceived in Canadian multicultural and social justice picture books (Courtland et al., 2009; Johnston & Bainbridge, 2013). That research informed us about how few Canadian authors and illustrators were known to pre-service teachers prior to their participation in the study, and how many teachers felt reluctant to address critical or uncomfortable issues in their future teaching. This latter finding was supported in research reported by Philpott and Dagenais (2013), who followed teacher candidates enrolled in a social justice teacher education program into their early years of teaching. Many teacher candidates perceived that they had little support or mentoring in their schools, and some were reluctant to address critical social issues in their classrooms. One of the researchers' recommendations was to promote collaborative inquiry among colleagues so that teachers had the support to implement their goals of social justice education. This book is a fulfillment of that recommendation.

Social Justice Education

> Words, literature, books, because of their very nature relentlessly chal-
> lenge the right of those in power, ask unsettling questions, put in doubt
> our assumptions. Literature may not be able to save anyone from injus-
> tice, but something about it must be effective if every dictator, every
> totalitarian government, every threatened official tries to do away with
> it, by burning books, by banning books, by censoring books, by taxing
> books. (Manguel, 1993, p. xi)

Teachers in social justice education recognize and seek to redress the marginalization of traditionally disadvantaged students, including those who are immigrants and from the working class. The purpose of social justice education is to deliver "full and equal participation of all groups in a society that is mutually shaped to meet their needs" (Bell, 2007, p. 1). This includes the representation of minority students' culture, language, and identity in textbooks and classroom learning. Christensen (2009) explained that students' home languages are the most valuable aspects of their culture, as they represent their family lineage and ties to their homes. Consequently, using students' home languages and cultures are two primary ways of valuing students' "lifeworlds" and instituting social justice in the classroom.

Practitioners of social justice teaching aspire to fight the deficit model of education, which positions students' failures as "inherent in the students or their families, not in the social ecology, grade, or classroom" (Weiner, 2006, p. 42). From a social jus-tice perspective, teachers envision a more holistic picture of students' performance, taking account of students' metacognitive state, mental health, and school culture. Educators' teaching practices and their attitudes toward students are also influential in determining whether or not a student succeeds in school.

Social justice education builds on concepts of multiculturalism. Banks (2003) recom-mended that "in addition to mastering basic reading and writing skills, literate citizens in a democratic multicultural society should also develop multicultural literacy" (p. 18). According to Banks (2003), multicultural literacy, which is foundational in social justice education, consists of the skills and ability to critically analyze texts for biases—assump-tions that can permeate textbooks. Multicultural literacy also recruits students to view knowledge from diverse ethnic and cultural perspectives. "A literacy education that focuses on social justice educates both the heads and hearts of students and helps them to become thoughtful, committed and active citizens" (Banks, 2003, p. 18).

Postcolonial theories of reading practices emphasize the hybrid nature of negotiating cultural identities and citizenship in a "third space" of literary engagement (Bhabha, 1994; Bradford, 2007; Gunew, 2003; Hall, 1997; Kanaganayakam, 2005; Spivak, 1993), and address the role of literary texts in "revisiting, remembering and interrogating the colonial past" (Gandhi, 1998, p. 4). These theorists critique liberal notions of multi-culturalism in which cultural and ethnic identity is seen as fixed and static. Bhabha's theory of hybridity in particular challenges notions of an "authentic" identity, suggesting instead that identity, like culture, is negotiated in spaces between the private and public, the psyche and the social sphere.

A complementary pedagogical theory for literacy educators to consider in teaching critical literacy for social justice is the notion of a pedagogy of discomfort (Boler & Zembylas, 2003). Challenging the myth of liberal individualism, Boler and Zembylas explain that "a pedagogy of discomfort recognizes and problematizes the deeply embedded emotional dimensions that frame and shape daily habits, routines, and unconscious complicity with hegemony" (2003, p. 5). They contend that by examining critically "emotional reactions and responses—what we call emotional stances—one begins to identify unconscious privileges as well as invisible ways in which one complies with dominant ideology" (p. 111).

Since the 1990s, Canadian authors and illustrators have published compelling texts that address a range of social justice issues across genres such as picture books, graphic novels, and novels. These literary texts provide a powerful lens through which children and adults can see themselves and come to appreciate social justice ideas and issues. Ching (2005) contends that literature is an instrument of power and offers readers "the power to narrate, the power to tell one's own story, the power to self-realize, the power to self-represent, the power to change inequity to equity, the power to articulate reparation for historical injustice" (p. 129).

Ching (2005) cautions that the selection of appropriate texts is critical for promoting students' understandings of social justice ideas and issues. He distinguishes between two different assumptions about multiculturalism underlying the themes in texts. One perspective, *assimilationist multiculturalism*, portrays images of diverse groups working in harmony. It is akin to a "food, festivals, and fun" approach that ignores the sociocultural and sociopolitical dimensions of social justice. The second perspective, *multiracial democracy*, "invites diverse groups to participate fully in the democratic construction of society" (p. 130). Ching (2005) observes that text selection is critical to teaching learners about social justice. Johnston (2013) also argues the importance of text selection in teaching for social justice: "postcolonial texts offer a more radical engagement with difference" (p. 197). She explains that "postcolonial texts invite teachers and students to consider the intersections of the aesthetic and political in the study of literary texts. Reading 'in-between' the aesthetic and political might be a fruitful position from which to consider the fluid boundaries of culture, race, and subjugated knowledges" (p. 197).

In exploring the potential of children's and young adult literature to promote students' awareness and understanding of social justice ideas and issues, educators must incorporate critical literacy and critical literacy pedagogies into their practices. Drawing on Paulo Freire's work *Pedagogy of the Oppressed* (1983), Naqvi (2015) explains that a focus on critical literacy represents a new emphasis on literacy instruction that was not practised in traditional approaches:

> Critical literacy reflects a fundamentally different view of knowledge and learning than has been seen in the past. Textual meaning is understood in the context of social, historic, and power relations. It emphasizes the importance of reading the world as well as the word. (Freire, 1983, pp. 80–81)

Vasquez, Tate, and Harste (2013) note that no text is neutral and emphasize the pedagogical imperative of teaching students to read critically and to engage them in developing a "justice-oriented citizenry" (p. 8). Drawing upon the work of colleagues, Lewison, Flint, and Van Sluys (2002), who articulated a comprehensive framework for critical literacy instruction, focus on four dimensions of critical literacy:

> With a "justice-oriented citizenry" as our end goal and using the research on critical literacy as our base, we will make the case that critically literate individuals demonstrate some specific dispositions relative to their world view. In short, they show an affinity for disrupting commonplace thinking, interrogating multiple perspectives, unpacking issues socio-politically, and taking social action for purposes of creating a more just and equitable world. At the same time, they understand and (are able to critique) their own complicity in maintaining the status quo. (p. 8)

What distinguishes Vasquez et al.'s interpretation from their colleagues' earlier framework is the increased emphasis on the explicit commitment to social action and the reflective stance on learners' "complicity in maintaining the status quo" (p. 8).

Literary texts offer powerful insights into social justice issues and the sociological and sociopolitical motivations underlying historical and contemporary issues. The implementation of critical literacy pedagogies supports students' growth as literacy learners and human beings in relation to issues, and considers their own situatedness in relation to issues and how they might begin to take action to make a difference in the world.

The Canadian Context

The social concerns of Canada in the early 21st century are evident in this book, whose purpose is to support teachers in identifying and helping their students think deeply about current issues. Canada officially adopted multiculturalism as a policy in 1971: "Multiculturalism ensures that all citizens can keep their identities, can take pride in their ancestry and have a sense of belonging" (Government of Canada, 2012). Although the 1971 policy also affirmed the rights of Aboriginal peoples, many First Nations did not accept their inclusion in the multicultural mosaic, affirming their differentiated rights as the original inhabitants of Canadian lands. More recently, Canadian federal, provincial, and First Nations governments have paid serious attention to the importance of Indigenous peoples in the foundation of Canada.

John Ralston Saul, in *A Fair Country* (2008), calls on Canadians to acknowledge their shared history of living alongside Indigenous peoples and building families together, especially in the early years of settlement. Saul claims that much is owed to our long association with the original peoples of this land; in his view, this initially reciprocal association was damaged by an increasingly colonial mindset, which is only now being recognized as a negative aspect of our development as a country. During the colonial period, Indigenous peoples were subjected to forced assimilation, deprived of their freedom to live and hunt on traditional territories, and endured physical and cultural privations. The infamous Indian residential schools were one tool for linguistic and cultural assimilation, and land reserves where First Nations were expected to live were another.

In the 21st century, Canada is finally acknowledging the cultural genocide of Indigenous peoples that took place in the 19th and 20th centuries. The Truth and Reconciliation Commission of Canada, which submitted its final report in December 2015, was an exhaustive effort to hear from Indigenous people about their experiences in residential schools. The Commission, which travelled across Canada over a six-year period, heard from more than six thousand witnesses. The writers of the report note: "The stories of that experience are sometimes difficult to accept as something that could have happened in a country such as Canada, which has long prided itself on being a bastion of democracy, peace, and kindness throughout the world. Children were abused, physically and sexually, and they died in the schools in numbers that would not have been tolerated in any school system anywhere in the country, or in the world" (p. v–vi). The two-fold purpose of the Commission was to open up the truth about what happened to Indigenous peoples in Canada, and to then embark on a course of reconciliation. As the writers point out, this is a major challenge for Canadians: "Reconciliation is not an Aboriginal problem; it is a Canadian one." A number of the teacher-researchers featured in this book have begun to take on this challenge in their classrooms.

There are other challenging issues taken up in the book. Canada is a multicultural country, but immigrant students and their families may still struggle to feel included in communities and schools, and not enough of our students see their own lives reflected in the literature they encounter in their classrooms.

> Unreflective gestures of multicultural inclusion in Canada will not automatically lead to systemic change of hierarchies of social power. What is absent from current articulations of multiculturalism is the profound potential of multiple and dynamic knowledges to mutually and substantively transform the national space. (Saldana, 2000, p. 175)

Teachers in this project chose to teach Canadian books to support immigrant students in feeling more included by their peers. In more monocultural classrooms, students expanded their worldviews by reading about those whose lives seem more precarious than their own. Participants in this study encouraged their students to imagine the lives of peers with physical and cognitive challenges, and to become sensitive to issues of gender and sexuality. All chapters in the book introduce the reader to engaging Canadian books and ideas for inclusive pedagogy.

Purpose of the Book

We hope to engage educators at all career stages to consider theoretical and practical issues in social justice education. In this book we explore the potential for multicultural literature to promote social justice, intercultural understanding, and more diverse notions of citizenship in Grades 4 to 12 classrooms. Through inquiry groups with prac-tising elementary and secondary teachers in six Canadian provinces, we investigated, alongside teachers, perspectives on the development of culturally sensitive curricula, pedagogies that address issues of individual equity and structural inequalities, and the role Canadian literature might play in promoting a greater sense of social justice in classroom settings. The research team members were active learners with the teach-ers in our project; together we explored global concerns around curricula related to social justice.

Jogie (2015) argues that "there are educational benefits for students who engage with texts from other cultures" (p. 288). Selecting appropriate texts is critical for promoting students' understandings of social justice ideas and issues. One method to choose texts is to take a postcolonialist approach. This approach "would enable texts to be selected considering a broad range of global and contemporary issues that can be reflected and discussed by individuals from diverse cultural backgrounds, in a time of proliferating globalisation" (Jogie, 2015, p. 303). Thus students would be exposed to different places, cultures, and ideas. Johnston (2013) also argues the importance of text selection in teaching for social justice: "postcolonial texts offer a more radical engagement with difference" (p. 197). These texts coerce readers to move beyond their comfort zones, allowing them to encounter, to understand, and to appreciate diversity.

The book also illustrates the challenges for teachers as they selected contemporary Canadian literary texts from different genres (appropriate for the age and level of their students), written and illustrated from a range of ethnocultural and linguistic backgrounds. The reflective questions at the end of each chapter encourage readers to think about what teaching for social justice means in diverse settings. After reading this book, educators should feel more confident introducing Canadian literature into their classrooms, as a catalyst for important conversations about historical and cur-rent injustices in local, national, and global contexts. Classroom conversations about the experiences of First Nations, for example, both current and historical, can begin with a story, as several authors note. Literature provides an opening for activities that encourage students to be more inclusive of differently abled peers. There are examples of creative activities, including multimodal responses, in many chapters of the book.

Section One: Unsettling Our Sense of Place through Reading Canadian Literature

In a settler country such as Canada, physical spaces may be contested. In particular, First Nations peoples' access to traditional lands has been constrained through treaty processes; this has contributed to cultural as well as physical loss for Indigenous peoples, leading to social alienation and marginalization. In chapter 1, Geraldine Balzer describes how teachers at her site negotiated the relationship between their own ideals for social justice and their perceptions of constraints within the evolving dynamics of a religiously conservative community. Historically, the communities had not been ethnically or religiously diverse; the larger community had denominational diversity, but was strongly shaped by "Christian" values. In recent years, the demographics of the communities changed as people relocated from urban centres, churches sponsored refugees from a diversity of countries, and there was more contact with First Nations from neighbouring reserves. Teachers participating in this inquiry group considered the following question: What literary texts can be used that support a social justice focus without offending community members? Teachers were committed to teaching for social justice, but were concerned that conservative community members would challenge chosen texts, resulting in censorship. Negotiating the middle ground, exposing students to new ideas, and discussing these concepts without creating defensiveness was a central concern. The teachers were also aware that the most religiously conservative members of the community saw themselves as marginalized in the broader society. Teachers debated the ways in which their own worldviews influenced the books they choose and the perspectives they advanced, determining that it was impossible to sever their personal views about social justice from their pedagogical choices.

Angela Ward and her co-researchers live on Vancouver Island, in the traditional territories of Coast Salish peoples. None of the teachers in the project came from First Nations backgrounds, but most had extensive experience working with Indigenous students and a strong commitment to social justice. The inquiry group meetings became places where teachers built social connections with each other, several developing teaching partnerships through their connections with the project. Chapter 2 includes significant contributions from the teachers themselves, so that the reader is drawn into the myriad classroom activities created by teachers as they explored their own knowledge of First Nations experiences. Cross-curricular integration was a powerful tool when teachers juxtaposed the histories of Aboriginal peoples in Canada alongside stories of Japanese internment in British Columbia during World War II and experiences of the Holocaust. Teachers' immersion into non-canonic literature, and consequent discussions and knowledge building about First Nations and other issues, was a key aspect of this group.

Section Two: Encounters between Readers and Challenging Texts

In chapter 3, Johnston, Jacobsen, and Howe focus on the teaching of controversial multimodal texts (a graphic novel and a play) with secondary students. The chapter provides a subtle reading of encounters between readers and challenging texts, going beyond aesthetic response to "visceral" experience. The discussion is framed by the potential for teachers to develop a "pedagogy of discomfort" (Boler & Zembylas, 2003) that challenges them to select new and less familiar texts for their increasingly culturally diverse classrooms, and to develop new pedagogical approaches that address the evolving multimodal nature of literacy today.

Burke and Young in chapter 4 consider the challenges and successes in the establishment of diverse reading selections focusing on LGBTQ content explored by the inquiry group. The chapter captures the voices of teachers in their struggle to build and diversify the novel selections in a middle school library. Social justice teaching is complicated in classroom settings and often constrained by political, social, and community forces. Students need to discover that "change occurs only when individuals act to create it" (O'Neil, 2010, p. 48). Emancipatory actions can encourage students to write, read, and rewrite the world and the word, linking literacy to human agency and the power to "effect social transformation" (Janks, 2010, p. 161).

In chapter 5, Yoder and Strong-Wilson reflect on the role of memory and understanding in one teacher's pedagogical approach to residential schools. The authors deal with the complexities of listening carefully to Indigenous voices in teaching "from stories that, as tragic and horrific chapters in our history, resist our 'understanding.'" This section takes account of ways in which participants' sense of self, as well as their curricular and pedagogical choices and attention to social justice, have been mediated by the discourses of school and shaped through socialization. In exploring the potential of children's and young adult literature to promote students' awareness and understanding of social justice ideas and issues, educators must incorporate critical literacy and critical literacy pedagogies into their practices.

Section Three: Opening Minds: Pedagogies for Social Justice

Throughout the book, there are examples of reciprocal learning for teachers and students. Teachers developed their own knowledge through reading and discussing Canadian literature for children and young people before selecting particular texts for the classroom. In chapter 6, Burke and the teacher-researchers with whom she worked (Powell, Hardware, and Butland) engaged with the educational history of Indigenous peoples in Canada after contact with European settlers. One of the focal teachers juxtaposed documentary evidence of abuse at the Mount Cashel orphanage in Newfoundland with literature about the treatment of First Nations children in residential schools. Examples of children's multimodal response to *Fatty Legs* (Jordan-Pokiak & Fenton-Pokiak, 2010) demonstrate the high level of student engagement with this challenging topic.

The inquiry group itself was a powerful site for learning. In chapter 7, Wiltse and LaFramboise-Helgeson analyze the learning supports provided by their community of practice. In this chapter, the authors highlight the way in which the teacher inquiry group supported teachers in moving out of their comfort zones, as they selected literature with which they were unfamiliar and engaged students in discussions on structural and social inequities in Canadian society. The research is grounded in contemporary theories of social justice that see teachers as agents of social change (McDonald, 2007) and in studies that emphasize the role of literature in advocacy research in literacy education (Bender-Slack, 2010; Cherland & Harper, 2007). Throughout all our research sites, there was obvious reciprocity between teachers' own learning through inquiry groups and their subsequent implementation of shared teaching ideas. Inquiry groups supported teachers as they drew on theories of social justice and multiculturalism to enhance their students' encounters with Canadian literature.

References

Banks, J. A. (2003). Teaching literacy for social justice and global citizenship. *Language Arts, 81*(1), 18–19.

Bell, L. A. (2007). Theoretical foundations for social justice education. In M. Adams, L. A. Bell, & P. Griffin (Eds.), *Teaching for diversity and social justice* (pp. 1–14). New York, NY: Taylor & Francis.

Bender-Slack, D. (2010). Texts, talk and fear? English language arts: Teachers negotiating social justice teaching. *English Education, 42*(2), 181–203.

Bhabha, H. (1994). *The location of culture.* New York, NY: Routledge.

Boler, M., & Zembylas, M. (2003). Discomforting truths: The emotional terrain of understanding difference. In P. P. Trifonas (Ed.), *Pedagogies of difference: Rethinking education for social change* (pp. 110–134). New York, NY: RoutledgeFalmer.

Bradford, C. (2007). *Unsettling narratives: Postcolonial readings of children's literature.* Waterloo, ON: Wilfrid Laurier Press.

Cherland, M. R., & Harper, H. (2007). *Advocacy research in literacy education: Seeking higher ground.* Mahwah, NJ: Lawrence Erlbaum Associates.

Ching, S. H. D. (2005). Multicultural children's literature as an instrument of power. *Language Arts, 83*(2), 128–136.

Christensen, L. (2009). Teaching for joy and justice. In I. Johnston & J. Bainbridge (Eds.), *Reading diversity through Canadian picture books: Preservice teachers explore issues of identity, ideology and pedagogy* (pp. 136–154). Toronto, ON: University of Toronto Press.

Courtland, M. C., Hammett, R., Strong-Wilson, T., Bainbridge, J., Johnston, I., ... & Shariff, F. (2009). Curricular landscapes: Preservice teachers' perceptions of place and identity. *Journal of the Canadian Association for Curriculum Studies, 7*(1), 135–179.

Gandhi, L. (1998). *Postcolonial theory: A critical introduction.* New York, NY: Columbia University Press.

Government of Canada. (2012, October 19). Canadian multiculturalism: An inclusive citizenship. Retrieved from http://www.cic.gc.ca/english/multiculturalism/citizenship.asp

Gunew, S. (2003). *Haunted nations: The colonial dimensions of multiculturalisms.* London: Routledge.

Hall, S. (Ed.). (1997). *Representation: Cultural representations and signifying practices.* London: Sage.

Janks, H. (2010). *Literacy and power.* New York, NY: Routledge.

Jogie, M. R. (2015). Too pale and stale: Prescribed texts used for teaching culturally diverse students in Australia and England. *Oxford Review of Education, 41*(3), 287–309. doi:10.1080/03054985.2015.1009826

Johnston, I. (2013). What are the benefits for teachers and students of reading post-colonial literature in contemporary secondary English language arts classes? In K. James, T. M. Dobson, & C. Leggo (Eds.), *English in middle and secondary classrooms: Creative and critical advice from Canada's teacher educators* (pp. 196–199). Don Mills, ON: Pearson Canada.

Johnston, I., & Bainbridge, J. (Eds.). (2013). *Reading diversity through Canadian picture books.* Toronto, ON: University of Toronto Press.

Jordan-Fenton, C., & Pokiak-Fenton, M. (2010). *Fatty legs.* Toronto, ON: Annick Press.

Kanaganayakam, C. (Ed.). (2005). *Moveable margins: The shifting spaces in Canadian literature.* Toronto, ON: TSAR Publications.

Levine, K. (2002). *Hana's suitcase: A true story.* Toronto, ON: Second Story Press.

Lewison, M., Flint, A. S., & Van Sluys, K. (2002). Taking on critical literacy: The journey of newcomers and novices. *Language Arts, 79*, 382–392.

Manguel, A. (1993). Introduction. In C. Stephenson (Ed.), *Countries of invention: Contemporary world writing* (pp. viii–xi). Toronto, ON: Addison-Wesley Publishers.

McDonald, M. (2007). The joint enterprise of social justice teacher education. *Teachers College Record, 109*(8), 2047–2081.

Naqvi, R. (2015). Postcolonial approaches to literacy: Understanding the "Other." In J. Rowsell & K. Pahl (Eds.), *The Routledge handbook of literacy studies* (pp. 49–61). London: Routledge.

O'Neil, K. (2010). Once upon today: Teaching for social justice with postmodern picturebooks. *Children's Literature in Education, 41*(1), 40–51.

Philpott, R., & Dagenais, D. (2013). Grappling with social justice: Exploring new teachers' practice and experiences. *Education, Citizenship and Social Justice, 7*(1), 85–99.

Ralston, J. S. (2008). *A fair country: Telling truths about Canada.* Toronto, ON: Viking Canada.

Saldana, L. (2000). Bedside stories: Canadian multiculturalism and children's literature. In R. McGillis (Ed.), *Voices of the other: Children's literature and the postcolonial context* (pp. 165–176). New York, NY: Routledge.

Spivak, G. C. (1993). *Outside in the teaching machine.* London: Psychology Press.

Truth and Reconciliation Commission of Canada. (2015). *Final report of the Truth and Reconciliation Commission of Canada, volume one: Summary. Honouring the truth, reconciling for the future.* Toronto: James Lorimer & Company.

Vasquez, V., Tate, S., & Harste, J. C. (2013). *Negotiating critical literacies with teachers.* New York, NY: Routledge.

Weiner, I. (2006). Challenging deficit thinking. *Educational Leadership, 64*(1), 42–45.

Unsettling Our Sense of Place through Reading Canadian Literature

The space in which we live, which draws us out of ourselves,
in which the erosion of our lives, our time and our history
occurs, the space that claws and gnaws at us, is also, in itself,
a heterogeneous space ... we live inside a set of relations.

—FOUCAULT (1961/1997, P. 65)

BOTH CHAPTERS IN THIS SECTION DESCRIBE A CONTEXT WHERE FIRST Nations and settlers share spaces in schools and communities. Most teachers in these two project sites are middle-class white educators whose sense of social justice permeates their teaching. The co-researchers in British Columbia and Saskatchewan spent time in their inquiry groups themselves reading books by Indigenous authors, and wrestled with unsettling concepts of shared place and space.

Understanding the intersections and parallel lines between Indigenous and settler experiences is evident in both chapters in this section. Recognizing diversity in responses to space and place is one element in working toward social justice for Indigenous students and their communities.

Chapter 1

Aren't We All the Same? The Challenges of Choosing Multicultural Literature in Historically Monocultural Communities

Geraldine Balzer

Occasionally in our journeys as researchers and teachers, we are privileged to hear a story, a story that resonates with us, that echoes in our thoughts for extended periods of time, that is always there, below the surface. Kate's[1] story, told to me as part of my dissertation research, is such a story—a story that shapes my ongoing research and a quest to use literature for social justice teaching:

> You asked me, Geraldine, what I hoped to gain from this study. This and that, I answered, truthfully, but not completely. That evening, I knew—it reverberated—what do I hope? To give Rosie George a voice.

> In his forward to Maria Campbell's (1994) *Stories of the Road Allowance People,* Ron Marken writes, "To have voice is to have power ... to be dumb or voiceless is synonymous with being ignorant." So I tell you about Rosie George.

> My first five years of school were spent at Queen Anne School. My Grade 5 teacher was Mrs. Jacques. On the playground I played with my white friends like I was supposed to. I was white after all. In the classroom were three Aboriginal kids as I recall. The boy, an absolute loner, was an artist. Yes, it was Christine Baker, with the pack of 64 pencil crayons (or was it only 32 back then?) and her pastel ponies, that was generally acknowledged as the class artist. But I recognized it—didn't we all?—that this boy's art was of a different sort—the eagles, bears, and wolves. Then there was this girl whose name I can't recall. She must have

been less troublesome to Mrs. Jacques than Rosie, or maybe it was just Rosie's presence that causes me to recall her so distinctly. She was tall, obviously older than the rest of us—a young woman, it seems to me now. Maybe it was also the matronly clothes she wore—the pink shell and maroon—what were they?—stretchy pants or jumper. I suspected the clothes came from the Salvation Army—where my mom worked. They helped the unfortunate kids from the residence.

I never knew what the residence was (were they orphans like my mother?), knew only that they weren't like us; they were quiet, and, for some reason, they—especially Rosie—made Mrs. Jacques angry.

Now that I think of it, everyone I knew in town with "Jacques" as a surname is Métis, but I don't remember what Mrs. Jacques looked like (they were neighbours, but he died early, leaving Mrs. Jacques alone), and I didn't know her maiden name. She thought I was wonderful, though. My parents were good people—Salvation Army—I was a neat obedient child who loved to read and write.

My clearest memory of Grade 5—apart from that boy's art—was Rosie being called upon in class (did this happen once or regularly?). She stood by her desk, tall, round-shouldered, head bowed—couldn't or wouldn't answer, and Mrs. Jacques ridiculed her. I don't remember the words, barely recall the tone, but I see it—FEEL it—all so clearly. I've relived this moment, wondered what happened to Rosie, felt the hot shame and indignation in my head and chest many times. Say something, Rosie! The next year we moved to Meadow View and I went to John Alexander School—white, no Indians, higher standards of marking, a teacher told me. Alexander and the Bill of Rights. Today John Alexander School is a "community school"—that raises fear in some of the whites who send their kids there—will they get lice from all those kids in the apartments nearby? You have to move to Meadow Heights and to a different school to avoid that. Queen Anne is now an office complex, the Indian Student residence is part of a reserve, and Mrs. Jacques, who lived across from Queen Anne, is dead. I don't know where Rosie George is, and I wouldn't dare speak for her, but I want a space for her voice. (Kate, quoted in Balzer, 2006, pp. 78–80)

While Kate's experience as a Grade 5 student occurred 40 years ago, teachers in Saskatchewan are still seeking spaces for the voices of Rosie George and other Indigenous Canadians. This is particularly true in rural Saskatchewan, in communities that have been historically monocultural and religiously conservative. While demographics have changed, community attitudes have not, and selecting literature that gives voice to the voiceless remains a challenge for classroom teachers. The teachers who chose to be part of this research study grappled with this challenge.

The Research Site and the Participants

Six teachers who taught in two rural communities participated in this research study. Both communities are within an hour's drive of a larger urban centre, and that proximity is part of a shifting demographic. Forestview, population 1,000, describes itself as "offering a lifestyle that rivals any community in Saskatchewan." Settled by Russian Mennonite immigrants in the late 19th century, Forestview was founded on the principles of "faith, toil of the land, industry and hard work, vision for the future, and strong community leadership." Ongoing immigration of German-speaking Russian Mennonites shaped the community in many ways and their presence is still felt today. The three Mennonite churches in the community attest to the diversity of faith perspectives within the denomination, but overall, the community norms remain rooted in traditions of hard work and strong faith. In the last decade, the demographics of the tidy little town have begun to shift. The altruism of the community has led to the sponsorship of several refugee families through the Government of Canada refugee sponsorship program; most of these immigrants are from Colombia, fleeing the threat of violence in their home country. Like many refugees, they arrived in Canada with no knowledge of English and a range of educational levels. Adding to the demographic diversity of the community are foster children, predominantly Indigenous, who live with local families. These two groups are visible minorities in the historically white Euro-Canadian community and one reason that the teachers feel that there is a need for a social justice pedagogy. Two additional groups have also contributed to the demographic diversity of Forestview: conservative Mennonites and urbanites. The conservative Mennonites are visible by their dress; girls always wear long skirts and do not cut their hair. The proximity to a large urban centre means that some families see Forestview as a bedroom community—an opportunity to live in a small, safe community with low housing prices.

Forestview has one K-12 school that serves the town and the surrounding farming community. Four teachers from this school took part in the study, and all four commuted to Forestview from the larger urban centre. Robert, the principal, taught senior history and was challenged by these questions: What's our responsibility as individuals to society as far as rights and freedom for others and acceptance of others? How can individuals play a role in society? Do we as individuals have a responsibility for others and not just ourselves? Through the teaching of history, he engaged his students in this challenge and hoped to expose them to a diversity of viewpoints by incorporating literature in his classroom.

Simon, a mid-career teacher, taught senior English. Simon had very personal reasons for promoting an anti-racist perspective in his classroom: "My niece's mother is from the Blood reserve south of Calgary and Rebecca grew up in Forestview as someone who appeared Native, but was culturally Mennonite. Seeing her struggle with identity issues as a teenager heightened my awareness of, and sensitivity to, racial issues." Robert and Simon worked together with Daniel, a teacher candidate who was doing his extended practicum in this school. Daniel hoped that his involvement in this project would expose him to a wider variety of Canadian literature that "would provide students with examples of justice or injustice that might be familiar to them and will be relevant to them."

Jessica taught English Language Arts in the junior high classrooms and worked with the English Additional Language (EAL) learners and provided support for special needs students. Jessica was drawn to this research study because of her interest in social justice issues. She spoke of including a range of issues in her classroom, such as human rights, environmental concerns, and developing world issues. Jessica was interested in being more purposeful in her teaching of these issues and expressed concern that she was not necessarily presenting the issues that were of greatest concern to her community. She also wanted students to become thoughtful inhabitants of the world rather than becoming unthinking followers. One of her greatest concerns was that she provide well-rounded exposure to issues rather than jump on a soapbox and present a limited or one-sided view.

Fifty kilometres from Forestview is Redstone, the second community involved in this research study. Like Forestview, Redstone is a small community surrounded by agricultural lands. Unlike Forestview, Redstone has become a regional centre with many amenities including a hospital, art gallery, and theatre. Light industry and agricultural services provide employment opportunities. The population is larger, approximately 1,700, and much more diverse. Like Forestview, settlers began arriving in Redstone in the late 19th century. However, while the European population that immigrated to Redstone included Russian Mennonites, it also included immigrants from Ukraine, the British Isles, and Germany. The predominance of European Christian immigrants from different backgrounds is made evident by the ten different denominational churches listed on the community website. As a result of these foundational roots, there is a perceived conservatism in the community, which, just as in Forestview, impacts teachers' literature choices.

Like Forestview, the demographics of Redstone have changed markedly over the last few decades. The area churches have worked together to sponsor refugee families, adding Colombians, El Salvadorans, and Karin (Myanmar) persons to the population. Employment opportunities have drawn immigrants from the Philippines and Russia to the community. Redstone also has a large First Nations reserve and several Métis communities in close proximity. Parents have a range of educational choices for their children including the two public schools, a K–5 elementary school, and a 7–12 high school. Parents of Francophone/Métis ancestry can elect to have their children bused to a nearby French school; two private schools, a K–9 Seventh Day Adventist school, and a 10–12 Mennonite high school with a residence, are also options. Two teachers from the public high school participated in this research study.

Lisa and Barbara are both experienced teachers and live in the community. Both women are long-term residents of the community, involved in various recreational and religious organizations. Their commitments are extensive, making them well-respected community members with a strong sense of the community's values.

Lisa teaches senior English and is an administrator in Redstone High School. Lisa had begun her teaching career in First Nations communities and through that experience recognized how intolerant Canadians actually are. Her own intolerance was exposed, but she did not understand what was wrong with her approach to teaching or why it was wrong. She believed that the communities were the problem, and her role was to fix things through the education system. Since then, Lisa has learned to look inwardly and recognize the ways in which she, as a member of the settler community, was part of the problem.

Barbara teaches intermediate English Language Arts and provides special education support to the students at Redstone High School. Barbara has a strong sense of social justice that is closely tied to her Mennonite heritage, beliefs, and values. She wanted her students to develop empathy and, therefore, chose literature she hoped they could relate to and could imagine themselves walking in the shoes of the characters. It was important to her that students knew where she stood on issues and why she took that stance. She identified the key social justice issues in the community and in her class-room as racism, poverty, and gender. Barbara was comfortable working with the first two, but was struggling to find an appropriate way to talk about sexual orientation.

The six teachers who participated in this study chose to do so because they were interested in developing pedagogies and using literature that introduced social justice issues to their students. Over an 18-month period, they met as a teacher inquiry group every four to six weeks and engaged in discussions of literature and articles. Some of our meetings had a book club format where we discussed Thomas King's *Inconvenient Indian* (2013) and *A Short History of Indians in Canada* (2006). Teachers also partici-pated in individual interviews. Data include the transcripts of those interviews and notes from the inquiry group conversations.

All six of the teachers involved in this study care deeply about the teaching profession and the academic success of their students. They are, however, aware of the conservative value systems present in Redstone and Forestview, and would like to challenge those biases and expose their students to other viewpoints. Addressing unacknowledged racism and blatant homophobia without alienating students and parents became the challenge in these schools.

Whitewashing: Contesting Our Sameness

The teachers involved in the research project grappled with definitions of social justice and identified the many injustices evident in the larger world as well as in the local communities. While they recognized the need to address a wide range of issues including the challenges women, individuals who identified as LGBTQ, and the disability community face in society, they all agreed that racism was the most obvious social justice issue in their communities and the one that impacted the most students. They also observed that racist attitudes toward Indigenous people were more prevalent than toward immigrants; Simon explained that "the history of racism against Aboriginal people is so deeply ingrained and historic that it is not seen or questioned where[as] a new immigrant is exotic. It is so difficult to get around that racism." Countering that racism became a central objective for the teacher participants, and through their interrogation of the roots of this social justice issue, they came to understand the important place systemic racism against Indigenous people has in the foundation of Canada. Calderon (2014) contends that "settler societies, as opposed to colonial societies, build new societies independent of their countries of origin and institute political institutions that maintain settler rule over the Indigenous peoples they displace. From this we can see that Indianness is central to the conceptualization of settler societies" (p. 317).

Verna St. Denis and Carol Schick (2003) identify three popular ideological assumptions held by many students: race doesn't matter; everyone has equal opportunity; and by individual acts and good intentions, one can secure innocence as well as superiority. St. Denis and Schick note that the statement "race doesn't matter" frequently indicates a reluctance to discuss race and racial identities. The authors are concerned that this denial "supports differences of power reflected in historical, social, political, and economic practices" and prevents the examination of institutionalized racism (pp. 62–63). The second popular assumption views Canadian society as a meritocracy, a view that "ignores how dominant group identifications facilitate access to social and institutional power" (p. 64). Again, this view denies the existence of institutionalized racism. St. Denis and Schick claim that the third assumption is the most difficult to deal with because it forces students to examine "the production of their own identifications" and the realization that "the notion of innocence and goodness depends on the marginalization of the *other*" (p. 65; emphasis in original).

The examination of anti-racist education by Schick and St. Denis (2005) identifies curriculum as "one of the significant discourses through which white privilege and 'difference' are normalized" (p. 298). They are concerned that terms such as "multiculturalism" facilitate the "whitewashing" of Canada, drawing attention away from racially constructed identities and connecting cultural difference to lack of school success (p. 306). The work of Schick and St. Denis is particularly relevant because it is based in Saskatchewan, where Indigenous Canadians are included in the racialized Other. Their experience as anti-racist educators has revealed the extent to which whiteness is normalized in Saskatchewan society and discussions of race are avoided.

St. Denis and Schick have grounded their work in the discourse surrounding the construction of whiteness. Christine Sleeter (1993a, 1993b) examined the language used to discuss racism and found that "we semantically evade our own role in perpetuating White racism by constructing sentences that allow us to talk about racism while removing ourselves from the discussion" (1993b, p. 14). Through the use of passive sentence constructions and making racism rather than racists the subject of the sentence, speakers are able to abrogate their responsibility in the perpetuation of racism. Sleeter also examines the focus on ethnicity rather than race as a method of minimalizing the restricted access to opportunity afforded non-whites in American society. Sleeter contends that ethnicity theory supports the concept of an open social system where success is dependent upon the work ethic of the individual. Her concern with this theoretical framework is that it denies the significance of visible, physiological marks of ancestry and of the history of colonization and harsh subjugation that Europeans and Euro-Americans extended over other peoples. In so doing, it denies white social institutions any complicity in the subordinate status of people of colour (1993a).

The focus on ethnicity rather than race is a hallmark of our current education system as we celebrate the multicultural mosaic that we believe represents Canada. Multicultural days are an annual occurrence at Canadian schools and universities as we celebrate diversity by sharing food, fashion, and festivals. February marks "Black History Month," when we celebrate Canada's role in the Underground Railroad and applaud the successes of Afro-Canadians. In each of these cases, we focus on the individuals who have achieved success in a Eurocentric context and applaud our open-door policies, blaming racist practices on the individual rather than the collective. However, according to Pillay (2015), "the rhetoric of multiculturalism conceals racist, discriminatory, and exclusionary attitudes and prejudices within the myth of the tolerant nation" (pp. 70–71). As well, she contends that "multiculturalism discourse veils relations of power in which one group has the power to tolerate other groups" (p. 71). Contesting this power imbalance is one goal of social justice education.

Additional studies by researchers such as Beverly Tatum (1992), Aruna Srivastava (1997), Leslie Roman and Timothy Stanley (1997), and Gary Howard (1999) consider the role of the education system in combating racism. Tatum, while concerned with all racist attitudes, focuses on the attitudes of white students who carry with them the "social power inherent in the systemic cultural reinforcement and institutionalization of those racial prejudices" (p. 3). Recognizing power differential is central to combating racism, and the members of the dominant group need to "identify and interrupt the cycle of oppression" (p. 4). Tatum's experiences as a college professor teaching anti-racism led her to understand that white students needed to be able to define themselves as white before they were able to hear and understand others' stories of racism and before they could become agents of change.

Srivastava (1997) describes the difficulties of leading anti-racist education in the academy, where personal narratives of students and teachers are met with general distrust. In order to arrive at self-actualization, Srivastava believes we need to understand history and how our actions are "complicit in the academic structures of oppression" (p. 115). We can expect the anti-racist classroom to be "chaotic, confusing, and disordered, a place of pain, denial, anger, and anxiety" where students and teachers are vulnerable and often physically, emotionally, and intellectually exhausted (pp. 120–121).

Recognizing the "asymmetries of power and historical/political and cultural contexts that define and redefine the borders of nations, nationalist pedagogies, and curricula," Roman and Stanley (1997, p. 205) draw attention to the role played by students as agents of cultural production as they attempt to make "sense of the hegemonic struggles" and "the contradictions of inhabiting places of neocolonialism and racism while at the same time striving for languages and community identification that challenge their effects" (p. 205). Although educators can learn from, and with, their students, they need to provide a supportive environment where these struggles can take place.

White teachers play an important role in multiracial schools. Howard (1999) recognizes the potential for intense emotional experiences that can occur in the classroom. He feels that white teachers can "contribute to the healing of dominance by demanding honesty in the teaching and construction of history" (p. 71). Again, he underscores the complicity of our educational institutions in the perpetuation of power imbalances. Howard feels that the work of advocacy has too often "fallen on the shoulders of people of color" and the burden of re-educating whites needs to be shared. Howard challenges white educators to open the circles of power and become involved in "re-educating many of our White colleagues who are not ready for such inclusion" (p. 76).

Educators involved in anti-racist education recognize the power imbalance that supports a Eurocentric status quo. St. Denis and Schick (2005) contend that, by focusing on ethnicity rather than race, many Canadians have avoided confronting racism and challenging the colonial power structures that support our current society. Anti-racist educators recognize the difficulty inherent in challenging ingrained attitudes but understand the necessity of doing so in order to decolonize classrooms. They also recognize the difficulties students have accepting this new interpretation of society, and anti-racist educators are prepared for students' resistance. Not all students will accept the challenges and become advocates of change and challenge the dominant discourses, but some will and therein lies our hope.

The Challenge: Choosing Literature

The number of Canadian multicultural texts available to the teachers was extensive, but choosing texts that unsettled the prejudices of the students without challenging the mores of the community was difficult. Lisa and Barbara, as teachers in a larger and more diverse community, had greater latitude than Robert, Simon, and Jessica. All six teachers read a significant number of texts in their search to find literature that they felt could be used in their classrooms. Robert, at one point, half joking and half serious, asked if it would be appropriate to go through the novels with a black marker and eliminate all the swear words. The challenge, as articulated by Lisa, is to "choose literature that promotes social justice awareness without offending conservative sensibilities." Challenging the ways in which community members held power while seeing themselves as marginalized in the broader society continually influenced the literature choices of the teachers.

Educators interested in calling attention to the power imbalances inherent in our society and exposing racism have approached the issue through a variety of channels. For teachers of English literature, the preferred channel has often been the inclusion of multicultural literature and the quest to open the Western canon. The introduction of multicultural literature has frequently been met with resistance from fellow educators, parents, and teachers. Just as anti-racist education enables participants to examine the ways in which power is constructed, multicultural teaching enables participants to examine the ways knowledge is constructed. James Banks (1993) believes students should be given opportunities to investigate and determine how cultural assumptions, frames of references, perspectives, and the biases within a discipline influence the ways that knowledge is constructed. Students should also be given opportunities to create knowledge themselves and identify the ways in which the knowledge they construct is influenced and limited by their personal assumptions, positions, and experiences.

Mary Louise Pratt (1996) labels one of the ways in which knowledge has been constructed as the "colonization of the imagination" and identifies current educational reforms as a "process of *decolonization* of culture and the national imagination" (p. 14; emphasis in original). In choosing literature that exposed the colonization of the imagination and the ways in which knowledge has been constructed by a settler colonial society, the teachers were opening themselves to resistance from students and their families. As Robert noted, "challenging those beliefs is particularly difficult if what you're saying is contrary to what they have heard at home. So now you are challenging the opinions their parents have been telling them their whole lives and now you're telling them something different."

The need for constructions of new knowledge and beliefs can be achieved, according to Jacqueline Royster (1996), through "compassion, communication, cooperation, and courage" as we learn to tell new stories (pp. 141–143). Royster identifies classrooms as political places and feels that educators and students need to be aware of the ways in which these spaces are negotiated. Drawing attention to the values and assumptions embedded in the curriculum draws attention to the power structures that support those values and assumptions. Although Royster advocates new ways of "doing," she also advocates new ways of "being" in the classroom. Royster hopes that a new sense of community will emerge from the "multiplicity of perspectives," one which preserves humanity, not Western authority (pp. 151–152). However, for the dialogue to occur, the voices need to be heard; just like Kate in her tribute to Rosie George, these teachers were looking for the spaces to introduce a multiplicity of perspectives.

For students to enter into the dialogue, they must be able to identify and acknowledge their ideological orientations, which Richard Beach (1997) describes as the beliefs and attitudes they apply to texts. Beach found that middle-class students responded negatively to texts that challenged their privileged perspectives of the world. Beach contends that students are socialized within their communities and by discourses of gender, class, and race. Students who were exposed to literature that challenged their socialized stance were "resentful of implied challenges to their sense of white privilege" and often denied the existence of racial difference (pp. 75–77). At the same time, many students had a "voyeuristic fascination" with "the other" (p. 79). Beach found that students needed to move beyond empathizing with the characters in literature and connect those experiences to their "real-world perceptions." Beach concluded that "some students are able to move beyond stances of resistance to explore how experiences in their own lives, and with texts, are shaped by ideological forces. These students then examine how their own behavior as well as those [sic] of characters are shaped by institutional racism" (p. 88).

One of the most powerful socialized stances that the teachers confronted was conservative Christianity. The teachers at Forestview were very cognizant of the dominant viewpoint of the community and were unsure of what challenges they might face should they introduce literary texts that were seen as offensive. Their use of canonical texts, validated by historical usage, had not prepared them for text challenges. They believed that novels with swearing or sexual acts, implied or actual, would upset members of the community and damage relationships. The danger of alienating students and parents could stop social justice conversations before they began.

Challenges to literary texts grounded in religious beliefs are common in North America, and teachers have to be prepared to defend their text selection on pedagogical grounds. Glanzer (2005) summarizes the advice of religious scholars who suggest that these books can be used "as a springboard for intelligent discussions about religious faith" (p. 168), providing teachers have "the necessary knowledge in this sensitive area" (p. 168). Balancing the aims of curricula, the increasing diversity of the community, and the concerns of conservative parents caused the teachers great consternation. However, they realized the power of a good text to promote discussion and agreed with Agee (1999), who observed that "one disturbing aspect of censorship is its power to deny students in one class or an entire school system the right to read particular texts" (p. 61). Lisa and Barbara were confident that their text selections would not be challenged as long as they didn't introduce explicitly LGBTQ literature; they hope to do this someday, but realized that issues of racism impacting Indigenous and refugee students were a current and pressing issue that had the potential to make a difference in the lives of many students. Jessica, Robert, and Simon were much more cautious about pushing too hard on the boundaries of their conservative community. Ultimately, they echoed Bindewald's (2015) concern about the limitations placed on schools by fundamentalist Christians and the need for open dialogue in our current pluralistic society:

> The type of authoritarian and indoctrinating education advocated by fundamentalist Christians is clearly not the sort needed to prepare citizens for life in a 21st century, pluralist democracy. What type of education, then, is needed for students in American public schools? Pluralist societies need schools that prepare young people with the knowledge, skills, and dispositions for autonomous living and full participation as democratic citizens. In such societies, individuals and groups with competing visions of the good life must find, at a minimum, ways to peacefully coexist. A fuller realization of the liberal, pluralist, democratic ideal would call for an education that helps to prepare citizens with the ability and desire to navigate complex cultural, social, and political terrains, across significant differences, for the purpose of shared decision-making regarding common public issues. (Bindewald, 2015, p. 107)

Ultimately, Jessica's choices were simplified by the Grade level she taught; ten percent of her Grade 7 class were EAL learners. She chose a novel that would open conversations concerning immigrant experiences. Robert selected a diversity of texts connecting to Canadian history and introduced them as supplementary reading, enabling students to self-select texts. Simon made the riskiest choices based on his personal commitment to introduce Indigenous issues in his Grade 12 classroom.

Pedagogical Considerations

The opportunity to select novels that explicitly dealt with social justice issues provided teachers with much welcome freedom and accompanying tensions as they introduced topics that were potentially controversial and required them to expand their own knowledge base. The books chosen easily fit within the requirements of the Saskatchewan curriculum and enabled the teachers to initiate discussions of racism in their classrooms. Since this research study focused on the teacher inquiry groups and their experiences working with the literature they had chosen, student work is not part of the data collected. The teachers, however, reflected on the choices they had made.

Jessica used several picture books and one adolescent novel in her Grade 7 classroom. Her students had expressed interest in world events that impacted children, and for this reason, she chose *The Breadwinner* by Deborah Ellis (2000). Parvana, the central character in this novel, is a young Afghan girl who disguises herself as a boy in order to earn the money necessary to support her family in Taliban-controlled Afghanistan. Through the reading of this novel and ensuing discussions, Jessica's class considered the way in which geography impacts life stories. They began to realize the politics of an individual's homeland determine his or her lot in life, and through this growing awareness became more empathetic to the immigrants in their community. Jessica had not previously pursued this line of thinking and recognized her need to develop a greater understanding of the political forces that resulted in refugees and Canadian immigration. This storyline connected well with the immigrant history of the Russian Mennonite settlers and their continued involvement in sponsoring and supporting current refugees. Not only did the students gain a deeper understanding of social justice issues, Jessica gained a deeper understanding of Forestview.

Lisa also chose a text that dealt with cultural diversity: Yann Martel's (2003) *The Life of Pi* details the journey (actual or metaphorical) of a shipwrecked 16-year-old and a Bengal tiger. Lisa was teaching the Canadian literature semester of the Grade 12 curriculum, and this is one of the recommended texts. A feature-length Hollywood film based on the novel had just been released, and movie tie-ins are often a draw for reluctant readers. The novel also connected with one of Lisa's primary questions: How do we teach beliefs? Studying *The Life of Pi* provided opportunities to explore religion and spirituality, values and ethics within the public school system. Through the teaching of this novel, Lisa felt that students were able to connect to personal issues in their lives, developing the language necessary to articulate their own beliefs.

Barbara also gave her students the opportunity to explore their values and ethics through Mikaelson's (2002) novel *Touching Spirit Bear*. The central character of this novel, Cole, is banished to a remote Alaskan island by a Native sentencing circle following his violent attack on another teen. This novel exposed students to an alternative justice system and caused them to consider the merits of the Canadian court system and the Indigenous sentencing circle. Barbara felt that it was important that her students knew where she stood on social justice issues and felt that her choice of literature clearly indicated her values: "But if you are presenting literature about social justice, doesn't that imply a bias anyway? I didn't read a novel about a character that went to jail and everybody on the outside felt safe. They pick up on that is what they are supposed to think." Barbara felt it was important that her biases be made clear and encouraged students to articulate their own biases. She worked hard to develop an atmosphere of respect in her classroom so a diversity of opinions, belief systems, and worldviews could be shared safely. For Barbara, this novel challenged the Indigenous racism in her community as she asked the students to consider the possibility that sacred texts and traditions existed in non-Christian contexts. Her Grade 9 class was so absorbed in Cole's story that they asked to study the sequel, *Ghost of Spirit Bear* (Mikaelson, 2010), the following year.

Simon, like Lisa, was also teaching the Canadian literature semester of the Grade 12 curriculum and, like Barbara, wanted to challenge the racist attitudes students held toward Indigenous people. Simon noted that changing demographics of the community presented challenges: "they have been homogenous for so long that it is a challenge to our community to celebrate the diversity." Simon noted that while students welcomed the children of refugee families into the school, they were less gracious to the Indigenous foster children and families of lower socioeconomic status who had moved from the city.

Simon wanted students to understand the systemic racism Indigenous Canadians deal with and chose five books written by Anishnabe author Richard Wagamese. In selecting five books, Simon gave students the opportunity to self-select a book that interested them and was at an appropriate reading level; they were also able to self-censor and choose texts that did not have swearing, violence, or sexual content. Simon gave his students the choice of four novels, *Keeper 'n Me* (2006), *A Quality of Light* (1997), *Dream Wheels* (2007), and *Indian Horse* (2013), and one memoir, *For Joshua* (2003). The students appreciated the choices given to them, and a literature circle approach provided ample opportunity to test ideas in smaller groups before sharing them in the larger class. Simon noted that the autobiographical elements of the books gave them a veracity students appreciated. Through their engagement with these texts, they were able to problematize the norms evident in their preconceptions and promote acceptance and understanding based on racial lines. Simon acknowledged the difficulty students face in questioning the status quo: "Sometimes social justice requires quite a bit of courage to speak out about injustices that you see because it isn't always the politically correct or the safest thing for a person to do, to say what they think is right or wrong in these situations." Choosing literature with a social justice agenda gave students this courage in the safety of his classrooms.

Making Space for the Voices from the Margins

I began this chapter with Kate's story and her wish to provide a space for Rosie George and others who have been silenced to tell their stories. This research study gave an opportunity for teachers in rural Saskatchewan schools to find those spaces. Their greatest fear at the beginning of this study was selecting literature that would introduce students to social justice issues that were problematic in the communities. Identifying issues elsewhere was easy, but holding up a mirror was difficult. The danger of becoming defensive and further entrenching existing stereotypes was ever present. The concern that the literature would be considered offensive and immoral was continually present. The teachers were afraid their own biases would become evident and harm relationships that they had worked hard to build. But they came to realize that their personal convictions were known to the students through the literature they chose and the issues that they raised. The altruistic values of the communities provided solid ground to introduce new ideas in small increments, creating enough discomfort to generate questions without raising defences. These six teachers found that literature provided a doorway to other perspectives; Robert noted that

> Kids have universally held biases and then when you present another
> idea you're challenging them to question. It's the kind of thing that is
> perpetuated generation after generation. So you need to expose them

to text and to other thinking so that they have to challenge their own beliefs and they are not necessarily going to accept but at least they are going to pause to see if what they are believing could have another side to it.

The stories opened the doors; whether or not the students choose to walk through remains their choice.

Keywords

- censorship
- monocultural
- religiously conservative
- secondary English Language Arts (ELA)
- rural

Reflection Questions

1. How could you choose literary texts that challenge stereotypes and societal norms without alienating culturally and religiously conservative students and their families?
2. How do you deal with your own personal biases in the context of social justice teaching?
3. Who are the marginalized members of your school community and what literature might you choose that would promote understanding and inclusion?
4 What pedagogical strategies can you use to ensure that the students in your classes respect the diversity of values held by their classmates?

Note

1. All names of participants and communities are pseudonyms.

References

Agee, J. (1999). There it was, that one sex scene: English teachers on censorship. *The English Journal, 89*(2), 61–69.

Balzer, G. (2006). *Decolonizing the classroom: Reading Aboriginal literature through the lenses of contemporary literary criticism.* (Unpublished doctoral dissertation). University of Saskatchewan, Saskatoon, SK.

Banks, J. (1993). The canon debate, knowledge construction and multicultural education. *Educational Researcher, 22*(5), 4–14.

Beach, R. (1997). Students' resistance to engagement with multicultural literature. In T. Rogers & A. O. Soter (Eds.), *Reading across cultures: Teaching literature in a diverse society.* New York, NY: Teachers College Press.

Bindewald, B. (2015). In the world, but not of the world: Understanding conservative Christianity and its relationship with American public schools. *Educational Studies, 51*(2), 93–111. doi:10.1 080/00131946.2015.1015343

Calderon, D. (2014). Uncovering settler grammars in curriculum. *Educational Studies: A Journal of the American Educational Studies Association, 50*(4), 313–338. doi:10.1080/00131946.2014.92 6904

Campbell, M., & Rocette, S. F. (1994). *Stories of the road allowance people.* Penticton, BC: Theytus Books.

Ellis, D. (2000). *The breadwinner.* Toronto, ON: Groundwood Books.

Glanzer, P. (2005). Moving beyond censorship: What will educators do if a controversy over "His Dark Materials" erupts? *The Phi Delta Kappan, 87*(2), 166–168.

Howard, G. R. (1999). *We can't teach what we don't know: White teachers, multiracial schools.* New York, NY: Teachers College Press.

King, T. (2006). *A short history of Indians in Canada.* Toronto, ON: HarperCollins.

King, T. (2012). *The inconvenient Indian: A curious account of Native people in Canada.* Toronto, ON: Doubleday Canada.

Martel, Y. (2003). *The life of Pi.* Toronto, ON: Harvest Books.

Mikaelson, B. (2002). *Touching spirit bear.* Toronto, ON: HarperCollins.

Mikaelson, B. (2010). *The ghost of spirit bear.* Toronto, ON: HarperCollins.

Pillay, T. (2015). Decentring the myth of Canadian multiculturalism. In A. Abdi, L. Schultz, & T. Pillay (Eds.), *Decolonizing global citizenship education* (pp. 69–80). Boston, MA: Sense Publishers.

Pratt, M. L. (1996). Daring to dream: Re-visioning culture and citizenship. In J. F. Slevin & A. Young (Eds.), *Critical theory and the teaching of literature: Politics, curriculum, pedagogy* (pp. 3–20). Urbana, IL: National Council of Teachers of English.

Roman, L. G., & Stanley, T. J. (1997). Empires, emigres, and aliens: Young people's negotiations of official and popular racism in Canada. In L. G. Roman & L. Eyre (Eds.), *Dangerous territories: Struggles for difference and equality in education.* New York, NY: Routledge.

Royster, J. J. (1996). Literature, literacy, and language. In J. F. Slevin & A. Young (Eds.), *Critical theory and the teaching of literature: Politics, curriculum, pedagogy* (pp. 140–152). Urbana, IL: National Council of Teachers of English.

Schick, C., & St. Denis, V. (2005). Troubling national discourses in anti-racist curricular planning. *Canadian Journal of Education, 28*(3), 295–317.

Sleeter, C. (1993a). Advancing a white discourse: A response to Scheurich. *Educational Researcher, 22*(8), 13–15.

Sleeter, C. (1993b). How white teachers construct race. In C. McCarthy & W. Crichlow (Eds.), *Race identity and representation in education* (pp. 157–171). New York, NY: Routledge.

Srivastava, A. (1997). Anti-racism inside and outside the classroom. In L. G. Roman & L. Eyre (Eds.), *Dangerous territories: Struggles for difference and equality in education* (pp. 113–126). New York, NY: Routledge.

St. Denis, V., & Schick, C. (2003). What makes anti-racist pedagogy in teacher education difficult? Three popular ideological assumptions. *The Alberta Journal of Educational Research, 49*(1), 55–69.

Tatum, B. D. (1992). Talking about race, learning about racism: The application of racial identity development theory in the classroom. *Educational Review, 62*(1), 1–24.

Wagamese, R. (1997). *A quality of light.* Toronto, ON: Doubleday Canada.

Wagamese, R. (2003). *For Joshua.* Toronto, ON: Doubleday Canada.

Wagamese, R. (2006). *Keeper 'n me.* Toronto, ON: Doubleday Canada.

Wagamese, R. (2007). *Dream wheels.* Toronto, ON: Anchor Canada.

Wagamese, R. (2013). *Indian horse.* Toronto, ON: Douglas & McIntyre.

Chapter 2

"I Wouldn't Stand Too Close to This Story If I Were You ...": Vancouver Island Teachers Explore Social Justice Issues

Angela Ward, with Allison Balabuch, Lauren Frodsham, Dale Jarvis,
Tanya Larkin, Carol Nahachewsky, Katherine O'Connor, Devon Stokes-Bennett,
and Alison Preece

Teachers living on Vancouver Island, set in the Salish Sea, are surrounded by natural beauty and built reminders of postcolonial realities. Different First Nations groups on the island honour wildlife through their historic and current totemic images of the bears, frogs, whales, and eagles with whom we share this land. Increasingly, formal events in British Columbia begin with statements recognizing traditional territories, and First Nations artwork is prominently displayed in public buildings. This chapter describes how teachers in the Vancouver Island social justice project went beyond surface recognition of Indigenous peoples to develop their own knowledge and understanding of British Columbians' shared experiences through settlement, colonization, and early attempts at building a postcolonial society. As part of the project, we also considered other aspects of social justice teaching, including social inclusion of people marginalized by physical and cognitive challenges. Some teachers, in their thematic teaching, also studied "hidden" aspects of Canadian history, such as the internment of Japanese-Canadians during World War II.

The Power of Stories

The Vancouver Island teachers at this project site met 12 times over two school years, usually in Angela's home. We would come together at the end of a teaching day, share refreshments, and talk about experiences of teaching from various social justice stances. Throughout the project, we told stories of our own lives inside and outside school, and stories of students' struggles and moments of illumination. We became storytellers. In our search for books that would support students in considering issues of social justice, we read storied historical accounts of injustices imposed on Indigenous children in residential schools such as *Fatty Legs* by Jordan-Fenton and Pokiak-Fenton (2010), as well as imagined recreations of tragic moments in their lives (Campbell, 2005). We were thoughtful story readers.

Jerome Bruner (2002) reminds us that narratives are not transparent windows onto reality, but "offer alternative worlds that put the actual one in a new light" (p. 10). Writers of narrative fiction often set out to create new and possible worlds, but these creations are always built from what is already understood in our own lives. For many storytellers and writers, a story is a way of distancing the reader from the difficult or unpalatable circumstances of our day-to-day lives in order to think differently about previously ignored assumptions. Thomas King, in his introduction to *The Inconvenient Indian* (2012), admits that, despite his own background as a historian, "I'd rather make up my own world. Fictions are less unruly than histories" (p. xi). In First Nations storytelling traditions, listeners are responsible meaning-makers. The propensity to edit our own stories is a research concern for Ritchie and Wilson (2000), who note that we "often selectively recall past behaviours in order to make them consistent with our current situations, attitudes, and understandings. Also, most storytellers want to please their audience" (p. 21). In this study, we were constantly telling stories to help us make sense of our efforts to teach from a social justice perspective, constantly striving for honesty and awareness about what was chosen for sharing and what was kept unspoken. Ideas were shared and challenges were explored.

Thomas King's playful yet powerful use of story in delineating the consequences of First Nations colonization by Europeans became a touchstone for us. At one meeting, we turned ourselves into a "book club," discussing King's (2005) *A Short History of Indians in Canada.* King himself warns readers that even humorous stories have the potential to be explosive: "I wouldn't stand too close to this story if I were you. Coyote and the RCMPs might grab you" (2005, p. 67). But as teachers we recognized the potential power of stories to enable us as readers, as well as our students, to see multiple points of view; to learn histories from the perspectives of those closest to events; to inhabit, albeit briefly, experiences very different from our own. As King reminds us: "Most of us think that history is the past. It's not. History is the stories we tell about the past. That's all it is. Stories. Such a definition might make the enterprise of history seem neutral. Benign. Which, of course, it isn't" (King, 2012, p. 2).

Teachers in this project shared stories of their own literacy lives, read about stories, delightedly thumbed through Canadian books, took them away and read them, and came back to our discussion groups with new insights. They were then ready to share the books with their students, sometimes as a whole class, often in small groups and with individuals. The teachers' experiences in sharing Canadian literature from a social justice perspective in classrooms and their students' moments of illumination are the grand story of this chapter.

The study is framed by contemporary theories of social justice that see teachers as agents of social change attending to issues of race, ethnicity, class, gender, and language. Multicultural education has become more common in Canadian schools over the past 40 years. Teachers are accustomed to "teaching about" multiculturalism through activities considered to represent cultural diversity. For example, students and their families might be encouraged to share particular foods or demonstrate customs associated with their home cultures. This approach epitomizes the awareness stage of diversity education as described by Banks (e.g., 1993). What is missing from the "dance, dress, and diet" approach to diversity education is a commitment to asking hard questions about systemic exclusion in schools and in the wider society. Cochran-Smith (1991) poses these difficult questions from a critical framework, positioning teachers as potential agents for change. She argues that "prospective teachers need to know from the start that they are part of a larger struggle" (1991, p. 280) and need to teach through "critical dissonance" (calling into question current school practices) to "collaborative resonance" (linking critical theoretical understandings with their practical experiences in schools). This chapter is a case study of teachers who use literature to challenge the status quo in their communities and classrooms.

As Johnston (2003), in personal documentation of her own teaching journey in varied contexts and consequent research with two high school English teachers in Canada, reminds her readers, minority students in Canadian classrooms are "accustomed to looking at a map of the world from diverse and often contradictory viewpoints" (p. 147). Initiatives such as the Truth and Reconciliation Commission of Canada (TRC) have drawn wider attention to the marginalization of Indigenous students in Canadian classrooms and more broadly in Canadian society. The TRC describes reconciliation in the following way: "Collective efforts from all peoples are necessary to revitalize the relationship between Aboriginal peoples and Canadian society—reconciliation is the goal. It is a goal that will take the commitment of multiple generations but when it is achieved, when we have reconciliation—it will make for a better, stronger Canada." Members of the TRC travelled for six years throughout Canada, and gathered more than 7,000 pieces of testimony on the legacy of the residential school system for Indigenous youth.

The teachers themselves describe how, in our monthly discussions, we raised questions of historical perspective; contested "truths"; and came to the beginnings of answers through our explorations of Canadian literature, media, and primary resources. The writing of Thomas King, quoted in the chapter title, was a spur for us to think in alternative and non-conventional ways about the use of story to teach hard lessons. "Boy, that Coyote likes to tell stories. Sometimes he tells stories that smell bad. Sometimes he tells stories that have been stretched. Sometimes he tells stories that bite your toes. Coyote stories" (King, 2003, p. 58).

The Storytellers

As part of the project, Vancouver Island teachers connected with their own literacy histories, those complex backgrounds that drew them into teaching and social justice issues. As teachers, we connected with each other, developing affinity spaces and a community of practice that encouraged some of us to go beyond "safe" pedagogical practices. Although there were no teachers from First Nations backgrounds in the group, many were teaching students from Indigenous backgrounds. We brought a range of experiences to this inquiry group project; there were seven classroom teachers, one librarian, and one researcher who regularly participated in the group meetings. Four teachers were teaching in the upper elementary and middle grades, two teachers worked in an alternative setting teaching high school grades, another was a senior high teacher, and we had one curriculum librarian from the university working with us. Most teachers had completed graduate degrees. Angela was the lead researcher, joined by Alison, an academic colleague who took on a less formal role. There were ten of us: nine women and one man. Our group members had between 6 and 40 years of experience in teaching, with most having taught for more than 10 years. The stories of early reading and life in schools were remembrances of favourite books and teachers, but not always of homes where books were shared every day. Playing school was a favourite occupation, and typical North American series books were eagerly devoured. Only one teacher could recall being aware of Indigenous students from nearby communities. Reading was often an escapist pastime, especially in elementary school years. Teachers were struck that the books we were reading in the project demanded a different kind of attention from them and from their students. The books we chose supported awareness of others' realities, current and historical. Although this provided an opportunity for teachers themselves to learn about historical and current injustices, they often found themselves in an uneasy space.

Our own histories were reflected in the social justice issues that became our pedagogical themes. While a number of us were drawn to First Nations histories and issues, one teacher included a classroom study of the internment of Japanese-Canadians during World War II. Another in our group was passionate about working with teachers to joyfully include children with disabilities in their classrooms. We began our inquiry sessions by puzzling through our understandings of social justice before we embarked on themes and units in the classroom.

Questions That Intrigued Us

The questions behind this project were "What does it mean to 'teach' social justice?" and "How can we use Canadian children's literature to support students' learning about our province and country's First Nations history prior to contact with settlers, through contact and colonial times?" Ideals of truth and reconciliation were behind the teachers' interest in fulfilling the goals of the newly developed English Language Arts curriculum in British Columbia to "explore Canadian literature, including authentic Aboriginal texts and world literature, to strengthen their understanding of self, others, multiple perspectives, and diverse cultures" (British Columbia Ministry of Education, 2010).

Thinking about Social Justice

Of course, there were no simple answers to our large questions, but in discussions, teachers shared their daily experiences as we struggled to describe the role of books and stories in supporting difficult classroom conversations. As well as a commitment to social justice that was longstanding for many of our teachers, the group shared a love of books and a delight in discovering materials that would engage their students. Describing social justice teaching was simpler than defining it. Katherine linked social justice teaching with critical thinking, and saw her role as modelling it: "I think you can describe how you came to your conclusion ... including the process you went through, what aspects you looked at, and what made you question whether you had the right belief or not, or what makes you conflicted about your belief."

We were challenged by the difficulties of exposing students to historical events that might make them uncomfortable, without "blaming" mainstream students for their relatively privileged lives. Those teaching older students were particularly sensitive to this dilemma: "My real social justice goal with students is to get them to get more perspective on where they are in the world ... without saying to them 'aren't you lucky.'"

We frequently revisited our thoughts on social justice, and the ideas became increasingly nuanced. Teachers were concerned not to introduce yet another "politically correct" set of assumptions that might shut down freedom of inquiry. One of us put it this way: "I'm trying to sort out what I think social justice is ... I worry about the imposition of another ideology ... a bunch of more sanctified perspectives that are now more powerful to us."

Part of the discomfort we experienced came from our place as immigrants and settlers in Canada, members of a society that is now more aware of the negative effects of colonization on Indigenous peoples. We are acutely aware that we cannot speak for First Nations peoples, but through our work in social justice teaching we hope to bring some "unease and unsettledness" (Bradford, 2007) to teachers' and students' reading of literature. Bradford reminds us that we are both colonizers and colonized and benefit from a society that favours non-Indigenous institutions. However, teachers' immediate responsibilities are to provide their students with opportunities for thought-ful discussions about social justice; engaging and challenging books may be the most straightforward way of stimulating powerful conversations and unsettling assumptions. But above all, teachers in this project always considered their own students' educational needs.

Browsing through Books and the "Book Club"

Our inquiry group was very informal; we began somewhat awkwardly sharing ideas about social justice teaching, but as teachers realized that there was not just one answer secretly lurking in Angela's mind, the discussion became more open. And once we began to "make the political more pedagogical" (Giroux, 1988, p. 127), the group became more fully engaged in discussing imaginative possibilities for classroom activities. In the early meetings, we spent time getting to know each other, usually as we commented on the Canadian children's books we had been reading. At first, Angela supplied the books, but, as the meetings progressed, teachers brought in other materials to support their emerging pedagogical themes and questions. The books we used (not all of which are referenced herein) are listed at the end of this chapter for teachers' further exploration.

Discovering unfamiliar Canadian children's literature also inspired the group to revisit familiar books from a social justice perspective. As can be seen in individual teachers' descriptions of the classroom activities they introduced as the study progressed, several group members started with Canadian materials, and then added other texts to enrich their thematic teaching. Juxtaposition of contrasting texts was also a powerful pedagogical instrument.

The Ministry of Education in British Columbia has a renewed emphasis on First Nations content across the curriculum, including a new course called English 10 and 11 First Peoples, in which a key feature is "focus on texts that present authentic First Peoples voices (i.e., historical or contemporary texts created by or with First Peoples)" (British Columbia Ministry of Education, 2010). A number of our teachers chose to use books about the residential school experience, including books written by Indigenous writers. Jordan-Fenton and Pokiak-Fenton's *Fatty Legs* (2010) and *A Stranger at Home* (2011) are based on the life experiences of a young Inuvialuit girl as she was taken to residential school, suffered there, and the resultant confusion she felt when re-joining her traditional family. These books are highly accessible for upper elementary students, but are dark in tone and sombre in illustration. *Shi-shi-etko* and *Shin-chi's Canoe* (Campbell, 2005, 2008), also written by an Indigenous author, tell a similar story in a more Romantic vein, although the second book does provide telling details of the emotional deprivations and thoughtless cruelty experienced by First Nations children in residential schools. *Sugar Falls* (Robertson & Henderson, 2011) is a graphic novel that tells a grim story of residential schooling based on the remembered experiences of a Cree Elder. After reading these children's books, our group decided they themselves needed more understanding of the history of First Nations peoples in Canada. The teachers felt it important to first build their own knowledge of Aboriginal history:

"I want to expand my own understanding of First Nation issues before I work on this with my students."

Consequently, we decided to use Indigenous writer Thomas King's *A Short History of Indians in Canada* (2005) as a "book club" book that we would all read and discuss together. The book is a collection of stories where relationships between Indigenous people (usually called "Indians" by King) and whites are illuminated through strategies of humour and parody. Sometimes, stereotypical roles are reversed and surreal situations are developed (e.g., an Indian boy writes a school paper likening white people to various characters in *Star Trek*). The stories often try to explain "who white people are … which characters in *Star Trek* do they most resemble? Who wants a white baby as a raffle prize?"

One teacher commented on King's future scenario where white people have collections of "Indians": "That's close to the bone in a lot of ways; people still use the book *The Indian in the Cupboard*" (where the protagonist receives a plastic figure of an Indian as a birthday gift). The book club, with varied responses from our participants, reminded us how important the *emotional* response to literature is when dealing with tough realities. We also recognized that the role of information is important for students as well. Connecting with *A Short History of Indians in Canada* (King, 2005) would be difficult if the reader didn't have some historical knowledge already. Our teacher group found the stories enlightening, but challenging and disquieting. As the "book club" happened well into the second year of our project, we knew each other quite well and were able to acknowledge the discomfort. Alison describes her response: "I can't find the words to describe the kind of laughter: it's so pitched, and yet full and rolling and funny. It makes us say 'What are we laughing at?' and unsettles our conventional understanding."

The books we read and discussed became the basis for planning classroom activities that focused on social justice, but the challenges extended to classroom management and to multimodal teaching as well. Teachers were fully engaged, while their reporting back from the field is a rich collage of personal response and a range of classroom activities.

Stories of Classroom Life

Seasons and Themes of the Academic Year

The project continued for two years, so we learned that each academic year has its own rhythms and seasons. In September, teachers working with a different group of students need to establish trust between themselves and their class, and to build a classroom community where students feel comfortable in sharing ideas. The experienced teachers in our group were very aware that students need practice in respectful listening and small group work, and planned for lots of practice in these areas. As Lauren said, "I want to be open to multiple perspectives but need tools for dealing with such problems as negative pre-perceptions, attitude, language."

The teachers in the project wrote the following descriptions of their classroom experiences in teaching social justice. They used a range of approaches, strategies, and materials; there will be a summary of their ideas at the end of this section and a list of children's books at the end of the chapter. Although all the teachers were inspired by the Canadian literature we shared, most used other materials (books and digital media) in conjunction with the work of Canadian authors.

Devon—Creating a Safe Place for Difficult Discussions

Some teachers have an instinct for creating classroom norms such as respect and safety, but I have always preferred to use as a benchmark the *Universal Declaration of Human Rights* (UDHR; United Nations, 1948); it provides a language recognized and used in the real world, allowing relevant transfer and extension. Also, I find it empowers youth; adults listen when youth use this universal language to advocate for their rights, allowing authentic debate to occur. The UDHR is also general enough to allow the real life tensions between different rights and responsibilities to breathe. And those tensions are so very real.

Social justice education posed specific challenges in my classroom. My students were familiar with teen pregnancy, poverty, addictions, residential schools, domestic violence, crime, sexualized violence, discrimination, and mental illness. The common element among my students was that they had struggled in a mainstream educational setting and had chosen an alternative option.

Our classroom community used a common lens through which to examine social justice issues, not just to develop a common language and tool set but to form a healthy community that gave us a framework within which we could discuss personal issues. Beyond that, it was crucial for classroom management. If we could make meaning of the 30 human rights and apply them to our community, we could use them to explore the larger world and negotiate the constant tension between rights.

Using the Universal Declaration of Human Rights

A student wore a shirt sexualizing females.
When does Freedom of Expression violate another's Right to a Safe Place?

Students skipped class to demonstrate outside the parliament buildings.
When does a person's Right to Public Assembly trump the Right to Education?

A friend posted an inappropriate picture of someone else on Facebook.
Who owns the picture? When does the Right to Own Your Own Things violate another's Right to Privacy?

I chose *iLit Strength and Struggle: Perspectives from First Nations, Inuit, and Métis Peoples in Canada* (Mishenene et al., 2011) as it was a Canadian resource with fiction and non-fiction texts ranging from short stories and poetry to graphic art and essays. The range of materials allowed me to co-construct our thematic inquiry with my students.

I used multimodal short texts to start a theme along with an anchoring text; I would then co-create the unit with students. For example, in a Grade 10 interdisciplinary social studies and English unit, the "Truth and Reconciliation Speech" by Justice Murray Sinclair from *iLit* provided a portal from our broad thematic inquiry into "What are inalienable human rights?" and then to a more specific inquiry: "How is Canada's history inconsistent with how we currently see ourselves as Canadians?"

My lessons are mainly discussion based, blending structured and unstructured, paired, small-group, and whole-group conversations with space for personal reflections.

As a classroom community, we shared what we knew of residential schools. As four of my students had Indigenous family members who had attended residential schools, this was a deep, rich, and respectful discussion. We then read *Shi-shi-etko* (Campbell, 2005), which explores the experience of being taken from home and family from a child's perspective. My students could relate to this. With even more questions, we utilized the Canadian Broadcasting Corporation (CBC) archives and invited a First Nations Elder from our community to talk with us. At this point, the students wanted to do something to honour residential school survivors and remember those lost, so we connected with First Nations staff in our school. Together we decided to create a tile mural.

At this point, having explored what happened and the ongoing impact on Canadians, the "why" became important to students. So we moved into studying colonialism and economy. We had also been exploring what I call "PEGS" (political structure, economy, geography, and society), with the goal of understanding these terms and their interdependence. This led us to an analysis of the differences of PEGS between First Nations and settlers. We explored colonialism through the 2009 movie *Avatar* (suggested by some students who saw similarities). In my class, we approached movies as we would traditional texts: chunking with pre-, during, and post-viewing activities such as goal setting, predicting, inferring, and lots of discussion. We discussed the similarities between the *Avatar* plot tensions and Canadian colonialism and then used PEGS to analyze the differences between the indigenous population and newcomers in the movie. We continued our learning with a trip to the Royal BC Museum to compare the First Nations gallery and the Settlers' gallery, once again using PEGS as a lens.

As we revisited our research question, we decided to go deeper, carrying out a small-group research project in which students investigated Canada's human rights track record. Our topics for small-group research, a number of them initiated by students, included workers' rights, women's rights, Asian Canadians' experiences, First Nation peoples, and Canada's treatment of mentally and physically disabled Canadians. After this, our research became international and contemporary. The similarities between residential schools and boy soldiers (taken from families, re-educated, and assimilated, resulting in loss of identity and culture) led us to Africa and beyond. Our social justice learning just kept evolving.

Tanya—Learning about First Nations History

My teaching colleagues and I decided to immerse ourselves in reading local authors and exploring social justice issues, specifically related to First Peoples and residential school injustices. The majority of my English 11 students were open to learning about Canada's history and the First Peoples' experiences—or so I assumed at first, as there wasn't any complaining. When we had a class discussion and completed a pre-reading question set, the students, almost all from Euro-Canadian backgrounds, displayed very little knowledge about this topic and for the most part seemed uninterested. Many of the students were at a low literacy level, but didn't mind reading literature so long as it interested them; pictures and gore always helped!

We used a local graphic novel called *Sugar Falls* (Robertson & Henderson, 2011). I chose this book because it was a graphic novel that had a strong yet clear plot and could be read in one class period. It was perfect for starting a short story unit and, more importantly, it would engage my students on the topic of residential schools. On the first day of the short story unit, I had the class fill in a worksheet on their knowledge of residential schools; after this, each student found a partner or small group and did a pair/share activity to gather more information on the topic. After this we took a moment to review the artwork and analyze the cover and title of the graphic novel. I read the first pages of *Sugar Falls*, then had a few volunteers read, and after a few more pages, the students read the graphic novel quietly to themselves. Once the class finished reading, we did a brief analysis of the plot, identified the protagonist and antagonist, and discussed the issue of residential schools. I took this time to introduce a few plot definitions, and we brainstormed examples for these using the graphic novel. Before the class ended, I had each student do a "quick write" on a prompt I gave them—five sentences. And then they wrote a reflective journal entry. As class concluded for the day, each student was immersed in conversation with peers about residential schools. They were floored by what had occurred and what people could do to others.

For the remainder of the short story unit, I had the students' attention, so each day I brought in more Canadian literature on the residential school theme. We concluded the unit by watching the movie *Rabbit-Proof Fence* (an Australian movie)—it was slow-moving, but a definite hit nonetheless.

Dale—Making Connections through Drama

I was teaching at the upper elementary level and have a long history of considering social justice issues in my teaching. I worked with staff within my school and in my district to develop a story drama project along with the literature circles I was already doing. The story drama with my class involved the children thinking about how First Nations felt about the ban put on giving potlatches (ceremonial feasts), since the penalty was to risk having their children taken away or going to jail themselves. When my students were challenged to consider what celebrations they might give up, they mentioned Christmas. Although I had not particularly appreciated the Christmas skit the children had put together, when I asked them whether Christmas was something they would give up, the children became hysterical. They had, in thinking about their own cherished Christmas celebrations, recognized the equivalent importance of the potlatch for First Nations. The culminating discussion was to be in role as an Indigenous community deciding whether they would keep the potlatch. Throughout this unit, I was in contact with an Aboriginal consultant and staff member. As part of my unit, I also used *My Name Is Seepeetza* (Sterling, 1992) and *Shi-shi-etko* (Campbell, 2005), as well as music from a First Nations singer/songwriter. I also used the CBC (2011) production *The Eighth Fire*, hosted and written by Indigenous people.

During the literature circle activity, my Grade 4 and 5 students commented on similarities between Japanese-Canadian internment during World War II, as described in *Naomi's Road* (Kogawa, 2005), and the residential school experience in *Fatty Legs* (Jordan-Fenton & Pokiak-Fenton, 2010). Students also connected the Holocaust with both these Canadian experiences.

Allison—Thematic Teaching with a Range of Materials

I teach Grade 8 English classes in a dual-track English/French Immersion school. My students mostly come from homes where families discuss current events and issues with their children. Consequently, my students have the vocabulary to identify social justice issues, yet have only a thin understanding of what those issues might really mean to those in the world affected by social injustice. What I love about teaching Grade 8 is the students' ability to dive deeply into topics that can change their worldviews. Without personal connections, social justice issues become "other peoples' problems."

With my classes, I carried out a picture book study centered on the theme "Lost." At the beginning of each study, I asked the students to give an example of a time they had felt lost. We discussed different ways you could be "lost": socially, emotionally, physically, and spiritually. Leaving the question open provided each student with an access point to the theme. Their answers ranged from being lost in a shopping centre to being emotionally lost at the loss of a parent. We then read a selection of picture books together; from each, we extracted how the characters or society were "lost" and how that connected to their personal experience and understanding of the world. My goal was to have them think more deeply on each issue. We read *Tricycle* (2007) by Guatemalan-born author Elisa Amado as a platform to discuss class inequalities. What I love about using this book is the power of the small amount of text that is so well scripted. The students are left with space to make their own sense of right and wrong. In the book, Margarita's tricycle is stolen by her friends next door. It is clear in the book that Margarita is wealthy and her neighbours are poor. Margarita is torn between telling her parents who the thieves are and protecting her friends. It is obvious that the tricycle is "lost," but my students pulled out deeper meanings: the loss of innocence by Margarita, the loss of trust in adults as certain and always right, and the loss of trust in friendship and its implications for a child. Is it all right for her neighbours to steal because they are poor? Or is it fair to live in a society that has such an inequality of wealth? Our school has two very distinct demographics; my French Immersion students come from more privileged homes than many of their English-track schoolmates. This book seemed safe to the students because it is centered on class inequalities in a distant country. Once the discussion had started, we switched the focus to local issues of wealth and poverty. Many had never thought about our local situation and how poverty and difficulty at home could impact their relationships with other students in the school. Now, a stolen iPod from the change room has a different significance for the students. Students struggled with the same issue as Margarita: If someone else is needy, does that make theft more understandable or is theft always wrong?

Another book we used in the study was *The Stamp Collector* (Lanthier & Thisdale, 2012). This is a beautiful book about a writer who is imprisoned in China for writing a short story that is critical of the government. The book has two perspectives throughout: that of the prison guard who dreams of a better life, and that of the writer who has become ill due to his imprisonment. The prison guard needs to work, and the writer needs to write. My students all could define "freedom of speech," but in their limited understanding, they believed that it would be obvious why the writer would be imprisoned. The loss of freedom for both characters due to their government's policies and actions was easier for the students to connect with than the actual content of text that might be considered controversial. One of my students was so inspired by the book that she found the short story *The Wild Pigeon* by the Uyghur writer Nurmuhemmet Yasin, who was imprisoned in China for ten years for writing it. We read it as a class, and the students were shocked to see what had caused his imprisonment. The text reads on the surface as a simple story about pigeons, but when we researched further, we learned that it is a metaphor for the unhappiness of the Uyghur people under Beijing's rule. The student's initiative to find the story, as well as the history behind it, was inspiring to me as well as to other students. They said that they didn't even know that the Uyghur people existed, let alone that they suffered under their government. "I wonder what else I don't know is happening in the world," was the student comment that impacted me the most. The book inspired many to delve into their own inquiry about freedom of speech, and many came back with facts about countries that currently suppress the voices of their peoples.

A third book I used in the study was *The Arrival* by Australian author Shaun Tan (2006). The book doesn't have any text, only images. It shows a man who seems to be fleeing his home country due to war, leaving his family behind. The images in the book are very powerful as they express the sense of loss and loneliness experienced by many immigrants. Many of my students shared family stories of immigration to Canada. There is an image throughout the book that looks like either a vine or a creature (my students couldn't decide which it was) that is threatening the people in the book. It sparked a discussion of what could threaten people to the point of making them flee their countries or become refugees. This was an excellent jumping off point for a closer look at current events, as well as fostering empathy for new arrivals to Canada.

The students who began the study thinking about "lost" by applying it to a child in the grocery store were by now writing about poverty, oppression, and loss of freedoms. One of the most powerful pieces was by a boy who said he had realized through the study that it was he who was the oppressor in his interactions with classmates. He had felt uncomfortable because he was so much bigger than the other kids in elementary school and, to deal with this, he had turned his feelings of insecurity into aggression against his peers. He reflected that perhaps this was similar to governments oppressing their people out of fear, as he had bullied others out of fear of their opinion of him.

I found that using picture books with older students was a very effective tool to spark rich discussions on social justice issues. The smaller amount of text compared to a novel allowed for a wider variety of themes and discussions within the short amount of time we had. The books also had powerful imagery that helped the students respond visually to the themes. Each time I work with this theme, new ideas emerge and the discussion goes in unexpected directions because of the richness of student opinions, past experiences, and prior knowledge. Young adolescent students are in a perfect position to examine social justice issues as they are making sense of themselves and how they fit in the world.

Lauren—Teaching Reading Strategies to Support Deep Reading in High School

My approach to teaching, particularly when grappling with social issues, promotes student-led inquiry. I use scaffolding, high-inference tasks and open-ended strategies, and also provide appropriate content to anchor students' learning. My goal was to have students engage with the content through their own lens, find value in multiple perspectives, and make personal connections. Shaun Tan's (2010) *The Lost Thing* was the focus of study. I have used this book with several high school English classes, ranging

Strategies for Book Sharing: *The Lost Thing*, by Shaun Tan

- Pre-reading activity—"What makes a good society?" (describing current issues)
- Webs, word walls, quick writes, partner sharing
- During reading activity—Read in chunks of two or three pages
- Students work in twos or threes guided by "What did you notice?"
- Class share-outs, including response to visuals
- Post-reading activity—Students share thoughts, ranging from literal to speculative

from low level learners to advanced placement learners. All students were able to find an access point in the picture book, explore complex issues, and express their thinking.

To deepen the class's understanding of the text, Socratic seminars provided the framework. However, it was the students who developed the questions that would be used in the discussions, rather than the teacher. This meant that each class discussion was different depending on how the students valued and connected with the social issues they wanted to explore. As a culminating activity, students were asked to either use one of the questions evoked in the discussions or develop a new question to guide their writing of a synthesis from the text. Students frequently came back to the original question of "What makes a good society?" and used a variation of this to focus their critical analysis.

What I found most challenging about student-led inquiry was that my students were so programmed to "find a right answer" or to try to echo my interpretation that creating their own positions and exploring ideas was sometimes difficult. The next time I do this, I will front-load students' learning with strategies aimed at helping them find their own voices earlier in the study.

Katherine—Connecting Students to the World

By the time I took part in the current research project in my 6th and 7th years of teaching, social justice was more than a topic I covered once in a year or through a single exploratory project; it was the base upon which I tried to plan my entire cross-curricular program. I was teaching in a school with mixed demographics: Some students came from upper- and middle-class homes, and others lived in low-income housing and/or foster care. This mix was modestly reflected in my classroom, though my students, who were 11 to 13 years old, primarily came from middle-class homes. Most of their courses were delivered in French, their second language. For this study, I focused on introducing Indigenous history and content, specifically the difficult truths surrounding the residential school system, into my French, English, and social studies courses. Acknowledging the sensitive nature of the subject area, and my personal history as a non-Indigenous person, I sought guidance from my district's Aboriginal Education department in how to most respectfully approach this subject, working closely with an advisor throughout the unit of study.

Setting up a climate of respect and openness in my classroom was crucially important, and we undertook a multitude of community and trust-building activities before tackling any sensitive issues. These included such activities as using a four quadrants worksheet, where, after students had worked on their own for a few minutes, collaborative learning was encouraged through sharing and adding at least one idea suggested by a partner to each quadrant. We also engaged in peer editing, where students looked for the beauty in their partner's work, and then shared with them why they loved a certain word or phrase in that piece of writing. Students wrote community stories, where, upon finishing the introduction to their stories, they passed their work on to someone else in the class to continue the narrative. As a class, we celebrated student

Four Quadrants Worksheet

- Fold a piece of paper into four sections
- Label quadrants, depending on focus of activity:
  - New vocabulary
  - Feelings evoked in the reader and identified in characters
  - Questions about the text
  - Key ideas, sensory details, images

Source: Adapted from Susan Close, *SMART Learning Framework*.

achievements as representative of the entire class's success. I also explicitly taught strategies for sharing opinions and disagreeing respectfully.

The introduction to critical examination of social justice issues was gradual. We began by examining the imagery behind picture books, including the beautiful book *Shi-shi-etko* (Campbell, 2005). We then looked at the *Universal Declaration of Human Rights* (United Nations, 1948), and real-life, cut-and-dried instances where this declaration was upheld or violated. Together, we read and analyzed non-fiction historical artifacts in both official languages, and I made other related reading materials available for use during self-directed reading blocks. Robertson and Henderson's (2011) graphic novel *Sugar Falls* was powerful and highly sought after by students for independent reading. Next, we undertook a full class novel study using Jordan-Fenton and Pokiak-Fenton's (2010) *Fatty Legs*—which we read both in English and in French—as our text. This Canadian novel captivated my students' interest. Some of the most effective activities we undertook included maintaining character arcs that followed the changing opinions and actions of certain key characters in our readings; Venn diagrams comparing the views of characters representing opposing positions on a topic through imagery and symbolism; journal writing in the role of key characters; and, in groups, tracing an outline of a person and visually demonstrating which factors influencing the lives of main characters were internal, which were external, and which were more broadly societal. Finally, through the Aboriginal Education department, we invited guest speakers to visit our class to share their personal experiences.

Throughout the unit, I found that it was important for us to step back from difficult issues often to look for hope in the world. We undertook a weekly "random acts of kindness" challenge and shared what each of us had done to make someone's day a little brighter, as well as identifying personal strengths and action points. We also looked at steps that communities and governments were taking to make amends for past actions; and to improve equality and access to social services locally, nationally, and internationally. Ultimately, the students showed a deep appreciation for meaningful discussions about issues that really matter to the world. They showed that they were fully capable of contributing to these discussions with well thought-out and articulate views and justifying how they had developed their opinions. They shared how these discussions extended beyond the classroom and how they were having new kinds of conversations with their parents and family members. The growth and engagement I saw in my students was inspiring and well worth the leap of faith it took to tackle a daunting subject with them.

Carol—Team Teaching in an Elementary Classroom

Two stories were shared with the class at the beginning of the unit to illustrate the concept of social justice advocacy. The first story was an oral one, drawing on my son Aidan's classroom inclusion experiences. I explained that it took advocacy by people with disabilities (and their families) to believe that people of all abilities have a right to an education. We talked about current awareness-raising movements such as that calling for people to use people-first language (i.e., putting the person before the disability). We then turned to the picture book *Lily and the Paper Man* (Upjohn, 2007), which deals with issues of homelessness and poverty. Over the course of the unit, the classroom teacher read *Shin-chi's Canoe* and *Shi-shi-etko* (Campbell 2008, 2005) to the class, and the Grade 4 students read *Yeny and the Children for Peace* (Mulder, 2007) and *Fatty Legs* (Jordan-Fenton & Pokiak-Fenton, 2010) as part of their literature circle experience. As part of our unit, the children became Young Social Justice League Investigators, exploring the school to see if they could find signs that their school community cared about human rights. Students identified such initiatives as the Christmas Backpack Project, the Sensory Room, and the WITS Anti-Bullying Program in their logbooks, and identified reasons why these projects were important to them. The family homework project had families discussing human rights concerns that were important to them, and a long and diverse list was created out of the issues when the students reported back to the classroom. Neither the classroom teacher nor I ever taught a unit on social justice itself, although our teaching often incorporated the values of human rights education, and we were drawn to children's literature that raised awareness of social justice topics. In the end, our focus was not just to raise awareness of the issues but rather to communicate that people in a community like ours can all work to make our world a better and more just place.

Exploring Facets of Social Justice Teaching: Insights from Classrooms

Angela and Alison, as research leaders, had qualms about turning the research meetings into graduate classes. We did choose to offer questions that could be taken up in discussion if the group saw fit to do so, if the questions proved relevant or resonant, but we were also deliberately and simultaneously open to "what came up." The decision not to over-organize a structure was one of the reasons why the project actually worked; it left everyone room to shape their participation as they chose. This mirrored the open-ended strategies used by our participants in their own classrooms. As it turned out, there was added power and richness because of the range of contexts where our participants taught. Each participant found a personal way of shaping engagement in the group.

All teacher participants stressed the importance of creating classroom spaces for dialogue, and it was necessary to do this at the beginning of every school year. They used a variety of community and trust-building activities with students. Devon introduced the *Universal Declaration of Human Rights* as a neutral arbiter for her students' practical and moral dilemmas in life and in literature. Teachers made sure to teach interactive reading and discussion strategies (e.g., quadrant worksheets; pre-, during, and post-reading activities), as well as techniques for encouraging students to think deeply about their reading (e.g., revisiting ideas, Socratic seminars, demonstration of respectful discussion techniques. Another way to enrich the experience of reading Canadian books was to include them as part of an integrated theme (such as Allison's "Lost") and to find books and digital media from other countries to juxtapose with the Canadian materials.

Most teachers worked with a team of colleagues, either as a formal group in middle years, or with support from a librarian or district level staff. Our inquiry group became a support group for teachers trying new themes and strategies, and many participants were part of communities of practice in their own schools and districts. Their own interactivity and the joy the teachers found in discussion with each other was something that they wished to recreate for students in their classrooms.

Our group had discussions about the "authenticity" of texts, as well as the dangers of a group of non-Indigenous teachers appropriating knowledge. We tried as much as possible to use books written by Indigenous authors, whatever their country of origin. A number of teachers found it especially rewarding to juxtapose texts, comparing and contrasting voices. Toward the end of the project, the group did talk more about the books as texts, thinking about literary devices and visual aspects, although earlier on we focused more on content.

Teachers themselves learned First Nations history and information about human rights through the books we shared as teaching intellectuals, and also through our exploration of the children's books. When the planned teaching units were completed, our discussions became even livelier. Using books, especially picture books, as a slightly distanced gateway into new knowledge and difficult worlds gave teachers confidence to tread new paths. Discussing historic racism against First Nations peoples, for example, made it easier to talk about what students had noticed in their own schools. Allison's "Lost" theme emboldened her students to look for instances where human freedoms have been lost, and then to examine their own attitudes.

The Vancouver Island teachers in this project developed multiple creative, interdisciplinary pedagogical strategies for accomplishing their goals for social justice (including broad issues of diversity as well as First Nations issues), and themselves modelled the "lifelong sense of curiosity" they wished for their Canadian students.

Keywords

- Indigenous education
- interdisciplinary teaching
- social justice
- team teaching

Reflection Questions

1. Many texts about First Nations peoples are written by non-First Nations authors. How do we select texts that support respectful dialogue about First Nations issues?
2. Can you identify moments of "pedagogical discomfort" in your own practice? In what ways can you move outside your own comfort zone to support students in learning about social justice?
3. How might you communicate with colleagues and parents about your social justice teaching?

References

Amado, E., & Ruano, A. (2007). *Tricycle*. Toronto, ON: Groundwood Books.

Cameron, J., Landau, J., Worthington, S., Saldana, Z., Ribisi, G., Rodriguez, M., Lang, S., ... Twentieth Century-Fox Film Corporation. (2010). *Avatar*. Beverly Hills, CA: 20th Century Fox.

Banks, J. (1993). Multicultural education: Historical development, dimensions, and practice. In L. Darling-Hammond (Ed.), *Review of research in education* (vol. 19, pp. 3-49). Washington, DC: American Educational Research Association.

Bradford, C. (2007). *Unsettling narratives: Postcolonial readings of children's literature.* Waterloo, ON: Wilfred Laurier University Press.

British Columbia Ministry of Education. (2010). *English 10 and 11 First Peoples.* http://www.bced.gov.bc.ca/irp/pdfs/english_language_arts/2010efp1011.pdf

Bruner, J. (2002). *Making stories: Law, literature, life.* Cambridge, MA: Harvard University Press.

Campbell, N. I. (2005). *Shi-shi-etko* (K. LaFave, Illus.). Toronto, ON: Groundwood Books.

Campbell, N. I. (2008). *Shin-chi's canoe* (K. LaFave, Illus.). Toronto, ON: Groundwood Books.

Canadian Broadcasting Corporation (CBC). (2011). *The eighth fire: Aboriginal peoples, Canada and the way forward.* [Television series].

Cochran-Smith, M. (1991). Learning to teach against the grain. *Harvard Educational Review, 61*(3), 279-310.

Giroux, H. (1988). *Teachers as intellectuals: Towards a critical pedagogy of learning.* Westport, CT: Bergin & Garvey.

Johnston, I. (2003). *Re-mapping literary worlds: Postcolonial pedagogy in practice.* New York, NY: Peter Lang.

Jordan-Fenton, C., & Pokiak-Fenton, M. (2010). *Fatty legs.* Toronto, ON: Annick Press.

Jordan-Fenton, C., & Pokiak-Fenton, M. (2011). *A stranger at home.* Toronto, ON: Annick Press.

King, T. (2003). *The truth about stories.* Toronto, ON: House of Anansi Press.

King, T. (2005). *A short history of Indians in Canada*. Toronto, ON: Harper Collins.

King, T. (2012). *The inconvenient Indian*. Toronto, ON: Doubleday Canada.

Kogawa, J. (2005/1986). *Naomi's road*. Markham, ON: Fitzhenry & Whiteside.

Lanthier, J., & Thisdale, F. (2012). *The stamp collector*. Markham, ON: Fitzhenry & Whiteside.

Mishenene, R., Toulouse, P., Atcheson, J., et al. (2011). *iLit strength and struggle: Perspectives from First Nations, Inuit, and Métis peoples in Canada*. Toronto, ON: McGraw Hill-Ryerson.

Mulder, M. (2008). *Yeny and the children for peace*. Toronto, ON: Second Story Press.

Noyce, P. (Dir.). (2002). *Rabbit-proof fence*. [Film]. London: Hanway Films.

Ritchie, J. S., & Wilson, D. E. (2000). *Teacher narrative as critical inquiry*. New York, NY: Teachers College Press.

Robertson, D., & Henderson, S. (2011). *Sugar falls: A residential school story*. Winnipeg, MB: Highwater Press.

Sterling, S. (1992). *My name is Seepeetza*. Toronto, ON: Groundwood Books.

Tan, S. (2006). *The arrival*. London: Hodder Children's Books.

Tan, S. (2010). *Lost thing*. Sydney, NSW: Lothian/Hachette Australia.

Truth and Reconciliation Commission of Canada (TRC). (2015). *What we have learned: Principles of truth and reconciliation*. Ottawa, ON: Author.

United Nations General Assembly. (1948). *The universal declaration of human rights*. Paris: Author.

Upjohn, R. (2007). *Lily and the paper man*. Toronto, ON: Second Story Press.

Yasin, N. (2004). The wild pigeon. In *Caged: The writings of Nurmuhemmet Yasin*. Kindle: Amazon Media EU.

Other Literature Resources for Teachers

Heide, F. P., Gilliland, J. H., & Lewin, T. (1990). *The day of Ahmed's secret*. New York, NY: Lothrop, Lee & Shepard Books.

Heide, F. P., Gilliland, J. H., & Lewin, T. (1992). *Sami and the time of troubles*. New York, NY: Clarion Books.

Smith, I., & Nhem, S. (2010). *Half spoon of rice: A survival story of the Cambodian genocide*. Manhattan Beach, CA: East West Discovery Press.

Winter, J. (2009). *Nasreen's secret school*. New York, NY: Beach Lane Books.

Winter, J. (2009). *The librarian of Bashra*. Orlando, FL: Harcourt.

Encounters between Readers and Challenging Texts

A pedagogy of discomfort recognizes and problematizes the deeply embedded emotional dimensions that frame and shape daily habits, routines, and unconscious complicity with hegemony.

—BOLER AND ZEMBYLIS (2003, P. 5)

I N THIS SECTION, THE READER WILL FIND VIVID EXAMPLES OF TEACHERS' approaches to working with difficult knowledge. Our participants and their students together experienced the discomfort of recognizing their own privilege in the contexts of their classrooms and communities. In support of their students, teachers took challenging texts on topics such as sexuality and violence and transmuted them through multimodal pedagogical approaches. The teachers who describe their work in this section remind the reader of the importance of close reading in developing insights for teaching. These chapters take the reader on a meditative journey through the dilemmas of choosing and learning from difficult texts.

Chapter 3

Multimodal Perspectives on Teaching Canadian Literature for Social Justice

Ingrid Johnston, Karen Jacobsen, and Bill Howe

Just as there are multiple layers to everyone's identity, there are multiple discourses of identity and multiple discourses of recognition to be negotiated. We have to be proficient as we negotiate the many lifeworlds each of us inhabits, and the many lifeworlds we encounter in our everyday lives. This creates a new challenge for literacy pedagogy.

— THE NEW LONDON GROUP (2000, P. 17)

This chapter draws on findings from the inquiry group with secondary-route English language arts teachers in Alberta to consider possibilities for addressing issues of social justice in the classroom through multimodal literacy approaches to Canadian literature. Our discussion is framed by the potential for teachers to develop a "pedagogy of discomfort" (Boler & Zembylas, 2003) that challenges them to select new and less familiar texts for their classrooms, and to develop new pedagogical approaches that address the evolving multimodal nature of literacy today.

Literacy pedagogy, according to the New London Group (2000), has traditionally meant "teaching and learning to read and write in page-bound, official, standard forms of the national language" (p. 11). Literacy pedagogy, in other words, has been "restricted to formalized, monolingual, monocultural, and rule-governed forms of language" (New London Group, 2000, p. 63). Their use of the term *multiliteracies* explains the connections between the changing social environment facing students and teachers, and a newer approach to literacy pedagogy. The term highlights two related aspects of the increasing complexity of texts: (1) the proliferation of multimodal ways of making meaning where the written word is increasingly part and parcel of visual, audio, and spatial patterns; and (2) the increasing salience of cultural and linguistic diversity characterized by local diversity and global connectedness.

Multiliteracies circumvent the limitations of traditional approaches by emphasizing how negotiating the multiple linguistic and cultural differences in our society is vital to the pragmatics of the working, civic, and private lives of students and encourages them to make meanings from texts by selecting from, adapting, and remaking the range of representational and communicational resources available to them in the classroom (Jewitt, 2008, p. 263).

In this chapter, we illustrate the potential for developing multimodal pedagogical approaches to Canadian literature through stories of two teacher participants in our study who moved out of their comfort zones by selecting to teach Canadian texts that posed new pedagogical challenges. During her many years of high school teaching, Karen had developed a vast repertoire of teaching diverse international literature, but had paid less attention to visual aspects of literary experiences. Now she decided to teach a Canadian graphic novel in her high school classroom for the first time. Over the past decade, the notion that comics or graphic novels are merely recreational out-of-school reading has given way to an acknowledgement of the value of such texts for promoting broader understandings of literacy in the classroom. Jacobs (2007) has commented:

> Reading and writing multimodal texts, then, is an active process, both for creators and for readers who by necessity engage in the active production of meaning and who use all resources available to them based on their familiarity with the comics medium and its inherent grammars, their histories, life experience, and interests. In turn, every act of creating meaning from a multimodal text, happening as it does at the intersection of structure and agency, contributes to the ongoing process of becoming a multimodal literate person. (p. 24)

As Karen describes in her story of teaching, she discovered that the interaction of text and image in this literary genre promoted new teaching strategies and different ways of inviting student responses. The selected text engaged both teacher and students in new ways of thinking about issues of historical marginalization that relate to current Canadian contexts.

Bill's story of teaching highlights new challenges he faced in selecting a controversial play to teach in his Grade 12 classroom. Although experienced in teaching modern plays, Bill recounts how this particular Canadian selection tested the boundaries of what might be considered appropriate for the classroom. He explores how the play encouraged his students to read mindfully, taking note of how theatre is experienced in the body, and making sense of their reflexive reactions to a text that set out to create deeper understanding through moments of discomfort. His story highlights how literacy that moves beyond the realm of purely representational art to speak to a deeper form of bodily experiences can extend students' meaning-making of a written text, and he poses the challenging ethical question of the value or danger of introducing violence in a literary text to high school students.

Karen Jacobsen: Teaching *The Listener* by David Lester

> Because of television, advertising, and the Internet, the primary literacy of the twenty-first century is visual. It's no longer enough to read and write text. Our students must learn to process both words and pictures. To be visually literate, they must learn to "read" (consume/interpret) images and "write" (produce/use) visually rich communications. They must be able to move gracefully and fluently between text and images, between literal and figurative worlds. (Burmark, 2008, p. 5)

My growing personal fascination with multimodal literacy has been reflected in a variety of ways in my teaching practice, most recently in my choice of a graphic novel when I was given the opportunity to pilot a Canadian text with a social justice emphasis as part of a University of Alberta Faculty of Education action research project. At the time, I was teaching high school English and had been conscientious about the importance of moving beyond the traditional canon of classic texts in my International Baccalaureate (IB) classes, including, for example, contemporary novels such as *The Hour of the Star* by Clarice Lispector, *The God of Small Things* by Arundhati Roy, *Woman at Point Zero* by Nawal el Sadaawi, and *The Kiss of the Spider Woman* by Manuel Puig. These texts were carefully selected to represent not only a range of geographical and cultural contexts, but also diversity in gender, sexual orientation, political point of view, and socioeconomic status among the characters and authors. Because I agree with Bender-Slack (2010), who states in "Texts, Talk ... and Fear? English Language Arts Teachers Negotiate Social Justice" that "social justice teaching should study the values and politics behind educational decisions such as what texts are taught and why" (p. 189), I had engaged my students in discussions about my decision, within the broader category of world literature texts in translation, to study works by underrepresented female and gay authors. Choosing a graphic novel allowed us to expand on these previous class discussions of the rationale for text selection.

My students were sophisticated readers, and despite the fact that several of them read graphic texts for personal enjoyment, they expressed some surprise at the inclusion of a work in this format on their "serious" literature reading list. They were not the first to express such reservations. In our teacher inquiry group, several of us had proposed teaching graphic novels, but we were dissatisfied with what we perceived to be a lack of literary quality in the examples we had read, when compared to the texts we usually explored in class. Such assumptions were challenged when I encountered the assertion of Carter (2008) in *Comics, the Canon, and the Classroom* that "the construct of a literary canon as it has been interpreted as policy in schools constitutes a prime example of the racism, elitism, and classism that hinders visual literacy and visual material such as comics and graphic novels from occupying a greater space in the classroom" (p. 55). Carter goes on to state even more provocatively that "If we find ourselves refusing to accept comics and 189 graphic novels in our classrooms, or intentionally ignoring their potential, we are in reality making powerful political statements. These statements might suggest that we do not care much for others who think, read, and decode differently from the narrowest notion of reading and literacy" (p. 53). This made it even clearer to me that a graphic novel was an important choice of text for exploring social justice in my ELA classroom. My challenge was to overcome my own and my students' biases while selecting a text that offered sufficient thematic and stylistic complexity to foster insightful discussion and writing in an IB class.

Negotiating a balance between the requirements of the IB program and the provincial curriculum in Alberta, where I teach, provided an additional challenge. During their Grade 11 year in my class, students read at least three translated novels, in addition to a Shakespearean play and numerous works in other genres. This volume of international reading made it difficult to also fulfill the Alberta Education requirement that 30 percent of works studied be Canadian. Therefore, even prior to the focus of our research study, I was strongly motivated to add more Canadian texts to my syllabus. Beyond these external reasons, I was committed to introducing students to literature that might capture their own landscape—geographical, social, and cultural—in a way that could validate their reality through their own sense of place and time. To this end, for my urban students, I selected *The Listener* by Vancouver author and artist David Lester (2011). Perhaps a perfect example of a multimodal artist, Lester is a guitarist, painter, graphic designer, and publisher, as well as author. Throughout his career, Lester's albums, posters, books, and projects have consistently addressed issues of social justice, promoting the theme of the ongoing art exhibit, lecture, and performance event that he has co-presented since 2002, "How Art and Music Can Change the World." Like these other works, *The Listener* engages readers with questions about social justice within the familiar context of a contemporary Canadian city, while also extending their imaginative experience to other places throughout Europe and other times, depicting past events during Hitler's rise to power.

As one might expect, Lester does not steer clear of provocative content and imagery in his work, and as a result, school and community standards were also a consideration as I debated whether to teach *The Listener*. Lester depicts an incident of oral sex on page 100. This page was the subject of one of our first class discussions, in which I introduced the topic of text selection, including many of the issues addressed earlier in this chapter. We discussed censorship, appropriate versus inappropriate content for high school students, and whether this book should have been eliminated from inclusion in our course due to this single page. It was a very rich discussion, and the students were, perhaps not surprisingly, strongly in support of studying it—not because of the taboo nature of the content, as one might expect from high school students—but because including it in the program showed respect for their maturity. At the beginning of the year we had emphasized that, in choosing to register in this course, students were acknowledging that they were able to handle both the sophistication and mature content of post-secondary level texts, as demanded by an IB program. In addition, knowing my school's community to be generally extremely supportive of experimental, progressive art, and critical thinking about controversial topics, I was relatively confident that this text would not be seen as offensive in the way that it might in a more conservative community. I know that in a different context, with less mature students, I would make a different choice; however, in this situation, this graphic novel was an appropriate and thought-provoking text choice.

Beginning with the book's cover itself, on which appears the subtitle, *Memory— Lies—Art—Power,* and the Publishers Weekly review quote, "A dense and fiercely intelligent work," this book's potential to provoke educative discussion was apparent. It is a frame story, the introductory narrative of which depicts the internal conflicts of the protagonist, Louise, a sculptor who sets off from her home in Vancouver to travel through Europe after a tragic accident. She is propelled into a search for meaning by feelings of guilt when a young activist who is inspired by her work falls to his death

Figure 3.1: *The Listener*, p. 292–293

Source: Lester, D. (2011). *The Listener*. Winnipeg, MB: Arbeiter Ring Publishing, p. 292–293. Used by permission of the author.

while hanging a protest banner. Panels depicting this incident open the novel, interspersed with panels showing Louise on a typical day, sketching, listening to music, and talking on the phone. From the very first page, the book inspired thoughtful discussion about the place of social action in the students' own lives. Some of them were involved in social justice activism through the extracurricular group that I co-facilitated with a teaching colleague at our school, and many considered themselves to be developing artists; the book's treatment of contemporary questions regarding activism and the responsibility of an artist was very relevant to them.

On the title page of the book, Pablo Picasso is quoted as questioning, "What do you think an artist is? An imbecile who only has eyes if he is a painter, or ears if he is a musician ... He is at the same time a political being, constantly alive to world events" (as quoted in Lester, 2011, p. 3). This expresses a key theme of the story, powerfully "hammered in" (pun intended) by the final two-page spread depicting a massive hammer as part of an art installation; the ironic humour of the passerby's comment, "I don't get it," plays with the whole question of the messages that works of art convey to an audience.

Key ideas and themes are presented and reinforced in multimodal forms throughout the novel. Each chapter opens with a quote; my personal favourite, from chapter 1—"Ah, but the true protest is beauty," by musician Phil Ochs (as quoted in Lester, 2011, p. 9)—explores a recurrent motif, the link between aesthetics and social action. Not only is the main character an artist, but in her quest for self, she travels through dozens of European art galleries—venues that are portrayed in distinctive panels. Louise's occasional verbal comments and reflections in thought bubbles while in these galleries raise further interesting questions. Statements such as "Ideas are not always to scale" (Lester, 2011, p. 152) and questions such as "Should I just make art that people like?" and "Why didn't Bonnard paint all the way to the edge of the canvas?" (Lester, 2011, p. 150) served as invitations to fascinating class discussions about art and philosophy.

Studying stylistic choices and their effect is an important part of any literary study, and this graphic novel provided unique opportunities for such practice. In order to maximize students' investment in close reading and close viewing of the work, I divided the book's chapters among the students, assigning each a portion of the text to analyze in detail. Having already gained experience in close reading of poetry, short stories, and passages from novels through doing oral and written commentaries, the students had developed skills in questioning a text in intricate detail and analyzing the effects of a text creator's choices upon an audience. They practised transferring these skills to a multimedia text through detailed annotation of a single page of *The Listener*, then went on to prepare notes on assigned chapters. These notes were then used as each student facilitated a Socratic seminar-style group discussion of an individual chapter. These discussions were the heart of our study and proved to be my strongest confirmation of the merits of this text choice. All of the students actively participated, contributing insightful and perceptive comments about not only the parts that were their assigned responsibility, but about every chapter; discussions inevitably extended

Figure 3.2: *The Listener*, p. 77

Source: Lester, D. (2011). *The Listener*. Winnipeg, MB: Arbeiter Ring Publishing, p. 77. Used by permission of the author.

Figure 3.3: *The Listener*, p. 78

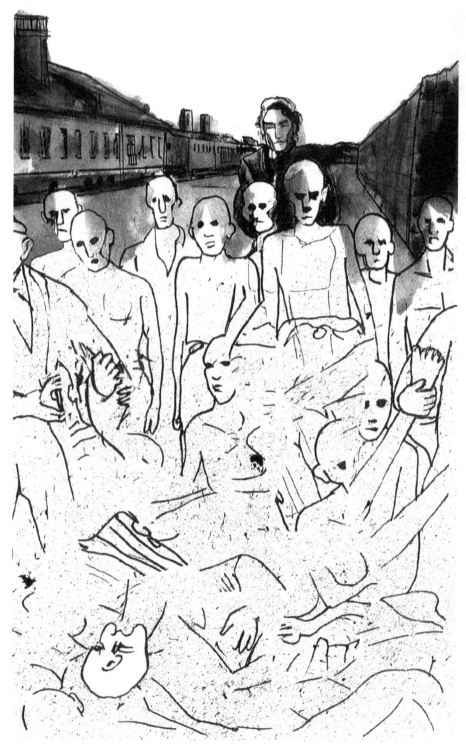

Source: Lester, D. (2011). *The Listener*. Winnipeg, MB: Arbeiter Ring Publishing, p. 78. Used by permission of the author.

over time. Despite the fact that some students were critical of Lester's artistic style, they were nonetheless able to interpret the story and analyze the ideas and stylistic choices, both verbal and visual, in great depth.

Particularly impressive was the students' demonstration of visual literacy through exploring the stylistic choices in Lester's art. We discussed a wide range of techniques that became evident upon close viewing. Interestingly, with this group of students, font design was one of the most heavily criticized aspects of the novel—I discovered that the students were far more sophisticated in their assessment of this aspect of graphic design than I was. While I hadn't previously paid much attention to the uniform, generic quality of the speech balloons, some of the graphic novel aficionados in the class found the font so disruptive that it was hard for them to see past this stylistic element to enjoy reading the book.

One visual technique that they agreed that Lester used effectively is the refraction of drawings depicting the typical image of Hitler in his pose as a powerful speaker (Lester, 2011, p. 166–171). Lester frames a less familiar depiction of Hitler's path to leadership within the story of Louise's quest through Europe. Lester emphasizes Hitler's ordinary humanity and lack of power in these sequences to reinforce the idea that the framed story portrays: There was a tipping point when Hitler could have been defeated if enough people had recognized both his potential danger and his vulnerability and had acted in time. Another series of images serves to undercut the iconic status that Hitler has held since World War II, even by those who revile him. It was only upon seeing Hitler portrayed on the toilet that my students and I reflected that the previous images of him that we had encountered, although they appeared in documentaries denouncing his evil acts, had been originally created by the Nazi party in carefully managed photos or video footage. We were struck by the power of imagery, and I found, like my students, that the drawings in Lester's book did more to detract from Hitler's mythical power than the narration of those documentaries—despite their critical message—ever had.

One student prepared a multimedia presentation for the class that explored the many ways in which Lester used another visual technique, superimposition, in this book. An example is a series of images that portrays Louise in a tour of a concentration camp; ghostly outlines of the former inmates take up increasing amounts of the image as reflections on their experience increasingly possess her thoughts.

The presentation powerfully conveyed one of the ways in which a graphic novel is unique as a literary/art form; this student's insightful ideas were alluded to frequently by other students in subsequent class discussions as they pointed out additional examples of superimposition in the chapters they had studied. Additionally, Lester plays with a wide variety of sequential art conventions: From splitting a single scene into a standard nine-panel format on page 128 to filling the frame with a single image on page 129, Lester juxtaposes different compositions, layouts, and drawing styles for a multitude of artistic purposes. One of our liveliest debates arose from our reading of the article "Alan Moore and the Graphic Novel: Confronting the Fourth Dimension" (Bernard & Carter, 2004), in which the authors argue that comics and graphic novels represent the epitome of postmodern art, transcending cubism and other styles by being able to bridge space and time in a way that is unique to sequential art. The idea that comics are a higher form of art than painting and sculpture drew outraged refutation by some of the budding artists in the class. Despite their impassioned arguments defending the skill and knowledge required for the various genres they studied in their art classes, they were intrigued by the authors' ideas about how comics graphically depict relationships in time (the fourth dimension). The article served to encourage us to focus our attention upon those ways in which graphic novels are a unique genre.

Studying *The Listener* also deepened the students' understanding of historical events, integrating well with what they were learning in other subjects, particularly social studies. Having recently studied dictators and the interwar period in their social studies class, this graphic novel provided a unique opportunity to deepen their understanding. At the end of the book, Lester provides a chronology of related events, from 1933 to 2010, and an appendix describing "Animators, Cartoonists, & Designers in the Third Reich." In the author's notes that follow, Lester details the historical references, quotations, and fictionalizing of actual events that appear throughout the book. Partway through the novel, while in Europe, the main character encounters an elderly couple, Rudolph and Marie, who recount the story of their experiences during the period of Hitler's rise to power in the early 1930s, focusing particularly on the Lippe election of 1933. The characters introduce the framed story, "a story with scars" (Lester, 2011, p. 57), about their experiences in the post–World War I German Free State of Lippe. Over several subsequent chapters, Lester portrays, through Marie and Rudolph's recollections, the period in German history during which Hitler's rise to power was by no means inevitable, and, in fact, even Josef Goebbels wrote in his diary, "It is high time we attain power, although for the moment there is not the slightest chance of it. All chances have disappeared" (Lester, 2011, p.115). The framed story conveys a theme that addresses the key question of agency in political and social issues. Reading a text that directly addresses agency naturally opened up the floor for discussion of this important topic.

Depicting a tour through a concentration camp, Lester takes us back to a time when Hitler's rise "could just as well be otherwise" (Lester, 2011, p. 3). Framing the historical narrative within the contemporary "travelogue" has the effect of heightening the reader's awareness of parallel concerns between the famous events of the past and experiences in the present, a theme that one of my students explored insightfully in a multimedia presentation that he made to the class; this proved to be an important culminating moment for our study.

In this pilot project, I did not encounter any administrative or parental resistance to the book's use, and student response to the graphic novel was generally positive. This is not the type of high-action, brightly coloured depiction of superheroes' adventures that one might expect of the graphic novel genre, though, and not all students found it engaging. Images are black and white, representing techniques drawn as much from traditional modes of visual art as from comic conventions, and the work is actually

Student Presentation

The class gathers expectantly; they enjoy being an audience for each other's IB oral presentations. Matthew opens by saying, "In my presentation, I am attempting to use some of what we have learned about the power of visual images to communicate my ideas about *The Listener*." He goes on to do this by showing a series of slides, each depicting a pair of photos without captions on a black background. He is juxtaposing pictures from the Nazi era and eerily similar images of events from Canadian history. For instance, on the first slide, the central focus of the first image is a shattered storefront; a uniformed officer stands to the left of the broken glass windows and door. Closer inspection reveals German signs above the window, a clue that this is a photo taken of the infamous *Kristallnacht*, "the night of broken glass," the massive coordinated attack on Jews throughout the German Reich on November 9, 1938. Beside it is a photo of shattered windows, with a uniformed officer in the exact same position to the left of the image. The students in the audience gasp as Matthew shows the next slide, which reveals the following caption: "Anti-Asian Riot 1907: British Canadians storm oriental businesses in downtown Vancouver, destroying signs and smashing windows. Rioters motivated by unemployment, blamed Asians for taking their job opportunities. Led by the Asiatic Exclusion League, which had gathered a mob of 9000 white people." None of us were previously aware of this event in our own country.

Other slides juxtapose images of Jewish families lined up entering concentration camps with Japanese-Canadians queued for transport to internment camps, and the poverty of pre-war Germany with the living conditions of the poorest residents of Vancouver's Downtown East Side. The power of Matthew's presentation comes from the directly parallel composition of the pairs of images that he researched, selected, and effectively displayed, and each slide draws a chorus of appreciation and amazement. The comparison between the two contexts is heightened and made poignant through the multimodal representation. His key message is communicated through the final slide, in which he concludes that there are "striking similarities between events in BC and Nazi Germany. Discrimination and poverty can be found in all nations and throughout history. Recognizing these connections gives us better insight and knowledge into and about the world around us." As the audience applauds, I reflect that my student has conveyed, far more effectively than I ever could, one of the most important reasons for studying texts such as *The Listener*. He has shown an understanding that it is not the writing style nor the images nor the thematic content alone that moves the audience, but the combined impact of the multimodal text or presentation.

in some ways quite cerebral and slow-paced. As such, it would not be a suitable text for less mature audiences, particularly considering the graphic sexual content previously mentioned. Discussion of the political implications of the genre could take place as part of the study of other graphic novels, and many aspects of visual literacy could be addressed through other works as well. The strength of using this particular text was that it provided an opportunity for exploring all of these issues in addition to the many artistic, political, and philosophical themes multimodally embedded in the book's content.

Bill Howe: Teaching *Scorched* by Wajdi Mouawad

I have struggled with questions of social justice and education from the day I decided to go into teaching. Like many teachers, I started my career many years ago vowing to make a difference ... to seek positive change in the world. And for years I held on to the belief that simple exposure and discussion, battling ignorance head on, would be all that was needed.

But more and more I've been forced to acknowledge the limitations of the purely cognitive domain of knowledge. Though unaware of it, perhaps I have always unconsciously known this as I recognized the distinctive role of literature from the beginning. Something happens in the encounter between text and reader that no activist or teacher, no didactic or pedantic lecture, and no list of facts or statistics can ever duplicate. When story meets audience, there is so much more going on than a simple coming to know or realization in the cognitive sense of the ever-present Bloom's taxonomy.

At this point in my career, much more than the immediately visible and readily articulated reactions and responses to text, I am interested in what goes on below the surface, under the skin, so to speak: the often delayed, often unconscious, and often invisible ruptures that occur at the molecular level within the mind and body of the reader. The shifts and changes that might take place without anyone knowing. Those which might be labelled the aesthetic effects of the literary encounter.

Such was my own experience when I had the opportunity to see the play *Scorched*, by Canadian playwright Wajdi Mouawad (2009), performed at the Citadel Theatre in Edmonton in 2009. As its title in both English and the original French, *Incendies*, suggests, it is a play that is not so easily forgotten. At the end of the play, after its rather shocking final revelation, I remember a stillness in the theatre unlike any I had felt before or have felt since. In contrast to the usual whisperings and rumblings of audiences making their way out of the theatre, everyone in the room remained seated for what seemed like several minutes. Something happened to me that day, something seared into my soul that I have yet to fully comprehend. In other words, something clearly "affected" me as I experienced the aesthetic forces of the play that defied language. Something felt in the body that was paradoxically both darkly discomfiting and yet warmly life-affirming. A beautiful ache that demanded my attention.

Needless to say, when the opportunity arose through the Teaching Canadian Literature for Social Justice project, after considerable deliberation, it was this text that I ultimately chose to work with in my classroom in the 2013–2014 school year with three separate classes, ranging from 23 to 39 students enrolled in English 30-1 (regular Grade 12). The reason for my initial reticence would likely be clear to anyone familiar with the text, as it raises a number of challenges for both students and teachers.

Admitting inspiration from the likes of Kafka and the Greek tragedies, *Scorched* follows the paths of a brother and sister who meet in the first scene to hear their mother's will. Both siblings have clearly borne the impact of growing up with the unspoken and unknown traumas of their mother in their own ways—with Simon entering the world of competitive boxing and for Janine, the contrasting world of university mathematics. With their mother having inexplicably gone silent five years earlier at the age of 60, the children have reacted in their own unique ways, perhaps in attempts, successfully or not, to control their own narratives. Within the will, however, they are both challenged by the mother's final wishes and, though reluctant, both embark on a journey of discovering their mother's story, which understandably, is inextricably tied to their own. In many ways, the play unfolds in a kind of Oedipal nightmare etched through the conflict-ridden landscape of an unnamed civil war and revolving around the mysteries of their mother's past and sudden muteness, as well as truths pointing to their own unresolved identities.

In keeping with the theme of this chapter, my approach from the very beginning was intent on multimodality. Students were able to read and reread parts of the play, imagine how these parts might be most effectively played out on stage, experiment themselves with scenes that stood out for them, listen as others took turns reading passages from multiple tonal perspectives, and ultimately try their hand at writing and representing the "truths" they took away from their felt experiences of the play.

It seems clear from both my own experiences and my observations of the various ways my students encountered the play that once we move beyond a purely cognitive focus into the domain of aesthetics and affect, we become aware of the various ways it is possible to receive a story. The nature of aesthetics encompasses the multiple ways in which a body senses or experiences affect, often without our awareness. And the play *Scorched*, already multimodal insofar as all theatrical experiences are, works on, through, or under the skin of the reader/audience as much as through the eyes and ears. As Beckett once said in a letter to Jessica Tandy, "I am not unduly concerned with intelligibility. I hope the piece may work on the nerves of the audience not on its intellect" (as quoted in Simone, 1988, p. 57). And while *Scorched* is frighteningly intelligible, it is first and foremost a visceral experience.

Although moving enough to keep even the most cynical students engaged, *Scorched* is not a simple play by any means. Much of this difficulty, aside from the obvious challenges of obscenity and violence, lies in the complexity of staging and the unique blocking of scenes, with different events and different time periods often crisscrossing the stage simultaneously. With so much happening at once, it is important that, should teachers choose to have students perform the scenes, each student's character is clearly identified. As just having characters read out their parts still left some students confused as to what was happening, I found it useful to clear a space in the room and try to create the scenes as theatrically true to the script as possible. Given the richness of the script, there are numerous opportunities for students to enter into fruitful discussions about how scenes might be presented, where characters should be positioned (blocked) relative to each other, and how these directorial choices might be justified dramatically or thematically. As an aside, the play, in French, was made into a film (with English subtitles), which was nominated for numerous awards. Though I chose, due to time restrictions, not to address it in my classes, it would have understandably added an additional mode for students to experience, compare, and contrast to those already discussed.

Much of the intensity within the play is opened through moments of silence. Not only does silence punctuate the play, literally as the playwright frequently inscribes "silence" within the stage directions, and dramatically as the flow of action, juxtaposition of time periods, and scenes of shock on stage evoke unscripted silences, the motif of silence within the play is mirrored by the dominant reaction to the play.

Considering the content of the play, in terms of language, sexuality, and violence—none of which I consider gratuitous—this was far from an easy decision. A justifiable caution surrounds many such literary selections, especially for teachers faced with restrictions or pressures within more conservative communities or under more austere administrative constraints. As my colleague Karen pointed out earlier in this chapter, the question of censorship is ever present.

And it is definitely warranted if one is to take seriously the risk of potential harm such a powerful experience might impart on students. To take up the questions of social justice in the classroom is, perhaps intrinsically, to practise a dangerous and risky pedagogy. Education that attends to social justice, that accepts a certain challenge to take acts of injustice seriously risks, I wish to argue, discomfort and even pain or anguish in the classroom.

In recognizing the principle that defines, in part, both the authority and responsibility of every teacher—"in loco parentis"—I am especially sensitive to both the obligation and the privilege of choosing "appropriate" literature. As our own professional body defines the principle, "the teacher stands, in relation to the student, in the position of a caring parent, as an unofficial guardian. This concept not only allows the teacher some of the privileges of a parent but also brings with it added responsibilities for the protection of pupils" (Alberta Teachers' Association, 2013, p. 24). As such, I am ever cognizant of certain imprecating fingers being pointed at me, exemplified perhaps by arguments such as that of Megan Cox Gurdon, whose article in the *Wall Street Journal* attacked teachers for bringing unreasonably "dark" literature into the classroom. Though primarily targeting young adult readers, the sentiments Gurdon expresses in her article are not unlike those many teachers such as myself either hear or fear on a regular basis:

> If books show us the world, teen fiction can be like a hall of fun-house mirrors, constantly reflecting back hideously distorted portrayals of what life is. There are of course exceptions, but a careless young reader—or one who seeks out depravity—will find himself surrounded by images not of joy or beauty but of damage, brutality and losses of the most horrendous kinds. (Gurdon, 2011)

In heeding my responsibilities as an educator, I am very much aware of the precarious blade upon which I walk. On the one hand, there is an opportunity to introduce a text which not only raises issues of social justice, but does so in a way that is deeply affecting and that might stand a chance of sparking real change. On the other, paradoxically its effectiveness lies in the very essence from which it draws its strength. In light of John Stuart Mill's harm principle, holding that a person's actions ought to be limited in so far as to prevent harm to others, is the choice of such a text defendable?

By all accounts, while I would argue that the portrayal of *Scorched* is hardly a "hideously distorted" one, it would certainly qualify as a text that, at least on the surface, might be challenged on the grounds which Gurdon questions and, in application of Mill's harm principle, would be a candidate for pulling from the list of school text options.

The question for me continues to be whether or not any real or lasting harm is actually instilled, or whether certain pain is ever justified. The longer I have dwelled on the choice and remembered how important the encounter with the play had been for me, the more I have interrogated the foundations of my hesitation. How often had I heard such cautionary statements shared between teachers: "This was a fantastic book, but I certainly wouldn't dare teach it in class!" Is such a caution actually grounded in real experience?

This question brought me to several additional questions: Is the experience of violence in the classroom justified in the context of a pedagogy for social justice? At what point does it become inappropriate, excessive, sensationalistic, or numbing, clearly antithetical to the ends of social justice education? In what ways is any education for social justice intrinsically violent?

And I wonder, too, whether or not we can actually end up doing more harm by avoiding the pain of experiencing certain works, in the name of safety, than we might by carefully and sensitively risking such experiences in the classroom, in the hopes that such works might affect the kinds of change that go beyond a well-crafted written essay. I realize, too, that at the heart of all education is a kind of violence.

As Mark Bracher explains,

> the whole purpose of education is to change students in one way or another, which means that education as such inevitably entails a certain amount of "pedagogic violence" [citing Warsham]. As currently practiced, literary pedagogy, like many other elements of education, contributes to the production of docile subjects for global capitalism

through, for example, enforcing classroom punctuality, reliability, obedience, and subordination. Moreover, any social criticism or peda- gogy that aims to contribute to beneficial social change must assume that it is both possible and justifiable to change students' behaviours. (2006, p. 465)

In the case of *Scorched,* it occurred to me, as we were working our way through the text, that there was a difference between the kind of violence conveyed in the text and that which saturates popular media, which many believe result in a kind of desensitization to real violence. And of course there is a difference, as noted earlier, between the level of violence described in this play and the somewhat muted or dulled narratives which generally pass as acceptable for school anthologies and classroom instruction, which is often felt to result in desensitization. As the Chilean artist Alfredo Jarr asks, "How does an image of pain survive in a sea of consumption?" (cited in Walker, 2010, p.76). Over the years, I realized that texts intended to raise issues of social injustice, but selected for inclusion in anthologies or syllabi so as to comply with what are no doubt imagined to be the most conservative of community standards of safety and acceptability, fail to arouse hardly a rise of the eyebrow, except in dismissal. Far too often, the issues in a text that I had anticipated would suffice to spark a shift of thinking, or even action, in students faded into little more than a glance at the clock.

Through the style, language, and imagery, not to mention a very complex but very moving series of parallel narratives, Mouawad creates an experience that far surpasses what is usually judged as "acceptable" for the classroom. But there is no question students leave the classroom deep in thought or feeling and wide awake. Though fictional, it is very visceral and very real, perhaps offering a kind of antidote to the widespread expressions of apathy generally accompanying communications of injustice in the news. As Jarr points out, "If I stick to the raw information, it's not interesting as art. I want to be able to move you, challenge you, touch you. I want to be able to irritate you, provoke you; that's a political task" (as quoted in Walker, 2014, p. 3). For the very reasons others might argue it should not be brought into the classroom, the violence of texts such as *Scorched,* so unlike and so unrepresentative of anything students have encountered elsewhere, may be one of the best justifications for actually doing so. In speaking of the aesthetic experience of reading, Iser reminds us of this challenge of the unfamiliar:

Every text we read draws a different boundary within our personality, so that the virtual background (the real "me") will take on a different form, according to the theme of the text concerned. This is inevitable, if only for the fact that the relationship between alien theme and virtual back- ground is what makes it possible for the unfamiliar to be understood. (1972, p. 299)

Although there are, of course, many ways of approaching this or any other work, within the context of social justice, I chose to consider *Scorched* as a work of testimony.

Mouawad's own life has clear biographical connections to the story depicted in the play. He was born in Lebanon, where he lived until the age of six. In 1975, the year the Lebanese Civil War broke out, after two bombs were dropped in close vicinity to his home, his family moved to Paris, and later to Montreal. As Dan Rubin explains, "His parents did not talk about the home they had left behind, or why they had left it." When Mouawad later read about the "horrors" of the war, he explained, "My parents weren't people with the emotional armour to deal with a civil war ... It was this silence that I have tried to name" (2012, p. 4).

In describing one of the sources of inspiration for the play, Mouawad recalls that in 2000, he encountered the story of Soha Bechara:

> Bechara, a Lebanese Christian with pro-Muslim sympathies, had attempted to assassinate the commander of the Israeli supported South Lebanon Army during the Lebanese Civil War and was subsequently incarcerated in the notorious Khiam prison for a decade. She was sentenced to solitary confinement in a cell adjacent to the room where inmates were tortured. "For ten years," Mouawad told CBC News, "she heard the crying and pain of the tortured. To try not to become mad, she began to sing. She sang the songs she knew, popular songs. The people in the jail, who heard this woman but never saw her, called her 'The Woman Who Sings.' She gave them hope and courage to survive." Bechara became Mouawad's inspiration for Nawal, the mother whose history is uncovered by her children in *Incendies*. (Rubin, 2012, p. 6)

Following the work of Shoshanna Felman, the witness/victim of the initial trauma struggles to convey the "truth" of the event, often sharing their testimony in the form of language or image understood in this case, as the work of art. The testimony of art manages to maintain the complexity and difficulty of the initial experience and itself evokes the reader or perceiver to become another witness who in turn will offer testimony to their account. These, I can only hope, will include the readers and audience members of *Scorched*.

In the footsteps of the highly influential French playwright Antonin Artaud, Mouawad seems to be exploring the difficult experiences of loss, identity, and cultural and personal trauma through his own generation of affect in *Scorched*. For my students, working through the running motif, both real and metaphorical, of silence, much of our classroom discussions focused on the constantly circulating air of judgement, both for the characters within the context of the play and for the readers and viewers observing the actions and words of the characters. What seems is certainly not what necessarily is, and as histories, both cultural and personal, are revealed, students are left struggling with their own shifting impressions. Often, in mirroring these revelations, such reflections in the play are generally expressed in silence.

In her work with trauma theory, Berlak, too, points out that

> if the major purpose of teaching is to unsettle taken for granted views and feelings, then confrontation, with its attendant trauma, and reflection on the trauma are necessary. Thus, confrontation and the intense emotional repercussions that are likely to follow may be essential to the process of eroding entrenched cultural acceptance of injustices such as racism. (2004, p. 123–124)

In my experience, this was most movingly affirmed with the story of one young student, who came to me at the end of one class bursting with emotion. Though I had provided plenty of warnings before we began the unit and reminded students of their right to choose to work on something else in the library, this student had chosen to stay, even though, unbeknownst to me, she had lived through her own trauma of sexual assault earlier in her life. Needless to say, had I known, she would have been the source of my greatest concern. Somewhat serendipitously, however, she explained how the play had allowed her to face her own trauma; it was the best thing she had experienced in years. She was somehow "free."

In the interest of aesthetic force, as opposed to cognitive, Twain's adage—"Don't say 'the old lady screamed;' bring her on and let her scream!"—speaks to the depth of impact of a play that more directly depicts the experience of injustice, even though such impact may come with a generous dose of discomfort. And when such encounters are marked by the flow and residence of affect in the body, it speaks to the residue of such experience held long after the reading or observation is completed.

Conclusion

Returning to the pedagogical challenge that was raised in the opening to this chapter, of negotiating the many "lifeworlds" that we and our students inhabit, we propose that one response may be to engage students in the reflective process regarding text selection and, within that process, to actively seek out multimodal works of literature for classroom study. Additionally, though it may be initially difficult for students, rich discussions often follow from having students share reflections around what content (and potentially what styles), what modes, and what combinations of content/style and mode affect them most directly or most powerfully.

As two secondary school teachers who encountered the inevitable challenges of pushing past previous boundaries of form and content, Karen and Bill also experienced unexpected rewards in the form of student engagement in deep, sometimes trans-formative discourses. When students participate along with teachers in a pedagogy of discomfort, the classroom becomes a space for honest discussion and validation of risk-taking. The teachers in this study modelled two levels of risk-taking, in their initial selection of controversial content and literary forms and further in their approaches to class activities and reflective discussion of those decisions and activities. By moving outside their own comfort zones, they nonetheless created a "safe space" where all members of the class could be authentically engaged in an embodied experience of literary themes. The risks of harm due to the pain evoked by powerful literature, the vulnerability necessary to subject our attitudes and decisions to shared evaluation, and the challenge to experience our own agency in contrast to a learned apathy—all of these require such a safe space. Although the affective and analytical experiences discussed are in some ways representative of all literature study, the results of this study indicate that there is great promise in exploring how transformative literary experiences can be particularly evoked through multimodal means.

Keywords

- art
- discomfort
- engagement
- graphic novels
- Lebanon
- multimodal
- multiliteracies
- plays
- transformation
- trauma
- World War II

Reflection Questions

1. How, and to what extent, can we engage our students in a sense of agency in social and political issues within the relatively cloistered environment of the classroom? What is the place for involving students in the text selection decisions?

2. How can teachers encourage students to move beyond superficial analyses of the differences among various modes of experience, for example, the difference between seeing a play live, watching the film version, or reading it in class as a script, novelization, or in graphic form?

3. What are various ways in which students can be encouraged to move beyond multimodal text analysis to multimodal text creation? What is the potential for this to have an impact on student engagement in social justice work?

4. How do teachers negotiate a balance between safe choices and risk-taking in text selection? What impact does censorship, particularly of a voluntary nature, have on teaching practice and student experience?

5. How might the different means by which texts are processed—hearing, seeing, feeling, thinking, reading, and conversing—provoke different audience responses and potentially motivate different levels of social engagement?

References

Bender-Slack, D. (2010). Texts, talk ... and fear? English language arts teachers negotiate social justice teaching. *English Education, 42*(2), 181–203.

Berlak, A. C. (2004) Confrontation and pedagogy: Cultural secrets, trauma, and emotion in anti-oppressive pedagogies. In M. Boler (Ed.), *Democratic dialogue in education: Troubling speech, disturbing silence* (pp. 123–144). New York, NY: Peter Lang.

Bernard, M., & Carter, J. (2004). Alan Moore and the graphic novel: Confronting the fourth dimension. *ImageTexT, 1*(2) .

Boler, M., & Zembylas, M. (2003). Discomforting truths: The emotional terrain of understanding difference. In P. Tryfonas (Ed.), *Pedagogies of difference: Rethinking education for social change.* New York, NY: Routledge.

Bracher, M. (2006). Teaching for social justice: Reeducating the emotions through literary study. *Journal of Advanced Composition, 26*(3/4), 463–512.

Burmark, L. (2008). Visual literacy. In N. Frey & D. Fisher. (Eds.), *Teaching visual literacy: Using comic books, graphic novels, anime, cartoons and more to develop comprehension and thinking skills* (pp. 5–21). Thousand Oaks, CA: Corwin Press.

Carter, J. (2008). Comics, the canon, and the classroom. In N. Frey & D. Fisher. (Eds.), *Teaching visual literacy: Using comic books, graphic novels, anime, cartoons, and more to develop critical thinking skills* (pp. 47–60). Thousand Oaks, CA: Corwin Press.

Gurdon, M. C. (2011, June 4). Darkness too visible. *The Wall Street Journal.* Retrieved from http://www.wsj.com/articles/SB10001424052702303657404576357622592697038/

Iser, W. (1972). The reading process: A phenomenological approach. *New Literary History, 3*(2), 279–299. Retrieved from http://www.jstor.org/stable/468316/

Jacobs, D. (2007). More than words: Comics as a means of teaching multiple literacies. *English Journal, 96*(3), 19–25.

Jewitt, C. (2008). Multimodality and literacy in school classrooms. *Review of Research in Education, 32,* 241–267.

Lester, D. (2011). *The listener.* Winnipeg, MB: Arbeiter Ring Publishing.

Mouawad, W. (2009). *Scorched.* (L. Gaboriau, Trans.). Toronto, ON: Playwrights Canada Press.

The New London Group. (2000). A pedagogy of multiliteracies: Designing social futures. In B. Cope & M. Kalantzis (Eds.), *Multiliteracies: Literacy learning and the design of social futures* (pp. 9–38). London, ON: Routledge.

Rubin, D. (2012). Wajdi Mouawad: At home with words. *American Conservatory Theatre Presents Words on Plays, 18*(4), 4–10.

Simone, R. T. (1988). Beckett's other trilogy: Not I, Footfalls and Rockaby. In R. Davis & L. Butler (Eds.), *Make sense who may: Essays on Samuel Beckett's later works* (pp. 56–65). Totowa, NJ: Barnes and Noble Books.

Walker, S. R. (2010). Artmaking and the sinthome. *Visual Arts Research, 36*(2).

Walker, S. R. (2014). Artmaking and the sinthome. *SYNNYT/ORIGINS: Finnish Studies in Art Education, 2.* Retrieved from https://wiki.aalto.fi/download/attachments/97623342/1. Walker%20Synnyt.pdf?version=1&modificationDate=1412238507891&api=v2/

Chapter 4

Challenges for Teachers and Schools: Creating Spaces for LGBTQ Literature in Schools

Anne Burke and Aedon Young

Teaching through a social justice lens often requires complex manoeuvring on the part of the classroom teacher. Teachers may need to negotiate between colleagues, parents, and other social communities' conflicting views about children's literature. As a result, the choice of resources, subject matter, and teaching pedagogical approach may be constrained. Some constraining factors are rooted in self-monitoring or censoring; others are related to specific and structural forces, such as mandated assessments or curricula; and still others are hindered by perceived opinions of others and the possible repercussions thereof. In this chapter, we consider what it means for schools to consider the gender marginalization of youth in their school and highlight challenges faced by teachers who choose to adopt an agenda allowing youth to find their voice. The chosen school, Jefferson Junior High School (JJH; a pseudonym), was one that was considered a leading school in social justice school initiatives. It was one of the first schools to take on the new LGBTQ community-building initiatives as outlined by the provincial government for schools. We view Jefferson Junior High School's project through two separate theoretical lenses: community of practice (Lave & Wengar, 1998) and critical literacy (Clarke & Whitney, 2009; Comber & Nixon, 2005; Jones & Enriquez, 2009; Macedo, 2005). Communities of practice are groups of individuals that interact on an ongoing basis due to similar interests or beliefs. Critical literacy in the classroom encourages students to think critically about the texts they encounter and relate them to their everyday lives both in and outside the classroom. These approaches reflect community intersections and the manner in which critical engagement with children's literature may not only bridge interests and questions but enable "voice and agency" through diverse children's literature, such as that of the emerging genre of Lesbian, Gay, Bisexual, Transgender, Queer (LGBTQ).

When students participate together on particular interests or issues, such as those concerning LGBTQ individuals or allies, they can learn from one another and from literature they encounter (which speaks to contemporary issues such as those of gender and sexual orientation) in order to enhance their personal engagement with a text. This reflexivity around identity cultivates in the reader a better understanding of current issues and may facilitate a challenge to society's prejudice. When we use a sociocultural lens to challenge prejudicial belief systems, we see how critical pedagogical openings can situate literacy in a transformative light where it is beyond "the mechanical learning of reading and writing skills" (Macedo, 2005, p. 12), to a political phenomenon that "must be analyzed within the context of a theory of power relations and an understanding of social and cultural reproduction and production" (Macedo, 2005, p. 13). In our society of multimedia, it is essential that children become critically literate in order to mediate the texts they encounter and resist stereotypes. Critical literacy mandates students to assume that "power relations within language construct inequalities and systematically marginalize particular groups in society" (Jones & Enriquez, 2009, p. 149). The school housed 800 students, with 30 percent of the school population being English as another language (EAL) learners. There were 55 teachers on staff with a large administration team. The library doubled as a classroom and housed a large collection of books of varied genres. We reflect upon critical choices made in the face of different types of marginalization, and how these were chosen to respond to the school community needs.

We began our discussion around communities of practice (Lave & Wenger, 1998), recognizing ourselves as an organized group of individuals or participants with a common interest in creating diverse spaces for diverse learning and acceptance in and out of the school context.

Our Passion and a Need for Literature

As a way to address the needs of the LGBTQ community within our school, our passion for children's literature guided the way. The research questions we addressed were the following: (1) How may we contribute to our students' understanding of LGBTQ knowledge and understanding through the use of children's literature?; and (2) What social, cultural, and political factors should we consider as we cultivate a library in our desire to address these needs? In particular, as a critical inquiry group of teachers who met monthly to discuss social justice issues and children's literature resources, we further discussed how to establish an ongoing collaboration in order to acquire new or deeper knowledge of LGBTQ issues within our school and through the use of the multiple perspectives brought forth by children's literature. We considered how we might work together to address the forces, which challenge us day-to-day, to provide an inclusive teaching agenda. We focus this discussion around a Newfoundland and Labrador provincial government mandate in 2012, which announced funding to create a new initiative to promote gay-straight alliances (GSAs) in schools through professional development and resource packages for teachers. We agree with Bell (2007) in that

> The goal of social justice education is to enable people to develop the critical analytical tools necessary to understand oppression and their own socialization within oppressive systems, and to develop a sense of agency and capacity to interrupt and change oppressive patterns and behaviours in themselves and in the institutions and communities of which they are a part. (p. 2)

In our professional learning group, we engaged in a book circle, which used children's literature as a bridge to address possible marginalization in our school, lending authentic and personal voices to the local and global issues around sexual identity—issues that are of primary concern to adolescents. Children's literature can, in turn, be shared with others as a way of engendering social change. Emancipatory actions can encourage students to write, read, and rewrite the world and the word, linking literacy to human agency and the power to "effect social transformation" (Janks, 2010, p. 161). As such, we share our stories of struggle, challenge, and success in making our school a safe and caring space, and more importantly, one of acceptance empowered through quality children's literature, which is based on our teachers' professional understanding of their school community and of an emerging genre.

Understanding Our School Context as a Community of Practice

In the early 1990s, Jean Lave and Etienne Wenger developed the theory of "communities of practice." Defined simply, a community of practice is a group of people that interact regularly for a common purpose. Communities of practice are found in everyday life—we are all members of groups either through our home, our work, or our leisure activities. A community of practice may be official, like a work group or a social club, or it may be informal. Although the exact nature may change, it is how the members develop similar values, beliefs, and ways of doing things that characterize a community of practice.

A community of practice has three defining commonalities. This first is membership. A community of practice requires that all members share a common interest. Schools need to take active steps in order to foster a sense of belonging and connectedness among their students. Students can be from a wide range of backgrounds and represent different cultural beliefs. Schools provide an environment where students can be exposed to diverse ideas that allow them to gain an understanding of the wider world. Schools are first and foremost a community to which students belong no matter a student's background. In this particular case, to foster a sense of belonging among students who identify as LGBTQ, Jefferson Junior High has an LGBTQ club where students can meet and spend time with peers. JJH has taken steps to ensure LGBTQ students feel a sense of membership and belonging to their school community.

How the community functions is the second feature of a community of practice. Members engage in discussion, share ideas, and interact to help each other. The LGBTQ club employs initiatives related to raising awareness, such as using posters to increase knowledge of the club, celebrating Pride Day, and inviting guest speakers to the school to share their experiences. One teacher aptly describes the partnership with Spectrum, a St. John's Queer Choir, by saying, "this partnership is centered on the importance of voice and community, and a queer choir is an apt symbol for a group that needs a voice."

The final feature is the resulting capability the community produces. Members develop communal resources such as routines, experiences, vocabularies, and stories. Through the sharing of resources, members not only increase their own awareness but also develop invaluable bonds. With the support of community behind them, community members are able to conceive and achieve far more than they may have imagined alone. There is, after all, strength in numbers, as seen at JJH as teachers and students work together in establishing a space for all students that is inclusive of LBGTQ youth voices.

The notion of situated learning, also proposed by Lave and Wenger (1996), argues that learning is a social process. Together, members combine knowledge, both old and new, to solve real-life problems and situations. The idea of communities of practice and, therefore, situated learning, has cultivated a new way of thinking for organizations and learning communities. Those involved in the development of learning organizations have come to realize the benefits of community. Having more perspectives and expertise from which to draw enhances the learning of all members involved. Kendra, a participant in our study, had been with the school for six years and taught sciences and was the designated resource teacher. She observed:

> Within JJH School, there are a variety of communities of practice that I consider myself a part of. First and foremost, I believe that my school as a whole is a community. We have a common interest—to help students learn. Regardless of job description, each staff member contributes to this goal by sharing his or her knowledge and expertise.

Although individual members and numbers are valuable, it is the combined knowledge of the group that helps a community of practice reach its full potential.

Critical Literacy

Closely related to the notion of communities of practice is the idea of critical literacy. Researchers and educators today are concerned with the pedagogical process of teaching children how to critically view the world around them and understand how they can make change for their community. Vasquez (2014) acknowledges the need for teachers to offer our students opportunities to participate in the world by contributing to social change; however, to do this we need not always look far. We may, in fact, use "everyday issues and everyday texts" (p. 2) and in so doing, the spaces we negotiate with our students become personally relevant. In one interview, Kendra explores this idea, saying

> There are many children who are marginalized for many different reasons, and there are plenty of books out there about that ... it seems a lot of YA literature these days is about exactly that: bullying, depression, family issues, drugs, even the uber [*sic*] popular dystopian fiction centers around marginalized groups. But there is a need for books that will not just act as a window into someone else's experience, but will mirror their experience.

Thus, we need books that reflect the social context and reality of our students.

Clarke and Whitney (2009) make use of Stephanie Jones' critical literacy framework. The first step in this process is interpretation, which involves breaking apart the layers of text—that is, "deconstructing issues of power, perspective, and positioning in a text" (p. 532). This means teaching children not to take texts at face value but to question both the words and their meaning. Reflection by a student upon the language and images in the texts aids in the acknowledgement of power relations. Clarke and Whitney suggest that by using texts with multiple perspectives we can help students to see an issue from many points of view. By allowing students to question the text and to construct their own ideas on the text, we allow them to build a critical eye. As students ponder, question, and challenge a given text, they often make connections to their own world in order to construct their knowledge. Furthermore, by investigating how the views of the text are different from their existing framework of knowledge and beliefs, students become truly reflexive.

Clarke and Whitney (2009) say that "it is not enough just to deconstruct a text, but we also have to give the students an opportunity to use this knowledge to create new ways of thinking" (p. 533). This can be evident from reading many established genres of literature, but also newer genres such as LGBTQ and Two-Spirit literature. The term *Two-Spirit* is the approximate Indigenous equivalent of LGBTQ, referring to a male or female-bodied person with a masculine or feminine essence. Two-Spirits transcend normative gender roles, expression, and sexual orientation (NativeOUT, n.d.).

By helping our students become avid readers of many different genres, we help them to see how words give voice to those who may be marginalized or oppressed. The power of the author's story and words is emphasized, and makes room for more discussions on the influence of texts on our understanding of issues of social justice. The cycle comes full circle. Comber and Nixon (2005) aptly commented:

> Critical literacy involves teachers exploring with children how texts
> work to have particular effects in particular situations. Teachers who
> take a critical approach to literacy understand that language and images
> involve power relations; that writers, producers, advertisers and every-
> day conversationalists use particular words and images and not others.
> Their products—texts—can exclude and include and position listeners,
> readers, and viewers in different ways. (pp. 127–128)

With this important realization, teachers have to consider where to begin. How can teachers build this awareness in students? Comber and Nixon (2005) suggest that teachers should "begin from children's everyday lives" (p. 131). They acknowledge that we should take student interests, popular culture, film, videos, television, computer games, and toys, as well as other variables, into account. What children know and can communicate in our world gives them social capital and can be empowering. We need to spark this social consciousness very early in their school learning process. Quality children's literature is one effective route to engage children's interest.

Yet even more important than personal interests are the students' individual iden- tities. In the case of LGBTQ/Two-Spirit students who are already marginalized, critical literacy offers the chance for differences to be valued and upheld without one identity being prized above others. Providing LGBTQ literature to students is a step in the right direction, but it needs to be done in an environment that is accepting. JJH created such an environment through their LGBTQ club, but also through the actions of their teachers. As previously shared, teachers may face disapproval from any number of school community stakeholders and must find a way to negotiate between all of them without jeopardizing the rights of LGBTQ youth. The resource teacher interviewed recognized this and explained how another teacher in the school was an advocate: "We have a teacher who is really active and is openly out as a lesbian. She sees the value of providing such a space for students in the school, and this has helped all of us to get to better understandings and openness."

School Community Constraints

While exploring literature in a critical manner is important for students, some par- ents oppose the availability of LGBTQ literature both for educational purposes and for reading pleasure. We found out while in a focus group that Kendra, while in a contract position in British Columbia during her early career received complaints about books in the school library that featured same-sex parents: "When I arrived, one day a vol- unteer parent cornered me and told me that if I brought that type of material into the school library, and her children found it, they would deface it and she would support them." From this early confrontation, the teacher's awareness and passion for advo- cacy grew. She and her school colleagues realized that in order for LGBTQ literature to be present in schools, they would have to make an effort to actively build libraries that contained diverse literature of all types. However, she conceded that although this incident occurred ten years ago, she was surprised to find some school employees still continue to express intolerant attitudes on this subject matter:

> When I did bring some LGBTQ books in Jefferson a few years ago when I had some money to spend, an administrator at the time took a look through them and "jokingly" said that those books were pornography. He knew that this was an initiative that was important to us, one that we were pursuing and so other than his one "comment," he didn't say anything else.

At the time, she chose not to discuss anything else pertaining to the building of the collection with him or try to convince him of the importance of the literature. This speaks to the courage of this teacher to continue in the face of political pressure. Not everyone has the courage to face dissent, especially in the hierarchy of a school. Although the teacher felt strongly about the activism in which she was involved, the disparaging comments of an authority figure were still very unsettling. This teacher continued her activities with students and with teachers who felt a part of the community.

Provincial Government and the Gay-Straight Alliance

In recent years, the provincial government of Newfoundland and Labrador has provided funding for MyGSA (My Gay-Straight Alliance), a school-based club for LGBTQ students to have a "safe space" in which they can talk to other students, teachers, and advisors about personal issues. Simultaneously, the alliance intended for schools to strive to unite LGBTQ youth with allies to "work together on making their schools more welcoming for all members of their school community, regardless of sexual orientation and gender identity" (Government of Newfoundland and Labrador, n.d.). As noted in a governmental news release, the resource is intended to "help us take an important step forward in recognizing that we all have a responsibility for ensuring that all of our students are accepted, and respected, for who they are" (Government of Newfoundland and Labrador, 2012). Moreover, upon announcing the creation of the program, the provincial government "asked school districts to re-examine their existing codes of conduct, and amend them to ensure there is specific reference made to protecting and respecting all students, including those with differing sexual orientations" (Government of Newfoundland and Labrador, 2012). This call to action confirms that LGBTQ issues should be relevant not only to individuals in their daily lives, but to society as a whole.

As part of the network of MyGSA community groups across Canada, this government resource provides guidelines, plans, and informative resources to educators so that they may successfully introduce such a club into their schools. These documents are available online for public access, and they help teachers assess how the club will work in their school climate, come up with engagement activities, and also detail numerous external resources and potential sources of interest—all while operating within curriculum guidelines. Step-by-step guidelines and schedules are provided in these documents, as well as examples that show educators how to overcome challenges they may face during the program. It is a tool that educators can use to create an inclusive teaching and social environment on a daily basis.

The funding for MyGSA groups is provided to junior high and high schools (Grades 7 through 12) by the Newfoundland and Labrador provincial government. In 2012, the first year the program was implemented, the province provided $90,000 for this initiative.

Development of LGBTQ as a Genre

Canadian children's literature featuring LGBTQ characters and themes is a growing phenomenon. These books allow children to see different types of family relationships and for these relationships to become normalized and more mainstream (DePalma, 2014). According to Flores (2014), "the terms LGBT and gay-themed children's literature refer to books that deal with gay familial awareness, such as families composed of two mommies and two daddies" (p. 115). It can also refer to the depiction of characters who identify as LGBTQ, even if gender and sexual orientation does not feature prominently in the plot (Dinkins & Englert, 2015). The introduction of this type of literature in the classroom can be beneficial for teachers and students alike, introducing students to concepts of identity, social justice, and fairness (Flores, 2014). Young readers, however, may not have access to such literature for a myriad of reasons. For example, given the controversial nature of the topic, some teachers may be hesitant to introduce LGBTQ literature in the classroom (William & Deyoe, 2015). As well, many library collections aimed at young readers lack diversity and contain few books with LGBTQ characters or themes (Hughes-Hassell, Overberg, & Harris, 2013; Williams & Deyoe, 2014, 2015).

Hermann-Wilmarth and Ryan (2014) underscored this lack of LGBTQ literature by looking at the limited number of chapter books that explore LGBTQ identities. Examining books written for children ages 8–11, they attempted to find literature that contained at least one LGBTQ character. Hermann-Wilmarth and Ryan (2014) explain that they

> believe layering multiple interpretive lenses creates possibilities for readers and invites interesting and nuanced conversations when seen together. Queer theory encourages us to look past categorical labels and look instead at the ways categories are constructed in the first place. (p. 15)

Based on their search criteria of LGBTQ literature, they were able to locate only ten books worthy of examination in greater detail. While LGBTQ characters played numerous roles in the books, they were predominantly either the parents of the protagonist, or friends or family of the protagonist. Shockingly, in only two cases did the books studied have protagonists who identified as LGBTQ. The significance of this is that LGBTQ is still being portrayed as "other" rather than first person. Lester (2014) also noted this phenomenon in his consideration of 68 children's books published over 30 years. He discovered that even though many of the books were attempting to challenge hetero-normativity, they unintentionally embraced it. Lester (2014) comments that there is a lack of diversity in LGBTQ-themed books. He states, "Queer characters are acceptable (less threatening to normative discourse) if they seem less queer and more 'normal,' which is read as heterosexual, gender conforming, monogamous, White, upper middle class, and reproductive" (p. 247).

In a fairly sizable project, DePalma (2014) had teachers incorporate children's literature with LGBTQ themes into the classroom in any manner of their choosing (e.g., books, drama, etc.). The project's intention was to "help educators plan not only which kinds of literature to use, but also how to incorporate such texts into the curriculum in ways that productively challenge prevailing heteronormative school discourses" (DePalma, 2014, p. 15). During the course of the project, although there was some opposition from outside groups (as LGBTQ is still considered a taboo subject by some), overall, teachers and students embraced the literature. Teachers and students explored literature that featured LGBTQ characters. They found that lesbian and gay characters were the most common, while bisexual and transgender characters were rare. Encouragingly, the results of this project indicated that children and teachers approached these books much like any other—looking at the content and quality of the literature, and not evaluating it based on the types of relationships and sexualities portrayed.

Flores (2014) explores her own personal experiences with introducing LGBTQ literature into the classroom. She details how both she and her colleagues had been met with resistance from parents who were unhappy about the introduction of books with LGBTQ themes. As educators, however, they recognized the importance of ensuring diverse literature is available for children. Flores (2014) states that "having a more inclusive multicultural curriculum reduces the invisibility of LGBT families and gay culture from mainstream curriculum" (p. 115). Families are becoming more heterogeneous, and it is important that children are given the opportunity to see that diversity and become socially aware. Overall, Flores (2014) recommends that teachers be professional and firm, and that they remember that they are teaching "tolerance and acceptance and providing the necessary tools and preparing the student population for the diverse world in which they will live and thrive" (p. 119).

Dinkins and Englert (2015) look at how a classroom reacted to reading a novel featuring a gay character. The authors identify some challenges associated with exposing young readers to LGBTQ themes in literature. For example, the school where the study took place was still very heteronormative in many of its activities, and representations of sexuality aside from heterosexuality ("the default") were viewed as being "other." Despite these challenges, Dinkins and Englert (2015) argue that the exploration of LGBTQ characters can aid students to develop an understanding of identity—including sexual identity and gender expression. Dinkins and Englert (2015) also express that the classroom teacher has a significant part to play in facilitating LGBTQ discussion in the context of literature: "The teacher's role in the classroom is perhaps most important in developing a safe and supportive environment with teachers serving as allies and addressing instances of hate speech, bullying and negative comments" (p. 402). Dodge and Crutcher (2015) make a similar argument, encouraging teachers to teach with a social justice lens and to build understanding. They suggest that while teachers may face adversity in introducing LGBTQ texts in the classroom, there are actions that teachers can take to overcome these challenges. Such steps include a profound consideration of the experiences of LGBTQ persons, researching the needs of the community, and involving students in the process of discovery and in the development of empathy.

Overall, research indicates that there is a lack of available children's literature featuring LGBTQ characters and themes. In our research, we found that Canadian titles were limited. Furthermore, there is some indication that the literature that does exist is fairly limited—that is, it focuses on lesbian and gay characters who are white and upper class, while leaving explorations of bisexuality and transgender issues on the periphery. Also highlighted by the research is the necessity for teachers to be committed advocates for LGBTQ literature in the classroom, while recognizing that there are practical issues, such as varying levels of school community resistance, to be overcome. Hermann-Wilmarth and Ryan (2014) highlight the importance of this process when they state that "teachers and students who think with a queer lens ... open the possibility of extrapolating that kind of thinking to interactions with LGBT people and topics, therefore interrupting the single homonormative story that currently circulates" (p. 18). Clearly, the teacher who views pedagogy through a social justice lens has a multifaceted job: to bring critical literacy to students for their own development and empowerment, to locate appropriately challenging literature in what seems to be a dearth of LGBTQ texts, and to manoeuvre between various school community stakeholders who may be resistant.

Building a Collection

As we have seen in the literature review, topics have a tendency to focus on stereotypical characters as they navigate social norms and cliques. We see this in *Athletic Shorts* by Chris Crutcher, which is a series of six short stories that follow a group of athletic teenagers as they deconstruct social norms. In the novels of James Howe, however, the protagonists are social outliers—they are the misfits. In his aptly titled novel *The Misfits* and its sequel *Totally Joe*, Howe's characters are described as quiet, overweight, nerdish, or just plain different from the norm, and they use this to their advantage. By embracing their individuality, they challenge heteronormative values much more poignantly than the typical, "normal" protagonists of many young adult novels. (The "normal," average ones appear as secondary characters.) Howe's characters are immensely self-reflective, and they challenge the values and standards of their peers, teachers, family, and society equally. Novels such as these are important assets in school curriculum and libraries as they have the ability to teach equality and issues of LGBTQ individuals to students and educators alike.

In our research site's school library, we find many books, Canadian and international authored, that pertain to the LGBTQ community. LGBTQ individuals appear as protagonists or secondary characters, and plots explore everyday teenage issues—as well as those exclusively related to LGBTQ issues. The concerns expressed in Canadian titles are applicable to a broad young adult community. For example, *Big Guy* by Canadian author Robin Stevenson tells a familiar tale: a young man, Derek, has an online boyfriend, Ethan, but he has not been entirely honest with his partner. The picture Derek sent to Ethan was taken a year ago—before his mom left, before he became depressed, and before he gained 80 pounds. Derek fears what Ethan might think if he learns the truth, and he is confused as to whether or not he should be honest with Ethan. In the digital age, young adults face issues of self-esteem, online identity, and sexuality on a daily basis. This book appeals to adolescents on a wider scale yet still address the concerns of LGBTQ youth. Meanwhile, Kristyn Dunnion's *Mosh Pit* is a coming-of-age story of a 17-year-old lesbian punk girl, Simone, living in Toronto. Her mohawk, her piercings, her concert-going lifestyle, and her sexuality are all taboo, but not to her love interest, Cherry, who is a punk girl too. When Cherry drops out of school, the two embark on drug- and alcohol-laden debauchery, and Simone watches Cherry's life spiral out of control. Realizing that path is not for her, Simone is forced to come to terms with her love for Cherry and Cherry's lifestyle. The themes of drug and alcohol abuse, unhealthy lifestyles, and love are teenage issues—not just LGBTQ ones. Both of these books address teenage issues through the lens of LGBTQ characters, which deconstructs heteronormative understandings of what it means to be a teenager. Bringing such characters, who are facing everyday teenage issues, to the forefront of young adult literature can allow for the creation of an inclusive school culture. This is particularly important when considering the importance of diverse literature for children and young adolescents to see themselves represented and to learn how others learn and cope with life challenges.

The resource teacher in our book circle also recognized certain limitations that became apparent as she began building a collection of LGBTQ-themed novels. The first of these was that while the novels may span a wide range of subjects, they tend to focus only on realistic situations as opposed to science fiction or fantasy or other subgenres of speculative fiction that are of keen interest to young adult readers. Kendra expressed concern, saying, "It is not balanced. I chose these books because I was given a list of LGBTQ-themed materials from the provincial department of education, which were mostly American, and I had some money to spend at the time so I purchased them all." Ideally, the collection would include more Canadian-authored choices and other genres such as graphic novels. However, the teacher expresses that this is a difficult undertaking: "I think one of my biggest obstacles is that picking out a balanced selection of books takes a lot of research and time." In her school, her library resource position was shared with another subject teaching assignment. Within the library, the LGBTQ-themed novels are dispersed among the other fiction books, not kept separately. This leads to an interesting dilemma, as creating a special LGBTQ section would reassert heteronormative standards and highlight otherness. Yet students interested in LGBTQ materials might have difficulty locating them. To address this, the librarian placed genre stickers on the books to identify the LGBTQ themes. The books may also have stickers to indicate mature content. Kendra shared that the books do get read: "Mostly they are signed out by students who are reading for pleasure or for their independent novel studies. I haven't had many kids ask for LGBTQ materials specifically." This approach clearly demonstrates how teachers instill critical literacy affordances to students, which materializes in the students' actions. Students are requesting to read books by a particular author they enjoy—the fact that they are LGBTQ materials has already been normalized.

Schools still need to consider challenges associated with the creation of an LGBTQ collection when the teacher librarian is unfamiliar with the topic area. However, the teacher was able to build a collection by drawing on the assistance of colleagues who had previously developed lists of relevant literature. Kendra asserted that it would be relatively easy to find books with LGBTQ themes on the Internet, "but that would most certainly exclude anything that was Canadian content, or even appropriate materials that are locally produced." The teacher further elaborates, drawing on her own literacy practices, "I was just reminded of an American-based science text that I used when I was in junior high that used a possum and a catfish to demonstrate some biological concept or other. Not only did I have no idea what these animals were, I also had no opportunity to learn that those biological concepts were not applicable in my local area." The teacher's point is that it is not just enough to select books with LGBTQ themes for a collection, but that books need to be chosen with care. Consideration of Canadian content is paramount. In the case of contemporary concerns, such as issues of social justice, we may be bound to books that exclude a relevant cultural context for our students—or in fact, that may not be engaging. Cultural and gender identity aside, books that are not interesting to students and to which they cannot relate will never make it off the shelf.

Another concern for the teacher librarian when creating an LGBTQ collection was the maturity level of the students. The teacher explained, "at the junior high level, there is quite a large difference in the maturity level of the students. At times, a child will bring a book back to me asking if they could have another one saying that one is inappropriate, for whatever reason. And I have other children who are looking for more mature themes." As previously mentioned, this led to the teacher placing stickers on the books when they believed that the content was "mature" (i.e., contained more explicit or descriptive mentions of sex or rape or heavy drugs, suicide, child abuse, etc.). Aside from the obvious differences between reading levels and emotional maturity, the reality that students find some literature inappropriate speaks to variances in social backgrounds and, perhaps, to what extent exposure to critical thought had been previously encouraged. In some instances, several LGBTQ books were classed as mature because of the type of content that was present within. Importantly, the teacher gives students the options to read books that may contain sensitive themes rather than refusing to purchase books, or undertaking other forms of censorship. This method puts the control of what is read in students' hands rather than in the teacher's and prevents one person's beliefs from influencing what ideas students are exposed to. According to National Council of Teachers of English (NCTE) guidelines (2009), "teachers must be free to employ books, classic or contemporary, which do not lie to the young about the perilous but wondrous times we live in, books which talk of fears, hopes, joys, frustrations people experience, books about people not as they are but as they can be" (p. 12).

Contemporary Realistic Fiction: No One Is an Island

Many of the LGBTQ books fall under the category of contemporary realistic fiction, "derived from actual circumstances, with realistic settings and characters who face problems and opportunities that are within the range of what is possible in real life" (Temple, Martinez, & Yokota, 2014, p. 228). The characters in these books tend to resemble real people; live in a place that is or could be real; participate in a plausible, if not probable, series of events; and are presented with a dilemma that is of interest to children and discover a realistic solution. According to another book circle teacher, this is important to children because

> just like an LGBTQ club supports children to let them know they are not alone so they don't feel marginalized, we need books that offer that same level of support. I'll never have enough books to represent all groups of children, but we can work on it.

Thus, these books help children to feel as if they are not alone, and this literature helps them to reflect on their own life and their own choices. Importantly, children can become more knowledgeable about people around them and can develop empathy for others. Children can discover that families are diverse, and this can help them navigate their identity, their relationships, and their notion of what constitutes a family. LGBTQ literature offers students an opportunity for self-discovery: "Many works of realistic fiction enable children to explore their own thoughts, feelings, and predispositions and to compare their inner experiences with those of others" (Temple, Martinez, & Yokota, 2014, p. 232). It is important for children to read contemporary realistic fiction, especially when the fiction has an LGBTQ theme. These books allow the reader to identify with characters that are his or her age, that expand the reader's horizons and interests, and enable the realization that his or her problems are not unique.

Conclusion

For the teachers in this study, the journey to build an LGBTQ young adult literature collection was one that was fraught with tensions. The school's various communities of practice encouraged teachers to press on to acquire diverse resources for students, thereby empowering a growing community within the school. The government's initiative to provide LGBTQ safe spaces and fund resources empowered the school community and teachers. This adds to the social justice initiatives in schools, voicing a need for more professional development for teachers in building greater understanding of LGBTQ supports in schools, and in particular how school context is paramount in understanding the challenges around marginalized groups, and curriculum resources. Without this type of professional development, administrators and teachers may continue to self-monitor and consider marginalizing the LGBTQ community and a growing genre in Canadian children's literature.

Keywords

- agency
- children's literature
- community of practice
- critical literacy
- gender identity
- inclusion
- LGBTQ
- social justice

Reflection Questions

1. Visit your school or local library and consider if the books in the collection represent the LGBTQ population in an empowering way that is not stereotypical.
2. Discuss what resources or curricula are sanctioned for use in classrooms in your school district. How many of the resources are Canadian?
3. Pick a tension or moment that a peer or one of the teachers quoted in this chapter shared about her desire to make LGBTQ resources more prominent and reflect on why it resonated with you.

References

Bell, L. A. (2007). Theoretical foundations for social justice education. In M. Adams, L. A. Bell, & P. Griffin (Eds.), *Teaching for diversity and social justice* (2nd ed., pp. 1–14). New York, NY: Routledge.

Clarke, L. W., & Whitney, E. (2009). Walking in their shoes: Using multiple-perspectives texts as a bridge to critical literacy. *The Reading Teacher, 62*(6), 530–534.

Comber, B., & Nixon, H. (2005). Children re-read and re-write their neighbourhoods: Critical literacies and identity work. In J. Evans (Ed.), *Literacy moves on: Popular culture, new technologies and critical literacy in the elementary classroom.* Portsmouth, NH: Heinemann.

Crutcher, C. (1991). *Athletic Shorts.* New York, NY: Greenwillow Books.

DePalma, R. (2014). Gay penguins, sissy ducklings ... and beyond? Exploring gender and sexuality diversity through children's literature. *Discourse: Studies in the Cultural Politics of Education,* 1–18. doi:10.1080/01596306.2014.936712

Dinkins, E. G., & Englert, P. (2015). LGBTQ literature in middle school classrooms: Possibilities for challenging heteronormative environments. *Sex Education, 15*(4), 392–405. doi:10.1080/14681 811.2015.1030012

Dodge, A. M., & Crutcher, P. A. (2015). Inclusive classrooms for LGBTQ students: Using linked text sets to challenge the hegemonic "single story." *Journal of Adolescent and Adult Literacy, 59*(1), 95–105. doi:10.1002/jaa1.433

Dunnion, K. (2004). *Mosh Pit.* Calgary, AB: Red Deer Press.

Flores, G. (2014). Teachers working cooperatively with parents and caregivers when implementing LGBT themes in the elementary classroom. *American Journal of Sexuality Education, 9*(1), 114–120. doi:10.1080/15546128.2014.883268

Government of Newfoundland and Labrador. (n.d.). MyGSA. Retrieved from http://www.ed.gov.nl.ca/edu/k12/safeandcaring/gsa/

Government of Newfoundland and Labrador. (2012, January 23). New education resource to support establishment of gay-straight alliances in province's schools. Retrieved from http://www.releases.gov.nl.ca/releases/2012/edu/0123n06.htm

Hermann-Wilmarth, J. M., & Ryan, C. L. (2014). Queering chapter books with LGBT characters for young readers: Recognizing and complicating representations of homonormativity. *Discourse: Studies in the Cultural Politics of Education,* 1–21. doi:10.1080/01596306.2014.940234

Howe, J. (2001). *The Misfits.* New York, NY: Aladdin Paperbacks.

Howe, J. (2005). *Totally Joe.* New York, NY: Atheneum Books.

Hughes-Hassell, S., Overberg, E., & Harris, S. (2013). Lesbian, gay, bisexual, transgender, and questioning (LGBTQ)-themed literature for teens: Are school libraries providing adequate collections? *School Library Media Research, 16,* 1–18.

Janks, H. (2010). *Literacy and power.* New York, NY: Routledge.

Jones, S., & Enriquez, G. (2009). Engaging the intellectual and the moral in critical literacy education: The four-year journeys of two teachers from teacher education to classroom practice. *Reading Research Quarterly, 44*(2), 145–168.

Lave, J., & Wenger, E. (1998). Communities of practice: Learning, meaning and identity. Cambridge: Cambridge University Press.

Lester, J. Z. (2014). Homonormativity in children's literature: An intersectional analysis of queer-themed picture books. *Journal of LGBT Youth, 11*(3), 244–275. doi:10.1080/19361653.2013.8794 65

Macedo, D. (2005). Literacy: What matters? *Language Arts, 81*(1), 12–13.

National Council of Teachers of English (NCTE). (2009). Guideline on the student's right to read. Retrieved from http://www.ncte.org/positions/statements/righttoreadguideline

NativeOUT. (n.d.). Two Spirit 101. Retrieved from http://nativeout.com/twospirit-rc/two-spirit-101/

Stevenson, R. (2008). *Big Guy*. Victoria, BC: Orca.

Temple, C. A., Martinez, M., & Yokota, J. (2014). *Children's books in children's hands: A brief introduction to their literature*. Boston, MA: Pearson.

Vasquez, V. M. (2014). *Negotiating critical literacies with young children* (10th ed.). London: Routledge.

Williams, V. K., & Deyoe, N. (2014). Diverse population, diverse collection? Youth collections in the United States. *Technical Services Quarterly, 31*(2), 97–121. doi:10.1080/07317131.2014.875373

Williams, V. K., & Deyoe, N. (2015). Controversy and diversity: LGBTQ titles in academic library youth collections. *Library Resources and Technical Services, 59*(2), 62–71.

Chapter 5

The Limits of "Understanding": Teaching Residential School Stories in the Classroom

Amarou Yoder and Teresa Strong-Wilson

"We fell in love with this character, this is such a loveable, happy character, and then it's kind of, like, foreshadowing his future. You already know what's going to happen to him. We don't feel the same connection with him anymore." Matthew, a Grade 6 student, shared these thoughts during a group discussion of Indigenous Canadian author Larry Loyie's (2002) *As Long as the River Flows*. This story recounts, in words and pictures, memories from Loyie's childhood leading up to his forced removal from his family to attend residential school. Matthew and his fellow Grade 6 students studied this book as part of a unit on residential schools. Matthew's loss of connection eloquently captures a paradox at the heart of reading and teaching stories that bear witness to great injustice and tragedy. Where the characters in the story go (to residential school, to concentration camps, to slavery, or to segregated schools), many contemporary students cannot follow or "understand."

Yet, perhaps some histories—especially the testimonies of violence, trauma, and suffering from which histories are made—should *not* be "understood" (Hilberg, 1996). This suggestion flies in the face of conventional pedagogical attitudes that take as givens the need for "comprehension" and "understanding." We *understand* a math lesson so that we might move on to the next lesson; we *understand* the reason that a friend hurt our feelings so that we might come to some closure over the hurt; we *come to an understanding* in making a contract or settling a dispute. In the face of tragedies of monumental scale, such "understanding" may not be ours to render. This creates a pedagogical problem. How do we teach about these stories, about these tragic and horrific chapters in history, which confound and defy our "understanding"?

Our subject here is the history and legacy of the system of residential schools for First Nations people in Canada, a shameful and ongoing chapter in Canadian history, especially as taught (or not) in history and language arts classrooms, and through the renewed focus of a Truth and Reconciliation Commission (Hoffman, 2015; Saunders, 2015). It is an ongoing chapter in as much as we, as a nation, repeatedly fail to recognize the extent of the trauma that victims and survivors experienced, and the implication of white settler cultures in such histories.[1] This leads us to ask, how might *recognition* rather than *understanding* serve as a more responsible pedagogical orientation when teaching stories of trauma? What might recognition look like in teaching and learning?

With these questions in mind, we explore the pedagogy of one teacher[2] from our research site in Quebec, Canada, where, over the course of two years, she took up residential school stories as an integral part of her fifth- and sixth-grade curricula. In planning her curricula, she used texts introduced to her through our research project, which, most broadly, explores teachers' engagements with Canadian children's literature of a variety of genres (e.g., picture books, novels, poetry, graphic novels) for teaching issues of social justice in an urban public school in Canada. We quickly noticed that teachers in our study were drawn toward books about residential schools (Strong-Wilson, Yoder, & Phipps, 2014). Gabriela[3] was one of the earliest to do so, and her engagement with the texts over a lengthy period of time, with the same students (she looped with her fifth-grade students), supported her development of a recursive and responsive approach to studying residential schools. Her pedagogical approach serves as the basis for our exploration in this chapter of the relationship between pedagogy and recognition in connection with residential school narratives for children.

Recognition

In the introduction to the chapter entitled "The Legacy" in the Truth and Reconciliation Commission of Canada's (2015) *What Have We Learned: Principles of Truth and Reconciliation,* the authors write: "Reconciliation will require more than apologies for the shortcomings of those who preceded us. It obliges us to recognize the ways in which the legacy of residential schools continues to disfigure Canadian life and to abandon policies and approaches that currently serve to extend that hurtful legacy" (p. 104). This passage identifies an obligation placed upon us to learn, where such learning is open-ended and continues to emerge through recognition. Other scholars wrestling with different histories and legacies of injustice and trauma also emphasize recognition in exploring what might be expected from learners of these histories. Holocaust historian Raul Hilberg embraces the observation made by Theresienstadt survivor H. G. Adler about Hilberg and his scholarship: That in learning about the Holocaust, "there is only recognition, perhaps also a grasp, but certainly no understanding" (Adler, as quoted in Hilberg, 1996, pp. 202-203). What Adler meant was that like Hilberg, those who learned about the Holocaust second-hand—even a close second-hand—could never fully take in and assimilate its magnitude and horrors. Recognition alone was possible. Students like Gabriela's are learning about residential schools second-, or even third-hand—quite possibly for the first time. It is to them—and us—that the Truth and Reconciliation Commission speaks when it urges recognition of the continuing legacies of residential schools, both for others and ourselves.

What makes "recognition" so different from "understanding"? Such a distinction is best drawn out by comparing the negative forms of both words, that is, *misunderstanding* and *misrecognition*. To misunderstand someone or something is to mistake meaning. To misrecognize someone or something is to take the person or idea for something that he/she/it is not. It is with recourse to truth, as Gadamer (1975/2013) notes, that recognition takes its particular potency. In light of this distinction, one can perhaps see why understanding—which is ever partial—might be considered insufficient or impossible in dealing with human suffering that calls out for an acknowledgement greater than any single person can give. By contrast, recognition is oriented toward truth. Indeed, the earliest appearance of recognition (1460) in the English language attests to the "acknowledgment of something as true, valid, legal, or worthy of consideration ..." (Oxford English Dictionary, 2015). Thus stories of trauma, while thwarting understanding in the sense of being "comprehended," might still be recognized as true. This is what makes the concept of recognition so important for our discussion, where the absence of recognition from all levels of Canadian society has obscured the truth of Indigenous peoples' experiences in residential schools and their continued legacies.

Excavation into the meaning and significance of recognition is not exhausted by any singular definition in the dictionary. Philosopher and narrative theorist Paul Ricoeur (2005) begins his exploration of the word by noting its different meanings. While he uses a French dictionary, *Le Grand Robert*, the *Oxford English Dictionary* reveals the same multiplicity of meaning. The "acknowledgement of something as true" is joined by other definitions: "admissions of achievement and/or appreciation" (1570), as well as "actions or acts of identif[ication]" (1748). It is Ricoeur's belief that the different meanings of recognition are connected with one another, as in a "course"—starting with identification of things in general, and reaching toward recognition between particular people, that is, mutual recognition. This progression happens through the intermediary station of *self*-recognition, which is central to learners in the classroom, as we shall see. Yet through each of these stations, the connection with truth remains key.

In teaching for social justice, recognition as a concept is often predicated on "being recognized" in a legal-political sense (e.g., Bingham, 2006; Taylor, 1994). The demand or "struggle" for recognition is especially urgent where there have been histories of marginalization, oppression, and/or violence. Such struggles for recognition are, as Gutmann (1994) and others point out, played out in discussions surrounding curricula, whether in public schools or in universities and colleges. In such curricula, the inclusion of reading materials becomes an occasion to recognize, with the imprimatur of the institution, stories, histories, and ways of knowing from people and peoples whose voices have largely been silenced, ignored, or *misrecognized*. We only have to remind ourselves of Gadamer's attestation about recognition to see the urgency behind such struggles: recognition makes a truth claim, acknowledging something as true or valid.

An institution like a school is representative of people, of a collective; however, truth must be felt or known in individual human consciousness. It is worthwhile recalling that the recognition between and among people is the third station along Ricoeur's course. It is preceded by two other iterations that locate recognition first in the identification of things in general, and in self-recognition. These are the tasks of the learner, of the reader, and the groundwork for mutual recognition. In reading these residential school stories, we suggest that students might experience recognition *both* of something/someone *and* of oneself (Gadamer, 1975/2013; Ricoeur, 2005). Furthermore, Gadamer (1975/2013) suggests that "in recognition what we know emerges, as if through an illumination, from all the chance and variable circumstances that condition it" (p. 102). It is not too much of a stretch to see in this contingency and variability (that condition recognition), the "biographic situations" that teacher and students bring to the classroom (Pinar, 2004): local and national identities, alignments, and ideals, as well as the occasion of the research project itself, which "by chance" brought this teacher and these texts together. Such apparently arbitrary features might comprise what Gadamer suggests is the "known already," which he separates from what is recognized. "Illumination" suggests a gradual recognition, but it may come in the wake of an initial shock. Gadamer calls "illumination" a "joy" whereas challenges to the "known already" may very well produce psychic pain or sorrow, such that recognition acts as a strobe light in an otherwise pleasantly lit living room. What is recognized as true might challenge what has been accepted, even revealing received understandings (as part of one's "biographic situation" or "self-recognition") as false.

The Pedagogical Challenge of "Difficult Knowledge"

However aspirational the work of recognition might be, its course is not a simple one. This raises the question of what challenges such a pedagogy might face. To theorize the various and complicated elements of this question, we begin with Canadian education scholars Deborah Britzman and Roger Simon.

Britzman (1998, 2000) makes careful study of the history and uses of *The Diary of Anne Frank* to formulate the concept of "difficult knowledge." We are drawn to this particular vein of inquiry because our study focuses on Canadian social justice literature, in particular, the literature that testifies to the—often first-hand—experiences of First Nations people in residential schools. She notes *Anne Frank*'s pre-eminence in many classrooms as an account of the universal and indomitable human spirit, and as such, is disembodied from the time and person of its origin. She suggests that such a reading is founded on idealization, on the teacher (and learners) making the effort "'to place some aspect of oneself or the group on a pedestal to then derive faith, hope, and sustenance from this idealized part'" (Freud, as cited in Britzman, 1998, p. 120). Such idealization can create distance, and elide the material and historical circumstances of Anne's life, death, and the conflicted history of the diary itself. Britzman continues, "When the vicissitudes of life and death cannot conform to the idealization of a life that should surmount the difficult, it becomes very difficult to live with, or in, loss" (1998, p. 120).

In pointing out the impulse of readers (teachers/students) to turn such "difficult knowledge" into an interpretation that comforts the reader and reinforces the conventions/understandings of his or her world, Britzman illustrates the limits of understanding where "making sense" is concerned. Yet, in the absence of "understanding," other alternatives like silence or recognition still exist, where the reader may be "summoned to become, in reading, 'the reader of his own self'" (Ricoeur, 2005, p. 68); that is, the reader might recognize the claim on him or herself of the narrative he or she has read.

In a previous paper (Strong-Wilson, Yoder, & Phipps, 2014), we considered the aesthetic effect of residential school stories on two groups of Canadian teachers, noting their attraction to the subject. We used Simon's (1992) adaptation of Walter Benjamin's notion of the dialectical image. Benjamin was interested in texts and images that would produce shock value by disrupting taken-for-granted beliefs. A dialectical image juxtaposes the past with the present, producing what Benjamin called "now-time"—a present moment invested with the hope of possibility because it was informed by critical reflection on past wrongs. We liken the images and texts of children's residential school picture books to Walter Benjamin's dialectical image, focusing on the image that most shocked the teachers: the concluding one of the cattle truck with Indigenous children inside. Cattle trucks were regularly used to "pick up" the children to bring them to the schools (Haig-Brown, 1998/2006), bringing them (by analogy) to "slaughter" (Strong-Wilson, Yoder, & Phipps, 2014, p. 87). Such shock might represent some part of Simon's (2000) suggestion that "remembrance becomes a practice that supports a learning from 'the past' that … unsettles the very terms on which our understandings of ourselves and our world are based" (p. 13). Note Simon's use of the preposition "from" when discussing this learning. Britzman (1998) also distinguishes between learning "about" and learning "from" these traumatic residuals, noting that "learning from" requires greater investment on the part of the learner; it "requires the learner's attachment to, and implication in, knowledge" (p. 117).

The loss or tarnishing of an idealization is, no doubt, an experience of profound recognition, where what was known is illuminated in a new and troubling light. This raises the question of the place of pedagogy in fostering recognition—the shocking and immutable alteration in how one sees the world and/or one's self—in light of historical and social episodes that demand and deserve recognition of a more political nature. Orange (2010) notes the recursive movement of recognition as "re-cognition." It is not possible to recognize what one doesn't know. It is a journey that, while admitting co-travellers, must be done by the self over time. In other words, it seems that recognition might best be approached in the fullness of time, with many returns and re-encounters. It is, finally, a process whereby the self becomes implicated in its own knowledge, as Britzman mentions above. It is not "something" that is understood and thus ushered into the past, but it (recognition) enacts a profound reshaping of how one conceives of the present and future. The pedagogical approach in this Grade 6 classroom was structured with precisely this kind of recursive movement, which we will discuss shortly, but situated in the teacher's reaching toward Indigenous perspectives, which we consider next.

Indigenous Perspectives

"How should I read these?" was Helen Hoy's (2001) question in coming to the literary writings of Native American women writers, Hoy being non-Indigenous. The same question applies to non-Indigenous teachers and students reading residential school stories written by Indigenous authors—even though such stories are arguably read primarily by a non-Indigenous audience. Indigenous peoples often already know, or know of, these stories: painful to tell, painful to hear. There are therapeutic as well as political benefits in their being told versus the alternative, of being silenced or ignored as part of a nation's past. They exist as counter-stories (Thomas, 2005), nowhere more than in childhood, which tends to be steeped in a storied "cauldron" drawn from the dominant culture (Bradford 2007; Strong-Wilson, 2007). The residential school children's literature, written by survivors of residential schools or their descendants, belong both within the genre of the testimonial, being stories drawn from personal experience (Daniels, 2013), as well as being creative responses to the "captivity narrative," which Sioux literary critic Elizabeth Cook-Lynn (2004) points out was seminal in constructing the Native as savage. Popular in the 19th century and often narrated by missionaries, captivity narratives told the stories of whites taken and held hostage or tortured and killed by marauding tribes. Strong traces of this genre have (not surprisingly) permeated into children's stories, from *Indian Captive* (the "true" story of Mary Jemison) to Laura Ingalls Wilder's *The First Four Years* (see Strong-Wilson, 2006), which, though lesser-known, have arguably influenced the larger, mythic story of the frontier (US) and of the bush/wilderness/North (Canada). As captivity or "kidnapped" stories, narratives published since the 1990s and by Indigenous writers tell a far different version of the tale, drawing attention to the unconscionable deed of spiriting away Native children from their families, communities, and ancestral lands, potentially leading to alienation and despair. It is vital, though, to contextualize these "Indian narrative[s]" (Cook-Lynn, 1998) within terms of reference set out by Native American intellectuals themselves (Tuhiwai Smith, 2012; Warrior, 1995) in which "community and land [are understood] as central critical categories" (Warrior, 1995, p. xxii) to a larger struggle for self-determination. The writings of Indigenous authors play an integral role in imagining and reimagining Indigeneity (Cook-Lynn, 1998; King, 2003; Warrior, 1995), where Indigenous stories and the tradition of storytelling itself need to be understood as powerful examples of resiliency (Laroque, 1996; Moses,

2012; Weenie, 2002) and "survivance" (Vizenor, 1994): of the refusal of victimhood and alienation; of stories that "create as they are being told" (Vizenor, as cited in McKegney, 2007, p. 3).

One distinguishing characteristic of the contemporary residential school children's literature/counter-story is its juxtaposition of a "before" with an "after," in which the "before" is granted greater reality and verisimilitude as an example of how to live in and with the world. This "before" takes place in what various Indigenous writers (of fiction and of academic writing) have depicted as a "traditional" world, namely a world informed by consciousness of Indigenous values and lived in close relationship to the land, animals, and extended family (e.g., Alfred, 1999; Deloria, 1997; Momaday, 1987; Ortiz, 1981). The "after" (viz., time spent in residential school) is a painful interval, an aberration from the conception of time and place created by the "before" narrative and to which protagonists ardently wish to return. Jordan-Fenton and Pokaik-Fenton's twin books of *Fatty Legs* (2010) and *Stranger at Home* (2011) stand out for their exploration of being away and of coming home; of the returning person being not the same as the one who left: with different thoughts, even different values, which contaminate and thus threaten an original balance. George Erasmus (Dene) places this problem in perspective when he says: "Our old people, when they talk about how the [traditional] ways should be kept by young people, they are not looking back, they are looking forward. They are looking as far ahead into the future as they possibly can" (as cited in McKegney, p. 173).

McKegney, who, like Hoy, like us, like the teachers and students in the research study, is non-Indigenous, persuasively argues (and this is endorsed by Ojibway author Basil Johnston, who wrote the preface for McKegney's (2007) book) that residential school experiences, in being subjected to fictionalization (stories), do not simply "represent" or "testify" to those experiences but in some way *transform* them, moving them out of the realm of feelings of paralysis and incapacitation to a larger vision of survival, in and through story. This argument is similar to W. G. Sebald's, as a German writing (belatedly) about the Holocaust, in which he suggests that fiction (which arises from and is partly embedded in "fact") can serve a redemptive function (Sebald, 2004), approaching difficult subject matter from an oblique angle that builds resonances rather than confrontations (Sebald, 2007). As McKegney (2007) suggests about the narratives:

> Although they depict historical disparities in power and often trau-
> matic personal events, they render these imaginatively, affording the
> Indigenous author interpretive autonomy and discursive agency while
> transcending the structural imperatives of proof and evidence embed-
> ded in historical paradigms ... they expose the failure of residential
> school social engineering by defining themselves in their writing, by
> "touch[ing] [themselves] into being with words." (p. 7; emphasis in the
> original, with Vizenor as cited in McKegney)

And what of the reader, especially the non-Indigenous reader, who is also a listener to a survivor's testimonies? Within the context of the classroom, at least the one in which we have been privileged to enter, the Grade 6 students were listening to the story as it was being read aloud by student volunteers, each in turn, with the teacher adroitly rereading certain parts aloud, drawing students' attention to the text. As Lyn Daniels (Cree; 2013) points out, the listener, as one who comes after, is in a difficult position. There is the interval between the experience and the narration of the experience; between its narration and understanding (which may not come); between hearing and recognizing what kind of story this is.

Daniels brings us back to "about" and "from" through her focus on looking, in relation to photographs of children in residential school. Looking can represent the colonial gaze, which further consolidates the alienation of residential school. In a school curriculum context, it has typically meant learning *about* "the Native."

Within an alternative mode of learning "from," looking can instead signify a wakeful interval, an interruption as well as a suspension of time, in which the person looking can wonder and ask questions such as, "What occurred inside the Indian residential school buildings that led to these [children's] expressions?" (Daniels, 2013, p. 38). Such questions can further propel thinking of the picture book, with its juxtaposed images of a "before" world and an "after" world, with the rupture from one to the other represented by the cattle truck, as dialectical image: as shocking, instigating a pause (as Benjamin likewise conceptualized it). Furthermore, the suspension (which may also take the form of silence) might thus be understood as an opportunity for recognition, especially when combined with hearing and listening to the words of Indigenous authors as narrators of their own Indigenous stories. As Daniels suggests, when addressing difficult stories involving deep trauma, "silence may be a necessary interval" (2013, p. 45).

Gabriela's Pedagogy

How do we teach *from* these stories, then? From stories that, as tragic and horrific chapters in our history, resist our "understanding"?

Gabriela has been using residential school stories with her students since the inception of the study in 2012 (Yoder, 2013). The first books she used were *Shi-she-etko* (2005) and *Shin-Chi's Canoe* (2008), both narrated by Nicola Campbell, who is a descendant of residential school survivors. *Shi-she-etko* is told from the point of view of the older sister, and *Shin-chi's Canoe* is from the point of view of the younger brother. Both stories tell of the children's journey to residential school, although *Shin-Chi's Canoe* focuses on the brother's time in the school while *Shi-she-etko* takes place entirely in a before-time, but in anticipation of what is to come. One would think that *Shin-Chi's Canoe* would be the more compelling story but teachers have been much more drawn to the first book, in which Shi-she-etko and her family are still living as they have been and would like to be, but their lives are overshadowed by a cognizance, a shadow, of something dreadful coming, for which Shi-she-etko tries to prepare by collecting her memories of home.

Most of Gabriela's Grade 5 students moved up with her into Grade 6 and continued to follow their interest in residential school stories by watching the video that has been made of *Shi-she-etko* and then reading Larry Loyie's *As Long as the River Flows*, which is similar in structure to *Shi-she-etko*, but a longer narrative suitable for a Grade 6 level. Another difference between the two texts is that Loyie himself is a residential school survivor. At the end of the story, the students find photographs from Loyie's life before, during, and after residential school. It is as if the students have returned to that interval of being in abeyance: of waiting, now with Larry, formerly with Shi-she-etko, for the shadow to fall.

Gabriela's engagement of the students with *As Long as the River Flows* began in January 2014 and lasted a full six months, until the close of the school year in June. We believe that the students' interest and attention could be sustained that long because of Gabriela's recursive pedagogy, which entailed reading the book aloud chapter by chapter, one chapter per class day, but distributed between literature notebook activities on that chapter and related historical and current events research. Students were grouped into six clusters of tables, three to five students per cluster; each cluster read a part. Gabriela had to choose among the two, sometimes three, students per cluster vying for a turn to read. Each cluster had a copy of the text, made available through the project.

- The reading aloud was punctuated by frequent discussion, or digression, which was the main pedagogical device for prolonging anticipation of the end, but also stretching and deepening possibilities for recognition (see next section).
- Once the chapter was read, the groups then worked more intensively on chapter vocabulary and questions, which involved a mix of literal and inferential questions. They used the text as well as Google searches conducted via iPads to do research (e.g., "what is bannock"). At the end of the period, one person from each group identified a question to put on the K-W-L chart (what we Know; Want to know; have Learned) with a sticky note, or a reaction on the Reaction chart. Background information on residential school was also available on a dedicated wall, which included various clippings, a residential school timeline, and a biography of Larry Loyie.
- Simultaneously, projects were developed; for example: totems that told the stories of residential school survivors, and a class book in which students investigated intergenerational learning of a skill, practice, or attitude; that is, students learned from someone in their family or immediate vicinity.

A Vignette: Silence as a Necessary Interval

During our classroom observations in January and February, we were struck by Gabriela's artful use of digression. Each class discussion of a chapter spanned about a half-hour; had the chapter been read continuously, from start to finish, it might have taken five to ten minutes, and the book itself, one period, perhaps two. The digressions were highly purposeful. From a pedagogical perspective, they accomplished the goals of guided reading (one of the practices adopted by the school board as part of a balanced literacy framework; for a discussion of balanced literacy as an aspect of effective teaching, see Allington, 2002). The teacher parsed challenging or unfamiliar vocabulary (e.g., particular to Cree/Indigenous life), scaffolded comprehension, and, most importantly, encouraged students to intellectually and personally engage with the story—from lively debates on how we obtain our food, now and then, to connecting the story to their own lives, locating sites of sympathetic similarity (e.g., Who knows the smell of mint? Does anyone have a root-cellar? Does anyone's family preserve fruits or vegetables?), as well as demarcating differences (e.g., Who is capable of distinguishing the smell of mint from many other herbs and plants growing in a field?). The density of detail provided by Loyie through both text and illustrations richly illuminate his "life before," that is, a life in keeping with the Indigenous values and practices of his family; it seems a sort of paradise, and in Gabriela's skilled digressions, the students raised questions and pursued inquiries spontaneously and urgently, often signalling their interests through several or many hands being waved at once. The respectful, admiring curiosity about Larry's way of life and the tragic impact of residential school spilled beyond the reading and discussions. Some students pursued inquiries on their own time. For example, one day, when the students were in the process of being dismissed for the day, Gabriela encouraged one of her students to show us her research journal, which showed a timeline of the history of residential schools in Canada. The student's journal was extensive, covering many pages in her notebook, with historical events interspersed with the student's reactions—many questions, interspersed with expressions of disbelief.

Subtly, Gabriela's digressive methods recursively probed the depths of the students' knowledge and perceptions, opening them to deeper and deeper connections to their own lives. At the same time students were being invited to enter into Larry's world, the conditions were being created for that moment when imagination might—and certainly would—fail. It was as if Gabriela was drawing a larger and larger net around the subject of Larry's life, in which certain nodes (like buoys) continually reappeared or emerged. Food gathering (for the Cree in 1940s Manitoba) was one such node: Larry's connection to the land (including plants and animals). Another, unsurprisingly, was residential school.

Perhaps most notably, the students responded in unison at the first reference to "residential school" in the text. Larry overhears mention of "school" and "prison" among the evening conversations of his family. It is only a brief hint, but foreshadows his forcible removal from his family. When the students, like Larry, "overheard" about residential schools, a sustained silence descended on the class. Why did they become so quiet? This silence happened again on another occasion, at a similar juncture in the story. Gabriela allowed for the silence. She then began to probe: Is this the first time this happens in the story? Does Larry's mom provide much information about the school? As 11-year-old children, the students then discussed the incident and why an adult (here, Larry's mother) would shield the child and refrain from telling the whole truth, speculating:

- She is trying to hide. Some of the questions she might not know the answer to.
- She wants to spend as much time as possible with him before he goes away, which he will.
- She has a natural instinct to cover it up so that the child will feel protected and safe. Not to panic. (paraphrased comments of students; field notes, January 30, 2014)

At the conclusion of Gabriela's study of the text, we collaborated with her to set up a focus group with the class, in the form of a whole-class discussion. We drafted some potential questions about the book and about residential schools, which we submitted to Gabriela; she revised them and added some of her own. On the day of the discussion, these questions formed the general focus for the class. For one of the questions, we asked Gabriela to ask the students if they remembered getting quiet, and if they could explain why. Again, the uniformity in their answers was striking and is perhaps best exemplified in the words of Matthew, one of the students: "We fell in love with this character, this is such a loveable, happy character, and then it's kind of, like, foreshadowing his future. You already know what's going to happen to him. We don't feel the same connection with him anymore." The last part sounds surprising, even shocking, and in need of elaboration. The students agreed that it was the background that Gabriela had given them that allowed them to know what was going to happen to Larry; however, Matthew poignantly articulates the occasion for silence: the loss of a meaningful connection built between them and the character of Larry (perhaps itself an idealization) based on the recognition that where Larry was going, they could not follow. During the same discussion, another student commented, "Not only have you left your family, which is traumatic, then you're brainwashed in residential school, and then when you come back you're a loner. When you're in that position, thinking about your future must be so hard." The students' words in Gabriela's classroom draw attention to the unsettlement that Loyie's text generated. Even as the children were attracted to the book, looking forward to every chapter installment, it was not without trepidation and vulnerability. At one point, the students lost their words, in a context in which we had witnessed words as being rampant. They lost the power of speech when they seemed to gain recognition of Larry's impending future—one of enforced separation from his family. But what might it mean to say that attachment was severed, even lost? In Sharon Draper's (2015) novel *Stella by Starlight*, set in a small town in the segregated South where the KKK are becoming active, family members have gathered around a fire to decide what to do about recent threats even as they are resolved on social change: on gaining the vote. The spectre of lynching hangs in the air. Stella, who is in Grade 5, listens. "For a moment, except for the roaring of the smoky flames, everyone went quiet. Stella wondered how silence could be so loud" (Draper, 2015, p. 180).

At one point in the same focus group discussion of the book, the students reflected on the purpose and place of the owl as a character in the story. *As Long as the River Flows* opens with an orphaned owl that Larry's family pledges to take care of and nurse back to health and freedom. As the students noted, Oohoo (as they call him) really becomes Larry's owl. We had already asked our question about the students' silence. The same student (Matthew) who made the observations about attachment seems to come back to this question of silence, but from another angle, asking about Oohoo. What happens to the owl in the story? The student thinks aloud: "I don't know if it's just the author's way of saying like, the audience, the people who are reading the book, are kind of like Oohoo—the story brought us [here] knowing they would have to let us go." There are appreciative sounds from those in the room—the other students, the teacher, us—as we ponder this possibility. Another student checks back and notes that in the last pictures of the story, the owl is in a tree as the truck drives away, taking Larry and his siblings to residential school. And then someone else adds, "There's another one where he is flying away." Matthew considers this new information: "I just realized. The point of keeping Oohoo was to keep him so that he could get educated to go back [to the wild]. And we were educated about the story" but, in the terms of this chapter and the students' engagement with the story, we understand Matthew's "about" as learning "from" the story. As a class, the students, and their teacher, were educated *from* the story: the story—and Gabriela's digressive, recursive approach to the story, which created openings for experiencing recognition *both* of something/someone *and* of oneself.

Conclusion

One might read in the students' silence an echo of that silence that marks the passing of the dead, signifying *their* loss and *their* mourning as readers of an attachment to Larry and his family and their way of life. The deep shock of the students' silence, though, might not signify an end, but instead a beginning, marking the place from which recognition—Gadamer's illumination—embarks. First there is shock, then silence, and then recognition. Through Gabriela's pedagogy, students were drawn into the ambit of Loyie's text, not through emphasis on "understanding"—and here we recall our earlier mention of Adler and Hilberg's rejection of understanding—but rather, as Matthew suggestively notes in his comments about the students being like Oohoo, in their parallel educations—through allowing authentic connections to accumulate between the students and the text which recounts Larry's story. This is not to collapse or ignore the vast differences between the students and Larry and his story: "The one is not the other" warns Ricoeur (2005, p. 263) in his concluding remarks about mutual recognition, the third stage in his "course" of recognition. However, such recognition might find as one of its early expressions the *inclination* toward the other, perhaps most powerfully through an inclination to listen intently. In our last visit to the class, two weeks following this focus group discussion and at the penultimate day of the end of classes and the beginning of summer holidays, we were accompanied by Dr. Elma Moses, a Cree residential school survivor, an accomplished traditional storyteller, and an Indigenous scholar, who graciously agreed to come to the class. She skilfully told the students traditional Cree stories of life, death, hardship, and survival, with the students showing grateful appreciation, but finally broaching, with tender care, their tentative questions about her painful experience of residential school. It was as if Larry himself were there to affirm to the students: I am still here. And the students were there to say: We now recognize better what to listen for, and how to enter a difficult but vitally important conversation.

Keywords

- Indigenous perspectives
- recognition
- recursive pedagogy
- residential school
- trauma
- understanding

Reflection Questions

1. Has there been a time in your life—as a student, teacher, or human being—where understanding seemed difficult or impossible? What was it about the situation or experience that made understanding so hard?
2. How might you describe the difference between "learning about" and "learning from" the stories of Indigenous peoples' experiences in residential schools? What makes this an important distinction?
3. What are some elements of recursive pedagogy that you've noticed in other classrooms or (would like to) include in your own classroom?
4. How can teachers help their students to independently extend their learning, such as by keeping a personal research journal? How might this strategy promote students' connections with the story and subject?

Notes

1. Some short attention will be paid to the different—but connected—meanings of "recognize" and "recognition" in the section devoted to this concept.

2. We would like to express our gratitude to Gabriela and her students, who welcomed us into their classroom and generously shared with us their work, ideas, and feelings.

3. All names of teacher and students are pseudonyms.

References

Alfred, T. (1999). *Peace, power, righteousness: An indigenous manifesto.* Oxford: Oxford University Press.

Allington, R. (2002). What I've learned about effective reading instruction from a decade of studying exemplary elementary classroom teachers. *Phi Delta Kappan, 83*(10) June, 740–747.

Bingham, C. (2006). Before recognition, and after: The educational critique. *Educational Theory, 56*(3), 325–344.

Bradford, C. (2007). *Unsettling narratives: Postcolonial readings of children's literature.* Waterloo, ON: Wilfrid Laurier Press.

Britzman, D. P. (1998). *Lost subjects, contested objects: Toward a psychoanalytic inquiry of learning.* Albany, NY: State University of New York Press.

Britzman, D. P. (2000). If the story cannot end: Deferred action, ambivalence, and difficult knowledge. In R. I. Simon, S. Rosenberg, & C. Eppert (Eds.), *Between hope and despair: Pedagogy and the remembrance of historical trauma* (pp. 27–57). New York, NY: Rowman & Littlefield.

Campbell, N. (2005). *Shi-she-etko.* Toronto, ON: Groundwood Books.

Campbell, N. (2008). *Shin-chi's canoe.* Toronto, ON: Groundwood Books.

Cook-Lynn, E. (1998). American Indian intellectualism and the New Indian story. In D. A. Mihesuah (Ed.), *Natives and academics.* Lincoln, NE: University of Nebraska Press.

Cook-Lynn, E. (2004). The Lewis and Clark story, the captive narrative, and the pitfalls of Indian history. *Wicazo Sa Review, 19*(1), 21–33.

Daniels, L. (2013). Expressions of policy effects: Hearing memories of Indian residential schools. In T. Strong-Wilson, C. Mitchell, S. Allnutt, & K. Pithouse-Morgan (Eds.), *Productive remembering and social agency* (pp. 31–48). Rotterdam, The Netherlands: Sense Publishers.

Deloria, V. (1997). Anthros, Indians and planetary reality. In T. Boilsi & L. J. Zimmerman (Eds.), *Indians and anthropologists: Vine Deloria Jr. and the critique of anthropology* (pp. 209–221).

Draper, S. (2015). *Stella by starlight.* New York, NY: Atheneum Books for Young Readers.

Gadamer, H.-G. (1975/2013). *Truth and method.* (J. Weinsheimer & D. Marshall, Trans.). New York, NY: Bloomsbury Academic.

Gutmann, A. (1994). Introduction. In A. Gutmann (Ed.), *Multiculturalism* (pp. 3–24). Princeton, NJ: Princeton University Press.

Haig-Brown, C. (1998/2006). *Resistance and renewal: Surviving the Indian residential school.* Vancouver, BC: Arsenal Pulp Press.

Hilberg, R. (1996). *The politics of memory: The journey of a Holocaust historian.* Chicago, IL: Ivan R. Dee.

Hoffman, K. (2015, June 6). Folio: Truth and reconciliation. *The Globe and Mail,* pp. A10–A11.

Hoy, H. (2001). *How should I read these? Native women writers in Canada.* Toronto, ON: University of Toronto Press.

Jordan-Fenton, C., & Pokiak-Fenton, M. (2010). *Fatty legs.* Toronto, ON: Annick Press.

Jordan-Fenton, C., & Pokiak-Fenton, M. (2011). *A stranger at home: A true story*. Toronto, ON: Annick Press.

King, T. (2003). *The truth about stories: A Native narrative*. Toronto, ON: House of Anansi Press.

Laroque, E. (1996). When the other is me: Native writers confronting Canadian literature. In J. Oakes & R. Riewe (Eds.), *Issues in the North* (vol. I, pp. 115-134). Edmonton, AB: Canadian Circumpolar Institute.

Loyie, L. (2002). *As long as the rivers flow*. Toronto, ON: Groundwood Books.

McKegney, S. (2007). *Magic weapons: Aboriginal writers remaking community after residential school*. Winnipeg, MB: University of Manitoba Press.

Momaday, N. S. (1987). *The names: A memoir*. Tucson, AZ: University of Arizona Press.

Moses, E. (2012). *Dancing with Chikapesh: An examination of Eeyou stories through three generations of storytellers*. Unpublished doctoral dissertation, McGill University. Available at http://www.worldcat.org/title/dancing-with-chikapesh-an-examination-of-eeyou-stories-through-three-generations-of-storytellers/oclc/845026205

Orange, D. (2010). Recognition as intersubjective vulnerability in the psychoanalytic dialogue. *International Journal of Psychoanalytic Self Psychology, 5*(3), 227-243.

Ortiz, S. (1981). Towards a national Indian literature: Cultural authenticity in nationalism. *Melus, 8*(2), 7-12.

Oxford English Dictionary Online. (2015). Recognition. Retrieved from http://www.oed.com.proxy3.1ibrary.mcgill.ca

Pinar, W. (2004). *What is curriculum theory?* Mahwah, NJ: Lawrence Erlbaum Publishers.

Ricoeur, P. (2005). *The course of recognition* (D. Pellauer, Trans.). Cambridge, MA: Harvard University Press.

Saunders, D. (2015, June 6). The reckoning. *The Globe and Mail*, pp. F1-F6, F7.

Sebald, W. G. (2004, December 20). Reflections: An attempt at restitution. *New Yorker*.

Sebald, W. G. (2007). A poem of an invisible subject (interview by M. Silverblatt). In L. S. Schwartz (Ed.), *The emergence of memory: Conversations with W. G. Sebald* (pp. 77-86). New York, NY: Seven Stories Press.

Simon, R. I. (1992). *Teaching against the grain: Texts for a pedagogy of possibility*. Toronto, ON: OISE Press.

Simon, R. I. (2000). The paradoxical practice of Zakhor: Memories of "what has never been my fault or my deed." In R. I. Simon, S. Rosenberg, & C. Eppert (Eds.), *Between hope and despair: Pedagogy and the remembrance of historical trauma* (pp. 9-25). New York, NY: Rowman & Littlefield.

Strong-Wilson, T. (2006). Bringing memory forward: A method for engaging teachers in reflective practice on narrative and memory. *Reflective Practice, 7*(1), 101-113.

Strong-Wilson, T. (2007). Moving horizons: Exploring the role of stories in decolonizing the literacy education of white teachers. *International Education, 37*(1), 114-131.

Strong-Wilson, T., Yoder, A., & Phipps, H. (2014). Going down the rabbit-hole: Teachers' engagements with "dialectical images" in Canadian children's literature on social justice. *Changing English, 21*(1), 79-93.

Taylor, C. (1994). The politics of recognition. In A. Gutmann, (Ed.), *Multiculturalism* (pp. 25-74). Princeton, NJ: Princeton University Press.

Thomas, R. A. (2005). Honouring the oral traditions of my ancestors through storytelling. In L. Brown & S. Strega (Eds.), *Research as resistance: Critical, Indigenous, and anti-oppressive approaches* (pp. 237-254). Toronto, ON: Canadian Scholars' Press.

Truth and Reconciliation Commission of Canada. (2015). *What have we learned: Principles of truth and reconciliation*. Retrieved from http://trc.ca.

Tuhiwai Smith, L. (2012). *Decolonizing methodologies: Research and Indigenous peoples*. New York, NY: Zed Books.

Vizenor, G. (1994). Postindian warriors. In *Manifest manners: Postindian warriors of survivance* (1–44). Hanover, NJ: Wesleyan University Press.

Warrior, R. A. (1995). Introduction. In *Tribal secrets: Recovering American Indian intellectual traditions* (pp. xiii–xxiii). Minneapolis, MN: University of Minnesota Press.

Weenie, A. (2009). *Resilience and First Nations students: A study of resilience in First Nations post-secondary students*. Saarbrucken, Germany: Lambert Academic Publishing.

Yoder, A. (2013). Something resembling hope: Notes on strategies for teaching Canadian social justice literature. *McGill Journal of Education, 48*(2), 435–442.

Opening Minds:
Pedagogies for Social Justice

The workings of power and social positioning in the pedagogical relation—especially a pedagogical relation with all good intentions—can be delicate and seemingly intangible.

—ELLSWORTH (1997, P. 6)

TEACHING FOR SOCIAL JUSTICE GOES BEYOND PROVIDING BOOKS THAT introduce multicultural themes and contexts; pedagogical approaches that support social justice support respectful discussion and use thoughtful conversations to dig deeply into issues and controversies. The teachers who were co-researchers in this project participated in inquiry groups at each of our project sites and engaged in powerful discussions about the literature they were using in their classrooms. As Wiltse and LaFramboise-Helgeson demonstrate, the inquiry groups enabled teachers to learn content and also to investigate new teaching possibilities as they shared ideas. Burke and her colleagues provide us with many examples of innovative pedagogy, including the use of "new media" to engage students in thinking about social justice.

Chapter 6

A Plurality of Voices for Social Justice: Implementing Culturally Responsive Pedagogies in a Grade 6 Classroom

Anne Burke, Theresa Powell, Shawnee Hardware, and Laura Butland

Residential schooling is a part of Canada's failures. It is hard to explain past injustices to children ... answering their questions is a first step.

—TEACHER-RESEARCHER

Teaching and creating classroom awareness of social justice is an ongoing challenge for teachers. Many classroom teachers strive to promote social and critical awareness, hoping to instill knowledge and empathy in students as they learn about historical wrongs. Teachers aspire to support children in taking agency for and redressing societal actions of the past. The quote at the beginning of the chapter was shared by one of the teachers at our research school, detailing that, despite how difficult a subject, the history of the residential school system must be addressed collectively, and we can instill awareness by engaging with children. This explains her philosophical/pedagogical approach to the difficult issue of the abuse many Indigenous children suffered in residential schools. It suggests how building a personal connection to their school community might offer children a closer understanding of social justice as they learn about the experiences of Indigenous students in residential schools across Canada.

During this project, teachers themselves read Indigenous picture books to explore these challenging issues, and then introduced the books to their classes. In this chapter, we describe pedagogical tools that have led to a heightened awareness of such historical injustices throughout Canadian history. Furthermore, connections are drawn between the abuses in residential schooling for Indigenous children with those of children left in the care of the Mount Cashel Orphanage in Newfoundland. Both of these historical incidents speak to the abuse of children; this is a controversial issue for the classroom, and a very sensitive one. Children's literature allows us to engage in such complex issues and further deepens student responses, while still meeting curricular demands. In this chapter, we share an exploration of historical time and place through high quality children's picture books and non-fiction resources. The tragedy of residential schooling was portrayed for Newfoundland teachers primarily through the reading of the novel *Fatty Legs* by Christy Jordan-Fenton and Margaret Pokiak-Fenton. The history of abuse at the Mount Cashel Orphanage was explored through non-fiction articles and narratives. A review of the literature related to the growth of Indigenous children's literature, multimodality, and culturally responsive pedagogy (Apple, 2011; Ladson-Billings, 1995; Nieto, 2006; White & Cooper 2012) will be used to expand concepts and research alongside the teachers' pedagogies. As well, student texts will be used to demonstrate how teachers were able to use Canadian literature to enhance the lived reading experiences of children from culturally and economically diverse backgrounds.

Laura's Story

Social justice issues permeate every facet of the school, and what a great way to help children reach new understanding around past injustices, through children's literature.

    —LAURA[1]

Bishop Academy (a pseudonym) is a two-stream school, one that offers instruction in both French and English. Students attend from Kindergarten through Grade 6. The current school population of 252 students has access to multiple facilities inside and outside of school, including a small park with play equipment, a gym, and a computer lab with 21 computers. Parents and guardians drop off children in the morning and are encouraged to enter into the school at dismissal to pick them up directly from their classrooms. This type of interpersonal connection allows time for the teacher to interact briefly with the adults who are significant in the students' lives.

    Our teacher-researcher Laura's beliefs about social justice, as voiced in the quote above, are representative of a school administration team that is seen on a daily basis to offer strong positive role models and advocate for the social issues that face this economically challenged school community. Marshall and Oliva (2006) write that the generation and production of a socially fit society requires such commitment, as well as on-going collaboration among the stakeholders. While the school draws much of its population from economically disadvantaged areas, it is also known for fostering coalitions both within the school community and the larger community, such as the Rotary Club of St. John's East. An annual stipend provided through the Rotary Club aids with needed literacy and mathematics resources. This partnership also led to the development of a much-needed playground. Within the community and the city at large, help is provided through the donation of blocks of theatre seats at the Arts and Culture Centre for orchestral and other performances, as well as money to cover the costs of bus transportation for field trips to local monuments and museums. Although the school has had its struggles with the social issues apparent in lower socioeconomic areas, a diverse school family continues to grow with children who are Indigenous, new immigrants, and large numbers of children coming from refugee camps. Most families in the school are drawn from nearby social housing projects, and parents are often working at several jobs to maintain basic living conditions. The school provides many types of services, from a family resource centre for early learning to English as a Second Language (ESL) instruction for parents, and includes a social worker and community medical supports. The school and teachers believe in the importance of understanding the culture of their students and making space for that understanding, and the school embraces cultural responsivity while showing a particular sensitivity to their school's cultural diversity.

Indigenous Literature and Social Justice

Social justice may be achieved through a conscientious commitment to addressing issues pertaining to inequality, including race, ethnicity, gender, and geography, among others. Much contemporary research has focused on the idea that literature can provoke a heightened awareness of social justice issues among children. There is general agreement among researchers that these stories can be morally instructive, have the potential to dismantle power structures, and entice children to become "global citizens." While social justice issues and agendas have become more salient in Canada, equality for Indigenous peoples remains elusive in the Canadian landscape. From early modern European exploration literature describing First Nations people as "savages" to the modern-day crisis of missing and murdered Indigenous women, Canada has maintained a culture of institutionalized racism and systemic marginalization. One of the greatest instigators of this is the former residential school system, which began in 1876 and ended in 1996. The system forcibly removed Indigenous children from their homes in a conscious effort to strip them of their cultural heritage and to have them assimilate into hegemonic Euro-Canadian society. In June 2015, the Canadian government's Truth and Reconciliation Commission (TRC) published a final report on the residential school system titled *Honouring the Truth, Reconciling for the Future: Summary of the Final Report of the Truth and Reconciliation Commission*. The opening line of the report states, "Canada's residential school system for aboriginal children was an education system in name only for much of its existence" (TRC, 2015, p. v). The system was not designed to teach. It was designed to solve "the Aboriginal problem" through assimilation to gradually eliminate the existence of Indigenous peoples in

Canada as a distinct entity of governance, culture, and nationhood. In the schools, "aboriginal languages and cultures were denigrated and suppressed. The educational goals of the schools were limited and confused, and usually reflected a low regard for the intellectual capabilities of aboriginal people" (TRC, 2015, pp. 4–5). The voice of the marginalized was silenced throughout the residential school system. Cultural genocide was the goal.

The legacy of the residential school system and reassertion of Indigenous rights in Canada remains a complex issue for all Canadians. It is only through the widespread recognition of injustices perpetrated through both negative actions and neglect by the Canadian government that reconciliation can be achieved. This must be addressed in all levels of society. On a primary level, Canadian classrooms are becoming increasingly diverse. Hegemonic Euro-Canadian culture is not representative of all students (and in some schools it is not representative of most). Given the history of Indigenous issues in Canada, it is logical to address multiculturalism and issues of social justice by first considering the local; in our project, we addressed these issues by reading about and linking the horrors of the Mount Cashel Orphanage in Newfoundland to the tragedy of Indigenous residential schooling. In particular, this was achieved through the teaching of Indigenous children's literature, as doing so allows the voice of the marginalized to be heard and hopefully embraced by students and educators alike. Many studies have shown, as we will see, that literature is not only a way to teach critical skills, but also allows for the instillation of empathy, moral values, and social understanding in students.

Children's Literature

Teachers can use children's literature as a vehicle to teach for social justice. "Stories that encourage children to develop critical thinking abilities, an appreciation for diverse cultures, and a sense of fairness are important for a child's development" (O'Neil, 2010, p. 41). Seidel and Rokne (2011) share that an

> interpretive and careful reading of literature in classrooms is one way
> to inspire contemplation and practice of peaceful and just ways of being
> together through a community of inquiry into the human condition.
> When shared with children [picture books] might offer comfort and
> hope, give words and names to children's experiences, and acknow-
> ledge and address their questions about human living. (Seidel & Rokne,
> 2011, p. 247)

To teach social justice in schools, educators must select works that are appropriate to the student body. Indigenous children's literature is a growing genre of literature, one that is both reflective of Indigenous cultures and children's learning practices. This literature, not unlike other culturally oriented literary genres, largely abides by the following specifications: It is created by, created within, and/or strongly affiliated with Indigenous peoples and communities. In Canada, some purveyors of the genre include Thomas King, Ted Harrison, and Lorraine Adams. The importance of this genre is that it consistently—whether explicitly or not—deals with issues of colonialism and social inequality. In a case study, Wiltse and colleagues quote Wolf and DePasquale, noting that "it is against a 'heavy colonial and neo-colonial history' that Aboriginal authors have had to 'adapt and redefine this Western literary form to tell their own stories'" (Wiltse, Johnston, & Yang, 2014, pp. 269–270). Indigenous writers must address the history of colonialism in order to create a space that allows their voice to thrive. Moreover, to do so through the genre of children's literature allows a wider audience reception and more ways of knowing—such as the accompanying images in picture books. With reference to Strong-Wilson (2007), Korteweg, Gonzalez, and Guillet (2010) address the potential that children's literature possesses: "Fictional narratives, including children's picture book stories, offer immersive 'perceptual horizons' or worldviews that run deep as 'touchstones': That is, they provide foundational or pivotal stories that impact perceptions and influence how we relate to the land and equally as important, to the peoples of the land" (p. 332). In this study, we found that children's literature was used to expand the cognitive horizons of teachers and students alike. For example, Thomas King's *A Coyote Columbus Story* retells the arrival of Christopher Columbus in what is now North America from an Indigenous perspective. Literature using conventions like these has the ability to change dominant historical narratives. For many of the teachers, including Laura, this was a new experience, which addressed a directive for cultural responsivity in the school. Furthermore, Indigenous children's literature is not a genre solely intended to set basic moral examples or to simply entertain. Instead, it is a sophisticated, complex genre of literature capable of addressing politicized, real-world scenarios that resonate in the lived Indigenous experience, thus making it the ideal mode through which to teach issues of social justice in Canada. Additionally, in our study, many of the educators felt uncomfortable challenging the history of schooling in Canada, or, rather, challenging the norm—in particular, finding ways to share such a horrific part of Canadian history in looking at child abuse through schooling. However, in an increasingly globalized and accountable nation, which now sees restorative justice as paramount, schools need to address and teach about these issues. Many of our teachers maintained that by "thinking outside the box" and approaching social justice issues even in a culturally responsive approach, educators can work within the constraints of time and curriculum to challenge inequality and the notion of power itself. In the simple act of assigning a work of Indigenous literature, the educator makes a stride toward conquering issues of social justice—that is, he or she starts a conversation with their colleagues and further to engage students as in this teacher case study.

What Is Culturally Responsive Teaching?

Ramirez and Jimenez-Silva (2015) define culturally responsive teaching as "a teaching philosophy that acknowledges students' cultural heritage and builds bridges of meaningfulness between home and school experiences in order to make academic learning accessible to all students" (p. 88). Culturally responsive pedagogy provides students with an education that is not only meaningful to that student's life, but does so in culturally appropriate ways (Toppel, 2015). In this case study, Laura and Sandra, the teachers, wished to connect the community experience with the national experience to allow children to develop a historical understanding of residential schooling and to further connect to the suffering of those within the school community. According to Mafuwane and Mahlangu, "diversity as a social construct manifests itself in a number of ways in any teaching and learning space and has the potential to affect what is taught, who is taught and how this is taught in a number of ways" (2015, p. 560). The important outcome and learning experience materialized in a number of multimodal texts produced by students. This was a validated outcome for teachers who, through the main teacher inquiry group, became introduced to the importance of Indigenous literature as a culturally responsive resource for Canadian classrooms. Many felt, alongside Laura, that our monthly meetings helped them to "recognize diversity in the classroom, but to respond to it in productive ways that can improve the educational outcomes of their students (Scott, Sheridan, & Clark, 2014). Next, we share a description of multimodality followed by an account of the teacher-researcher's experiences and students' texts in the classroom.

Multimodality

The integration of multimodal teaching practices in the classroom is a way to teach social justice in literacy in an engaging manner while still conforming to curriculum standards. Cunningham and Enriquez (2013) maintain that read-alouds, such as the use of the novel *Fatty Legs* by our teacher-researchers, are crucial to the learning of social justice, noting in particular that they "can provide the necessary scaffolding for the close reading of complex, powerful, and transformative texts" (p. 29). Using the graphic representations in the novel to extend the reading aloud showed how read-alouds that combine auditory and visual learning can be interactive events. Laura described that, in her read-aloud, she asked children guiding questions, which provided students with an opportunity to process and to reflect upon the novel. Although the content was not difficult, the tragedy of such an experience narrated through a child character's eyes was challenging for Grade 6 students to understand. She noted how sharing the illustrations in the book and revisiting them with passages around the pictures led to new questions and further inquiry. In many ways, the children deepened their connections because such questions provoked thoughts of social justice inquiry concerning issues of power, values, culture, and acceptance. Questions from the children, such as "Why didn't their parents check on them?," "Couldn't they have just run away?," and "Why did they have to leave their homes for school?," deepened their inquiry.

This reading process allows for a complex learning experience. The multimodal classroom is also addressed by researchers Groenke and Maples (2010), who discuss digital literacy. Referencing leading cultural theorist Henry Jenkins, the authors note that the convergence culture of 21st-century digital media is an arena in which "content flows across multiple media platforms, multiple media industries (e.g., music, film) cooperate with each other, and media consumers will go almost anywhere in search of the kinds of entertainment experiences they want" (Jenkins, as cited in Groenke & Maples, 2010, p. 39). When considering the classroom setting, this perspective suggests that students will choose the platform that suits their own unique preferences. Although students were given many opportunities to discuss in literature circles and to write in their journals, many found the culminating project of producing a digital postcard in the voice of a character to be the most liberating experience. Perhaps, as one child shared, "it feels more real" while composing the digital postcard as a part of the reflective response. While the authors refer to digital literature as "marked by sophisticated literacy engagement, rather than something that might displace traditional reading and writing skills," we can equally apply the concept to multimodal literacy in general (Groenke & Maples, 2010, p. 39). The heightened interaction and perceived proximity and reality that multimodality provides allows for a closer engagement with social justice for the student, as is illustrated later in the chapter concerning children's 3D postcards. With regards to teaching Indigenous children's literature, one of the perceived challenges of teaching is that minimal research has been undertaken on the genre. Such is true for Laura and her teaching peer Sandra. Educators may feel that they do not have adequate resources or understanding to effectively teach the genre. In this chapter, we show how multimodality comes into play. Visual, auditory, digital, or theatrical accompaniments can complement read-alouds such as the one offered in this classroom.

Using Indigenous Literature in a Grade 6 Classroom

You could hear a pin drop at the beginning of our daily read-aloud of Fatty Legs, children sat silently listening and contemplating on every word, as I read to them about Margaret Pokiak's experience.

—LAURA

The Grade 6 class, which participated in the unit on Indigenous literature and residential schooling, had 15 students from various social and ethnic backgrounds. Within this class of 15 sixth graders, there was one student who had immigrated from Cuba and two ESL students who had immigrated to Newfoundland from other provinces within Canada. The ESL students worked with an ESL itinerant teacher to learn English. The remaining students had lived in the area for most of their lives, and hailed from varying family backgrounds, ranging from two-parent and single-working-parent families to single-parent families receiving social assistance.

One research-teacher had been interested in the whole notion of residential schools since the closure of Mount Cashel, a Roman Catholic orphanage in Newfoundland, on June 1, 1990, following revelations of chronic child abuse by the Christian Brothers who administered it. Since her interest was first sparked, she followed stories in the newspapers, television documentaries, and other media. At the time of the research, a financial settlement had been made to many of the plaintiffs of the closed Newfoundland residential school. Sandra had a real interest in bringing to light the injustices against children in residential schools. Her belief that teaching children about atrocities within their local community deepens their understanding and empathy for others was one that she kept close to her heart, and at times she would share newspaper stories of children who had suffered unjustly, referencing the UN Rights and Freedoms of the Child in her Grade 6 social studies curriculum. Understanding the importance of being culturally responsive in taking agency and action, she and Laura chose to use the book *Fatty Legs: A True Story* (Jordan-Fenton & Pokiak-Fenton, 2010). This is a powerful story based on the personal narrative of the author's mother-in-law, the protagonist Margaret, who recounts her journey as a courageous eight-year-old Inuit child who aspires to attend school and learn how to read. The narrative recounts the abusive treatment she receives at school from one elderly nun and how she is later empowered by the kindness of another, showing others her bravery, dignity, and resilience against injustice.

The read-aloud was powerful for the children because it enabled them to visualize what was happening as the story was read with expression and emotion where applicable. The illustrations were shown to the children to help them envision the circumstances and the characters. For a great number of the students, the illustration of Olemaun burning her red stockings really struck home—it showed the character's strength in the face of adversity and, despite the harsh treatment she was dealt at the hands of her guardians at the residential school, the power she was able to maintain over at least one small aspect of her life. Laura reflected afterwards, "For the children, Olemaun avenged herself for the harsh treatment visited upon all the children at the residential school—the cutting off of the girls' hair, the strict rules against speaking their native language, and the chores the children were forced to perform."

Literature Circles

Before the children were given a writing prompt, they worked in literature circles. These are "small, student-led discussion groups in which group members have selected the same book or article to read" (McCall, 2010, p. 153). Deepening their engagement with the text and its issues, all students in the group must "critically observe their world to build academic knowledge, and [are] expected to observe and support each other as learners" (Mills & Jennings, 2011). To do this, students must read the text in advance and critically engage with it alone and later in circle with peers, providing the opportunity for discussions and collaborative learning (Süleyman et al., 2013). As Amy Heineke notes, literature circles "[support] facets central to students' reading" and "have been shown to boost reading engagement ... comprehension ... background knowledge, and critical literacy" (Heineke, 2014, p. 119). Sanacore (2013) further builds this idea suggesting that, "literature circles [act] as a vehicle for nurturing personal and critical responses to text" (p.117). Literature circles have also been shown to increase students' reading comprehension, helping students better understand and reflect on the texts they read (Süleyman et al., 2013). When used to teach important socio-historical topics, moreover, literature circles can be very informative as they help address various understandings of historical events or current affairs (McCall, 2010, p. 153). Thus, "teachers can encourage students to understand that primary and secondary sources are interpretations of historical events rather than a 'true account'" (2010, p. 153). With issues of social justice, literature circles foster a multiplicity of ideas, as a result of cultural diversity amongst group members and the collaboration of ideas. Differences in ideas among students also allow students to question what true accounts of history are, and how literature mediates them. The fact that literature circles allow children to share ideas is of the utmost importance. In these peer-led circles, engagement with each other encourages thoughtful discussions that are moderated by teachers (Sanacore, 2013). Whereas social studies instruction over the 20th century has focused on "a dominance of teacher talk during 'discussions,' individual seatwork interrupted at times with small group work, and the use of tests to measure student learning," literature circles allow students to lead and take on different roles, such as group leader or researcher (McCall, 2010, pp. 153-154; Süleyman et al., 2013). When students engage in group discussions with their peers, they are building a community where all members of the group are heard (Mills & Jannings, 2011). In a study conducted by Mills and Jennings (2011), students, "learned to take both reflective and reflexive stances and to pay attention to talk and their own engagement in it." (p. 597). Although students may feel challenged when faced with literature circles because of the necessity of reading in advance and sharing their critical thoughts, it is important, as Sanacore suggests, that "students' personal responses are encouraged, respected, and sensitively refined" (Sanacore, p. 119, 2013). The students in these circles are not only listeners—they are teachers for their fellow students, inside and outside of the classroom.

A Teaching Moment

One powerful moment for Laura and Sandra occurred when several of the children cheered for Olemaun, especially when they saw the illustration of her burning the symbolic red socks. One boy, in particular, recreated this illustration for his postcard because it vindicated her—to him, it represented the strength of a little girl trying to survive and maintain her cultural identity in a situation that was foreign to her. It was a transformative moment for the teacher-researchers because it showed how invested the students had become in Olemaun's story. Sharing stories opens channels to explore and understand one's own culture and historical disjuncture, offers ways to compare and contrast cultural expectations and behaviours, and provides opportunities to further engage in conversations about how we can reach some understanding of the past. The conversations throughout and following the reading of *Fatty Legs* were rich and insightful as the children made connections to the text and their personal experiences. In the meantime, Sandra had begun the discussion of residential schools, what they were, who was affected, and the atrocities that resulted. Discussion evolved around the different ways in which oppression occurs in cultures, which connected to central discussions around cultural responsivity in social studies classes. In the social studies curriculum, the students were learning about the atrocities happening to cultures in war-torn countries such as Serbia and Somalia and the resulting increase in numbers of refugees escaping these countries. Such discussions helped the children reach a better understanding of students attending their school who came as refugees from places such as Kazakhstan, Serbia, and various countries in Africa.

The Grade 6 social studies curriculum seeks to explore the concept of culture alongside the role it plays in all of our lives. Importantly, the curriculum document concerns itself with the relationship between culture and environment and how traditions relate to culture in a global perspective and in Canadian regions. Its goal is to have children reach a cross-cultural understanding of all Canadian peoples and of the way that multiple voices contributed to the shaping and development of Canada. In many ways, the use of such a real account begins with an understanding of the suffering of Indigenous peoples in the development of the Canadian cultural landscape. Like Laura and Sandra, many of the teachers in our study hoped that with the use of Indigenous literature, more opportunities would be given to explore and discuss such a tragic period in Canadian history.

When personal writings and narratives are used in the classroom, children can make connections on a more personal level (Hytten & Bettez, 2011) and can begin to reflect on their own experiences in relation to the narratives. In this study, children proved themselves to be more engaged by the chance to respond through journals, illustrations, and digital media because they were not confined to only one method of representing their understanding and responses to the book. Providing a variety of options allowed children to respond based on their interests and strengths. The students who experienced difficulty with written output were able to effectively share their responses to the book through illustrations and/or the digital postcard. This supported students who were not comfortable speaking out in front of their peers but were able to share their journal responses. Laura shared in an interview that her student Luke's emotional response to the treatment of the boys at the residential school was demonstrated through his illustration of a young Indigenous boy crying. He found it difficult to share his response verbally as he teared up explaining it to the teacher; however, the illustration spoke volumes. Often with historical narrative fiction, the plots are powerful and can be quite emotional and impact children. With this said, the powerful benefits include making children aware and connected to a past that may seem so far away or even fictional.

Fatty Legs can be described as "contemporary realistic fiction" that is "derived from actual circumstances," which, in this case, concerns the residential school system in Canada (Temple, Martinez, & Yokota, 2014, p. 228). The book provides "realistic settings" such as the classroom, a place with which the students are very familiar. The characters in the book "face problems and opportunities that are within the range of what is possible in real life," regardless of a child's cultural background (Temple, Martinez, & Yokota, 2014, p. 228). The authenticity of the characters in the book created significant connections with students, as we will see in our discussion of the digital postcard assignment. The characters are not so different from the students themselves: They resemble real people, and they live in a place that is or could be real. We felt that students shared a real sense of place with them. The characters act in ways similar to the children: They participate in a plausible series of events, they are presented with a dilemma that is of interest to the children, and they discover a realistic solution. The teachers observed that the children could feel themselves reflected in the individual characters. Although the teachers felt moments of discomfort during the read-aloud, both felt this type of literature teaches awareness of a Canadian social injustice and fosters cross-cultural understanding of Indigenous peoples. Laura talked about her and Sandra's awareness that the school population of children consisted of those who were Indigenous, alongside some of the children whose families could personally identify with the tragic outcomes of Mount Cashel Orphanage. This pedagogical choice to include a novel and other materials about residential schooling would invite the children's voices in the journal writing session. The journal entries were shared only within the comfort level of the children. Laura decided that she and Sandra would engage the children in writing postcards using an online app called 3D Postcard Generator, which allowed them to create digital postcards. With this program, students select a photo from the registry provided or upload a personal one of their choosing. The personal one can be found on the Internet by the student, created using a computer program such as Paint or Photoshop, or it can be drawn by hand and then scanned or uploaded to the app. The photo "should illustrate a multimodal understanding of the text (picture representation, connection, etc.)" (MyWebMyMail, n.d.). The photo is situated on the left-hand side of the digital postcard, and on the right-hand side appears a message of six lines that the student has written. In this message, students can write a letter, a poem, a work of prose, or perhaps a journal entry. Students are not limited to simply choosing their picture and message; they can also choose the colour of the postcard, frames, size, shadowing, shape, decoration, and so on. Ultimately, this multimodal medium allows students to express themselves in a complex way, particularly in a more nuanced fashion than writing alone.

With this journal assignment, children were asked to write a postcard home to their parents or to one of the adults or students at the residential school. Having been asked to take on the role of Olemaun, the students wrote from her perspective later in life, after her experience in the residential school system. Students reflected on what they thought Olemaun would say to her parents or one of the other characters at the school now that she was older, giving students the opportunity to think about Olemaun's personal growth and how she coped with her experience. This included how she felt about the role these other characters played in her experiences at the school and how that affected her life up to that point—students attempted to come to terms with Olemaun's past for her. Not only did students think about the effects of the residential school on Olemaun, but they reflected upon Olemaun's emotions: how she felt on the way to the school, when her braid was cut off, when she was bullied by some of the girls, as she stood up for herself and her fellow classmates, and how she was treated by the sisters. These "memories" provoked emotions of fear, apprehension, embarrassment, horror, pain, determination, and resilience, to name a few. Both positive and negative aspects of Olemaun's life were reflected upon, which suggests that students engaged with the literature and issues of social justice in a complex and comprehensive way.

Among the diverse student population, Sandra had children who struggled with oral and written composition. Both teachers were interested in finding an assignment that would engage a multiliteracies approach and multimodal composition, through both illustration and journal writing. The book evoked many reactions and emotions from the children—from shock and disbelief that children could be taken from their parents and sent to boarding schools, to anger for the parents and empathy and sadness for Olemaun, the main character. Many of the students drew depictions based upon the readings shared in class.

Multimodal Response in the Classroom

Through the use of literature circles for this book and in particular the personal narrative of Jordan-Fenton and Pokiak-Fenton's book *Fatty Legs,* we found that students were more engaged in the process of critical inquiry as opposed to explicit instruction. Students were asked to connect with a character at a critical point in the story. Sandra asked students questions to help them focus and connect with the character. The students' reactions varied, but were generally very powerful. Initially, the students expressed shock and disbelief about what had happened to the Inuit children at the residential school. Upon reading newspaper accounts and Sandra's sharing of articles from webpages, most children were horrified by such events and outwardly expressed anger. "Where were the police? Didn't her parents say something? What about the priests in the church?" Actions such as the cutting of children's hair off upon arrival were very disturbing for several of the girls in the class. One girl stated that if she had been there, she would have physically fought back and she wouldn't have let them cut her hair. In other forceful treatments, the boys shared in group discussions they would have either fought back, played pranks, or run away. As the literature circles evolved, empathy for the character of Olemaun grew with other statements, such as "I would try to be her friend," "I would be scared," and "it wasn't fair what they did to those people." The phrase *those people* also gently opened up discussions about inclusion and personal responsibility for others. Evidently, the students were moved emotionally by the powerful narrative.

The culminating digital postcard project provided students with an engaging platform through which to explore *Fatty Legs*. In the story, the children were told what to say when broadcasting a message home via the radio station and through letters. All had to be positive. The following is just a sampling of the diverse multimodal responses composed by the students in this creative exercise.

Character Postcard Responses

Leah used multiple modes—words, colour, and a picture—to illustrate the emotions in her card. The use of the colour pink as her postcard background expresses empathy, kindness, tenderness, and sensitivity. The depiction of the character places her in the future. This is demonstrated through the aesthetic of her clothes, hair, and lipstick. Most interesting, the character appears very calm and hopeful. Leah chose to write her postcard as a reflective response to Sister MacQuillan, also known as the Swan among the students at the residential school.

Dear Sister MacQuillan (Swan),

Thank you for being so nice to me while nobody else was. You helped me while I had nobody. Thank you for the stockings when I didn't have any. You and Agnes were kind to me.

Olemaun Pokiak

Bobby was quite engaged in the read-aloud, often asking critical questions for clarification of the plot, as well as questions about vocabulary and the historical period. He studied the illustrations and captured the personality of Olemaun in his illustration.

The most striking mode in his illustration of her personality is the use of curved, thick, and diagonal lines to depict her anger. These lines are normally used to depict a fight or to convey restless and uncontrollable energy. Finally, her facial expression also conveys her anger.

Alongside his visual, a very powerful journal response and emotional connection with the character is shared:

> Dear Raven (Yes, that's what I called you), You were always mean to me. You embarrassed me in front of everyone. You would have hit me if it wasn't for the Swan. I wanted to tell you how I really felt. I was scared then but no more. Olemaun.
>
> P.S. I burned the red socks!

Figure 6.1: Leah's Postcard

Figure 6.2: Bobby's Postcard

Figure 6.3: Phillip's Postcard

Although some students wrote their journal responses to show empowerment of the character's voice, others were saddened and distraught over the traumatic experiences of the character.

Phillip showed sadness through his character drawing, which used different shades of blue. Blue can signify sadness or depression, and other very strong emotions. Even Oleumaun's tears were created with a combination of blue and grey. The tears were drawn large as droplets, clearly delineated on the cheeks to express the magnitude of Oleumaun's seriousness. Additionally, her complexion is textured through the use of hard lines to enhance the character's confusion, defeat, and sadness. Phillip shares a narrative of the ill treatment and defeat of the character in her letter to her parents.

Dear Mother and Father,

I hate it here. Everyone treats me bad. One Nun makes me wash the floor and clean the chalkboard. She gave me red socks and now everyone calls me fatty legs.

You were right. I want to come home.
Your daughter, Olemaun

Both teachers chose this assignment to engage children in critical reflection on the past injustices suffered by children in residential schools. Laura talked about the difficulty of having children discuss and respond to content that was traumatic. She also believed that by introducing children's literature about residential schooling, they were enabling young children to identify and understand how both the provincial orphanage residential and the residential school Oleumaun attended were tragic points in history. These pedagogical approaches of read-aloud, literature circles, and digital journal responses were the beginning steps in sharing a culturally responsive pedagogy for educators to engage children in critical reflection of historical wrongs.

Culturally Responsive Pedagogies

Culturally responsive pedagogies provide a more nuanced understanding of culture beyond the superficial one advanced in many educational settings to one that sees culture as the "multiple social identities and ... ways of knowing and being in the world" (Ontario Ministry of Education, 2013, p. 1). The teachers in this study believed that a more nuanced discussion helped learners from all cultures to develop a deeper understanding of the socio-cultural lived experiences that informed their classmates' perspectives. Laura and Sandra hoped that this project would also develop a deeper sense of identity for racialized students within the school, in particular for students who could culturally relate more closely to the book. The teachers hoped their approach would support students in developing a greater sense of identity, which might serve to promote greater self-confidence, which in many cases increases students' in-class engagement (Nieto, 2006). Other scholars maintain there is also a correlation between students' engagement and students' academic success; hence culturally responsive learning might lead to more academic success among all students (Christensen, 2009).

Although the study did not measure academic success, the students in the study displayed a greater sense of engagement than they would normally using traditional forms of writing and non-culturally responsive means. The students' highlighted engagement can be observed through the care that they took to portray the selected themes from *Fatty Legs*. Moreover, students showed a greater understanding of Indigenous culture as exemplified by their references to the significance of such treatments as cutting off hair, loss of language, cultural knowing, and forced colonized schooling. Finally, by learning more about the abusive treatment of their community's Aboriginal population and students at Mount Cashel, they also learned more about their own selves and cultural identity.

Mafuwane and Mahlangu (2015) argue that the implementation of culturally sensitive teaching is a necessity, and suggest that such teaching practices are in line with a truly democratic society. Teaching using this approach means being cognizant of and able to respond to students of all different backgrounds and learning abilities (Mafuwane & Mahlangu, 2015). Additionally, culturally responsive pedagogy has been linked to improved self-concept and self-image in students as well as feelings of "empowerment, transformation, validation, comprehension, multidimensionality, and emancipation" (Scott et al., 2014, p. 3). Curriculum such as the unit using Indigenous literature in Laura and Sandra's classroom was designed with respect to this teaching practice and truly was intended to reflect the diversity of students and to "empower ethnically diverse students by making content knowledge accessible to them by connecting it to their lives and experiences outside of school" (Toppel, 2015, p. 557). Both teachers felt students had become more aware and knowledgeable about residential schooling because it was made relevant to their lives.

Conclusion

In closing, the teachers' explorations of thematic activities around residential schooling and consequent abuse were successful in raising awareness of social justice. Teachers felt that children's understanding of the experiences of the main character made them more aware of controversial historical events. These stories helped students to become more understanding of types of abuse and intimidation used to hurt others. The critical questioning engaged in the literature circles and through writing response showed that students did seek more answers as to the Indigenous children's plight and the suffering of the Mount Cashel boys. This generated more critical inquiry about why such suffering happened, and opened a door to a deeper conversation. This in turn gave children a chance to liberate Olemaun through writing, helping them to walk in the shoes of another.

Keywords

- children's literature
- cultural responsiveness
- education
- Indigenous literature
- literature circles
- multiculturalism
- multimodality
- pedagogy
- postcolonialism
- residential schools
- social justice

Reflection Questions

1. How can Indigenous children's literature be used to teach ideas of social justice across cultures and history in Canadian classrooms?
2. What technologies or media can be used to allow children to communicate their feelings related to social justice?
3. How can literature help children understand the long-term effects of atrocities such as the residential school system (e.g., unequal opportunities for Indigenous people, continued marginalization, and incomplete reconciliation)?
4. Why is it important today to use non-stereotypical literature (such as Indigenous children's literature) to teach issues of social justice?

Notes

1. Pseudonyms are used in the chapter.

References

Apple, M. (2011). Global crises, social justice, and teacher education. *Journal of Teacher Education, 62*(2), 222–234. doi:10.1177/0022487110385428

Christensen, L. (2009). *Teaching for joy and justice: Re-imagining the language arts classroom.* Milwaukee, WI: Rethinking Schools Publication.

Cunningham, K. E., & Enriquez, G. (2013). Bridging core readiness with social justice through social justice picture books. *New England Reading Association Journal, 48*(2), 28–37.

Groenke, S. L., & Maples, J. (2010). Young adult literature goes digital: Will teen reading ever be the same? *The ALAN Review,* (Summer 2010), 38–44.

Heineke, A. (2014). Dialoging about English learners: Preparing teachers through culturally relevant literature circles. *Action in Teacher Education, 36*(2), 117–140. doi: 10.1080/01626620.2014.898600

Hytten, K., & Bettez, S. C. (2011). Understanding education for social justice. *Educational Foundations, 25*(1/2), 7–24.

Jordan-Fenton, C., & Pokiak-Fenton, M. (2010). *Fatty legs.* Vancouver, BC: Annick Press.

King, T. (2007). *A coyote Columbus story.* Toronto, ON: Groundwood Books.

Korteweg, L., Gonzalez, I., & Guillet, J. (2010). The stories are the people and the land: Three educators respond to environmental teachings in Indigenous children's literature. *Environmental Education Research, 16*(3–4), 331–350.

Ladson-Billings, G. (1995). But that's just good teaching! The case for culturally relevant pedagogy. *Theory into Practice, 34*(3), 159–165.

Mafuwane, B. M., & Mahlangu, V. P. (2015). Teaching practices responsive to cross-border education of learners from culturally diverse settings: A South African perspective. *Mediterranean Journal of Social Sciences, 6*(1), 560–567. doi:10.5901/mjss.2015.v6n1p560

Marshall, C., & Olivia, A. (2006). Leadership for social justice: Making revolutions in education (2nd ed.). Boston, MA: Allyn and Bacon.

McCall, A. L. (2010). Teaching powerful social studies ideas through literature circles. *The Social Studies, 101,* 152–159.

Mills, H. & Jennings, L. (2011). Talking About Talk: Reclaiming the Value and Power of Literature Circles. *The Reading Teacher, 64*(8), 590–598.

MyWebMyMail.com. (n.d.). 3D postcard generator. Retrieved from http://www.mywebmymail.com/?q=content/3d-postcard-generator

Nieto, S. (2006). Solidarity, courage and heart: What teacher educators can learn from a new generation of teachers. *Intercultural Education, 17*(5), 457–473.

O'Neil, K. (2010). Once upon today: Teaching for social justice with postmodern picturebooks. *Children's Literature in Education, 41*(1), 40–51.

Ontario Ministry of Education. (2013). *Student voice transforming relationships: Capacity building series.* Toronto, ON: Author.

Ramirez, P. C., & Jimenez-Silva, M. (2015). The intersectionality of culturally responsive teaching and performance poetry: Validating secondary Latino youth and their community. *Multicultural Perspectives, 17*(2), 87–92. doi:10.1080/15210960.2015.1022448

Sanacore, J. (2013). "Slow Down, You Move Too Fast": Literature Circles as Reflective Practice. *The Clearing House, 86,* 116–120.

Scott, K. A., Sheridan, K. M., & Clark, K. (2014). Culturally responsive computing: A theory revisited. *Learning, Media, and Technology, 40*(4), 412–436. doi:10.1080/17439884.2014.924966

Seidel, J., & Rokne, A. (2011). Picture books for engaging peace and social justice with children. *Diaspora, Indigenous, and Minority Education, 5*(4), 245–259. doi:10.1080/15595692.2011.606007

Süleyman, A., Nurdan B., Mehtap G., & Arzu, Y. (2013). The Effect of Literature Circles on Reading Comprehension Skills. *Journal of Theoretical Educational Science, 6*(4), 535–550.

Temple, C., Martinez, M., & Yokota, J. (2014). *Children's books in children's hands: A brief introduction to their literature.* Philadelphia, PA: Temple University Press.

The Truth and Reconciliation Commission (TRC). (2015). *Honouring the truth, reconciling for the future: Summary of the final report of the Truth and Reconciliation Commission.* Ottawa, ON: Government of Canada.

Toppel, K. (2015). Enhancing core reading programs with culturally responsive practices. *Reading Teacher, 68*(7), 552–559. doi:10.1002/trtr.1348

White, R. E., & Cooper, K. (2012). Critical leadership and social justice: Research, policy and educational practice. *US-China Education Review, A,* 517–532.

Wiltse, L., Johnston, I., & Yang, K. (2014). Pushing comfort zones: Promoting social justice through the teaching of Aboriginal Canadian literature. *Changing English: Studies in Culture and Education, 21*(3), 264–277.

Chapter 7

Opening Doors, Opening Minds: The Role of the Inquiry Group in Teaching for Social Justice

Lynne Wiltse and Shelby LaFramboise-Helgeson

> It was a good experience for me because it opened up doors that I may
> not have taken if I wasn't coming to the inquiry group. I may not have
> sought out a new novel and been forced to do something different with it
> rather than just the traditional way of teaching. (Ann)

> This project is opening their minds to what is justice ... It makes them
> think outside of themselves a little more and takes their narrow life
> and makes it a little bigger. It makes them think and have questions.
> (Collette)

These comments, made by two of the teachers in our research study, describe ways in which involvement in the project was opening up possibilities in their teaching for social justice. Ann was reflecting on how group membership helped her to break with tradition at the conservative school in which she taught.[1] In contrast, Collette's comment speaks to the ways in which participation in the project was providing her students with opportunities to broaden their views of life and justice. In both cases, the inquiry group was instrumental. In this chapter, through two illustrative teacher stories, we will highlight the role of the inquiry group in opening doors and minds to social justice teaching and learning. Before turning our attention to these teacher stories, we will provide pertinent background information about our research site, a brief discussion of the theoretical perspectives that inform our chapter, and the research questions that frame our illustrative examples.

Study Details

Our research site, situated within the Department of Elementary Education, was one of two sites in the Faculty of Education at the University of Alberta. Our inquiry group was designed for elementary teachers who were teaching in the intermediate grades (in Alberta, Grades 4–6). Teacher recruitment occurred in various ways. Our research team received news that our study had been funded just before Lynne taught her last graduate course in children's literature. During that class, she let her students, most of whom were practising teachers, know that she was looking for research participants for the new study. This proved to be a productive way to begin to recruit teachers for the inquiry group. A vice-principal of a charter school with an academic focus contacted Lynne over the summer to let her know that she would like the intermediate teachers in her school to participate; this resulted in four participants. A primary teacher recommended one of her colleagues; she joined the study and brought along two of her colleagues. Lynne invited two former students of the children's literature course and asked Shelby LaFramboise-Helgeson, also a former student of this course and, at the time of the study, a full-time M.Ed. student, to be the research assistant for the project.

Perhaps not surprisingly, the inquiry group membership shifted somewhat over the course of the three-year study. A French immersion teacher joined our group after learning about the study through a conference presentation. While most of the teachers participated for the duration of the study, two participants had to leave the study and were replaced by new members. The composition of our group included teachers from a range of schools and classrooms (public, Catholic, charter, French immersion). This representation of research participants from diverse teaching contexts is one of the factors that made our inquiry group unique; this contrast played out in interesting ways in the study, as will be seen in the chapter.

During the first term of the inquiry group, along with the teachers, we read and reflected upon academic articles and book chapters about Canadian children's literature and/or teaching for social justice. We also introduced the teachers to a variety of Canadian children's literature with social justice themes; we brought a wide selection of possible texts (picture books as well as novels) to the meetings, gave book talks, and collaboratively read some of the shorter books. At our last meeting before the Christmas break, we encouraged teachers to take some books home to read, in the hopes that this would give them time to read some of the longer texts. This proved to be a productive plan; book selection for our first teacher story happened in just this way.

Data for the teacher stories, in terms of the actual teaching, are from the first year of the study; however, in our follow-up discussion, we also draw on data collected from inquiry group meetings beyond the initial year of the project. Two broad research questions guided us in analyzing the data: (1) What is the role of the inquiry group in supporting teacher participants in opening up possibilities to teach for social justice? and (2) In what ways do teachers engage students with Canadian literature to promote social justice? Before proceeding to the teacher stories, we mention in brief the theoretical perspectives that helped us to answer these questions. Our inquiry group approach was grounded in the work of Wenger (2007) and Cochran-Smith and Lytle (2009), who encourage community members to engage in inquiry around their own practice as they attempt to improve curriculum, pedagogy, and student achievement. The research drew on contemporary theories of social justice that regard teachers as agents of social change who pay attention to issues of race, class, gender, and language (Cochran-Smith, 2004), as well as studies that emphasize the role of literature in advocacy research in literacy education (Bender-Slack, 2010; Cherland & Harper, 2007; Ching, 2005; Wolk, 2009). For the purpose of this chapter, Lave and Wenger's (1991) and Wenger's (1998) concept of communities of practice, in particular, informed our understanding of the teacher stories. The learning process, from a community of practice perspective, involves a shift from the traditional focus on individual learners to an emphasis on their shared membership in the community. Communities of practice may develop naturally when members share a common interest in a particular area, or they may be formed with the specific intent of acquiring knowledge related to their field; group members learn from each other as they share their expertise and experience. Over time, these communities develop a shared history. We came to think of our inquiry group as a community of practice, while keeping in mind that our research participants were also members of other communities of practice, for example, in their schools. As we will see, these two overlapping communities of practice were especially pertinent to the two teachers that we feature in this chapter.

Teacher Stories

Our study findings suggest that there were two key, interrelated aspects in terms of how teachers selected and taught the texts in a social justice framework. First, the project provided teachers with contemporary Canadian literature that, for the most part, they did not have access to; either they were unfamiliar with the texts and/or their schools, especially in times of fiscal constraint, did not have the funds to purchase the books. Secondly, the support of the inquiry group encouraged several of our teachers to move out of their comfort zones in terms of the texts they selected, as well as their approaches to teaching the children's literature. Ann, the first of the teacher participants to make her selection, provides a particularly powerful example on both counts.

Ann—Going against the Grain

At the start of the study, Ann had been at Dawnbreak Charter School for six years; prior to this, she had taught for two years in a public school in one of the local districts. In the following excerpt, made during an inquiry group discussion about how teachers navigated the teaching of potentially challenging topics at their respective schools, Ann explains a bit about her teaching context:

To me, I get the feeling that as long as the admin get their results and that there are no parent complaints, they don't really care. The only time they would come and talk to me is if the results were down to see why. I've never been talked to by the admin about what I'm doing in my classroom, ever. But, as a precautionary about teaching certain things, I don't really hold back on anything, just because I think the parents know me well enough and I've been there long enough that I feel like I can take those risks.

As we will see, this was no small concern for teachers at Dawnbreak School.

After having read the novel over the Christmas break, Ann chose *Elijah of Buxton* (Curtis, 2007), a fictionalized account of Buxton, Canada, a settlement of runaway slaves near the American border, for her two Grade 6 classes. Ann's students were primarily immigrant or second-generation Asian students, predominantly from India and China; students wore uniforms and were used to traditional teaching approaches. By and large, parents chose Dawnbreak because they wanted their children to achieve high academic results; the school was known for its highly structured environment, teacher-directed instruction, and strong home/school partnerships. Ann's choice of text marked a significant departure from her regular practice of teaching the same books every year: "When I taught *Elijah of Buxton,* it was helpful to have something fresh because I had been teaching English for four or five years and I'd done the same books for years." Here we return to Ann's comment, with which we began the chapter, that participation in the inquiry group was good for her as it opened up doors that she may not otherwise have taken. In the following excerpt, a continuation of her explanation, we see that this involved a measure of discomfort for Ann:

It was a little bit scary for me because some of the teachers at the school didn't really like what I was doing because I was going against the grain and they thought, "Oh you're being all fancy with what you're doing with your book, right?"

Opening up doors may have been good for Ann in some respects; at the same time, it was not easy, as it meant going against standard practice at her school. Ann's choice of the word *forced* likely speaks to her discomfort in doing something other than the familiar. While there was no coercion involved, there was an expectation that teachers teach their texts in ways that would encourage their students to reflect on structural and social inequities in Canadian society. Prior to her involvement in the study, Ann's approach to the teaching of novels had been reminiscent of traditional novel studies: vocabulary work, comprehension questions, and quizzes. Ann took advantage of her involvement in the project to try new teaching strategies. In the following excerpt, Ann refers to the effect of the inquiry group on her teaching practice:

> I found I became more open as a teacher to different ways of teaching
> and having the kids do different things rather than just, OK, sit down in
> your desk and do the questions, which is the way our school is. Even the
> students were just taken aback, like, "Oh, my gosh we're doing this, this
> is awesome. Are you sure we're allowed?"

Just how was Ann's teaching different? The first change was in the reading of the novel itself. Because *Elijah of Buxton* is written in a dialect other than Standard English, Ann thought that the language might pose challenges for some of her students, especially as several were English-language learners. For example, on the second page, Elijah, the main character tells his friend, Cooter, "You got me. I ain't never seen such tracks nowhere. Let's ask my pa once he comes out the field" (Curtis, 2007, p. 2). Accordingly, Ann read the first several chapters aloud so that students could become acquainted with the unfamiliar language variety. This in itself was not "business as usual;" Ann seldom read aloud to her students. Ann also engaged her students with more discussion than was her customary practice; during one of our visits to Ann's class, we were impressed by the way she was able to get students to draw connections between a text set in a distant time and place and with a foreign context—the first free-born child in a community of former slaves in the mid-1800s—and students' contemporary lives, something not necessarily easy to do. In the inquiry group meeting following this classroom visit, I was describing what we had observed to the participants. Ann elaborated:

> Yeah, I've been noticing with *Elijah of Buxton* that I do find it a lot eas-
> ier because I have many children who are first-generation Canadians or
> they're immigrants themselves. If I had a different group of students,
> I don't think I would be able to relate the novel to them as easily. I find it
> very easy to bring it into their own world. Like, I was talking about how
> Elijah is caught between being a free-born and he also has the world of his
> parents being slaves. Many of my students are caught being a Canadian
> citizen and fitting into this society, but they also have the traditional
> expectations of their parents, so they're kind of balancing both worlds.

Various historical and contemporary social justice issues were threaded through this discussion—from structural and social inequalities to discrimination and racism.

Another striking example of change in her teaching practice was the way that Ann involved students in a variety of multimodal representations. Students explored the website for the Buxton National Historic Site and Museum, which celebrates the Underground Railroad and early Black settlement in Canada, trying some of the offerings of the learning centre: an interactive CD-ROM; a game, *100 Steps to Freedom;* and a video, "The Many Roads to Buxton." The students also participated in "a choose your own adventure" webquest with a slavery theme. During one of our visits to Ann's class, Lynne joined two boys who were so eager to tell her about the choices they had made with their choose-your-own-adventure that they initially argued about who would get to talk first; without a doubt, the boys were engaged! As a culminating project to the reading of the novel, students created digital quilts, based on the freedom quilts used by slaves as part of the Underground Railroad. During one of our inquiry group meetings, Ann explained how she had introduced this activity to her students. In the following excerpt, Ann describes how she read *Patchwork Path: A Quilt Map to Freedom* (Stroud, 2007), a fictionalized account of the Underground Railroad; through a series of clues hidden in the quilt, the picture book tells the story of two of the thousands who escaped slavery by making the dangerous journey to freedom in Canada:

> Today I read them the *Patchwork Path* ... It was kinda funny the way they reacted when I said to come sit around my desk. They didn't know what to do—they were like, "What are you doing? Why are we listening to a story?" It was pretty cute, but it really made me realize just how structured my class is, and as soon as I messed that up they didn't know what to do, and they didn't know what to expect. But, they were really pleased with it.

The students had some questions following the reading of the book: "How did people know how to make the paths to freedom? Where did they get the stories from? How did they get that information back then? Do people still do real quilting nowadays?" Ann then explained her expectations for the digital patchwork project: "The patchwork had to relate to something they'd learned about slavery, or something from the book, *Elijah of Buxton*. They have to write up a report on what the symbol means and why they chose the colours and so forth. When both classes are finished, we'll put all the squares together and then there'll be 44 squares to make a big quilt. I'm interested to see what kind of ideas they've come up with as I've shown them a couple patterns, like the bow tie pattern, and the bear's paw." We were really excited by the results when we visited the class again to observe the completed quilts, prominently on display in the hallway. Visually, they were very striking—colourful and creative; we were also impressed by the written pieces that accompanied the quilts. As doors opened for Ann, she became more open as a teacher; this in turn opened up possibilities for her students, as evidenced in Ann's comments about the students' final projects: "It was kind of nice to see the kids spread their wings because they no longer were asking, 'OK, well is this right? Can I do this?' It was more of an expression, a way that they could express themselves."

Collette—Do(ing) It for Real
The second teacher we profile in this chapter is Collette. She had been teaching for ten years at two schools. At the time of the study, Collette was in her second year of teaching Grade 6 at Steven Powrie Elementary School in the local public school district. In contrast to Dawnbreak, at Steven Powrie, the focus was on developing the leadership

potential in all students—the school was known for valuing diverse voices and for being solution-focused and supportive. Collette described the class composition accordingly: "Vietnamese, Chinese, Korean, Somali, Cree, Métis, a mixture of White European like German and Irish backgrounds, some new to Canada families. In terms of socio-economic status, many of the students were lower end. A lot of children were living with grandparents, or single moms, some were hungry." As will be seen, Collette's teacher story provides a striking comparison to that of Ann's in various ways.

Collette had a deep interest in social justice issues and a significant amount of experience in teaching for social justice. During an interview following the first year of the study, Collette explained how she considered the dual focus of our research study on Canadian literature and social justice to be complementary: "I think Canadians are a socially just people—being that way is kind of our own culture and our heritage. So, with Canadian authors for young people, I think you'll find that in their writing, kind of the underlying theme." In the following interview excerpt, Collette elaborates on her comment, mentioned at the beginning of the chapter, that the project was opening her students' minds to social justice:

> For our future, we need to choose to be guardians of social justice and to spread that in an unjust world, and to challenge these kids to be leaders to promote justice, and you can start when they're 11. We talked a lot this year about Craig Kielburger who started Free the Children when he was 12. We were involved in *Me to We* and we streamed in We Day and watched that. That really got the ball rolling.

As teaching for social justice was familiar to Collette, involvement in the research study did not push the boundaries of her comfort zone as it did with Ann; rather, participation motivated her to become more deliberate in her teaching for social justice:

> I found the inquiry group really made me start thinking consciously about what maybe I would do instinctively. So, I started really thinking academically about how I wanted to teach this project, and what's a better way. And my plans worked really well for doing inquiry-based learning, as that is big in our district. Just really thinking carefully and having a conscious plan of approaching these social justice issues. Do it for real instead of as I went along.

Collette was the second teacher in the inquiry group to select and teach texts; this occurred during the spring of the first year of the study. Rather than a whole class novel, Collette chose to do a literature circle approach. In keeping with the social justice aspect of the study, her plan was to have her Grade 6 students create group advocacy plans related to their texts; the selected books would be used with her students as a starting point for further inquiry:

I explained to them that their novel study was their starting or their kick off point—it was their spark. When they got hung up in retelling the novel, I'd say, "No, that was just to get us started. What you need to find is the issue inside the novel and then go from there. So, it's not a book report. The novel is to give you an idea that you want to explore farther."

Collette selected four texts that would provide a range of social justice issues, both historical and contemporary: *Fatty Legs: A True Story* (Jordan-Fenton & Pokiak-Fenton, 2010); *The Heaven Shop* (Ellis, 2004); *Parvana's Journey* (Ellis, 2002); and *Caged Eagles* (Walters, 2001). Two of the choices deal with difficult aspects of Canadian history. *Fatty Legs: A True Story,* co-authored by Margaret Pokiak-Fenton and her daughter-in-law Christy Jordan-Fenton, is a memoir of an Inuit girl, Olemaun (Margaret), who attended residential school in the Canadian Arctic. The second historical text was *Caged Eagles* by Eric Walters, set on Canada's West Coast during World War II; it is a story of Japanese internment. The other two texts, both by Canadian author Deborah Ellis, were set in contemporary times, but in distant places. *The Heaven Shop* tells the story of Binti and her family, whose lives are affected by the AIDS epidemic in Malawi. *Parvana's Journey,* the second novel in the Breadwinner trilogy, tells Parvana's story in war-torn Afghanistan during the time of the Taliban. Collette created a detailed plan for this social justice unit, which she entitled *Children for Children.* She explained that she wanted the project to be "valuable, authentic, meaningful and exciting to the kids." In small groups, students read one of the four texts; following the reading, each group had to identify a social justice issue within their book and then "their job was to create a non-profit, non-governmental organization that would back the issue and present their solution or action; we called it an action because you can't necessarily solve these issues."

Collette allowed the students to choose their own issues from within the novels, but she provided guidance and structure: "It was all kind of laid out for them ... so first they had to define their issue. I asked them, 'What is the issue that you found in the novel that you want to explore farther?'" For example, a group of girls who read *Parvana's Journey* surprised Collette by their choice:

> With the *Parvana's Journey* group, they chose poverty and hunger, which is interesting because I would have chosen education. That the girls weren't allowed to go to school to me is appalling, but maybe their choice was closer to home. They've been hungry, so to them to be hungry is a bigger issue ... Yeah, to be an underclass person in your own country. We did talk about education, but I really wanted them to be allowed to choose what they wanted.

The importance of choice is well known to be an important factor if students are to have ownership of their learning (see, for example, Bainbridge & Heydon, 2013;

Wiltse, 2015). With *The Heaven Shop*, a group of girls focused on the issue of HIV and AIDS orphans in Africa, and a group of boys who read *Caged Eagles* concentrated on Japanese internment.

Given space constraints, we will highlight one of the four groups as an exemplar of Collette's teaching of the project. A group of three boys—Timmy, Sheldon, and Larry—read *Fatty Legs: A True Story*. Collette scheduled times for students to meet during their reading of the text: "They had to sit down together and they had little steps along the way of paperwork to keep them on track." She noted that "it got pretty exciting—when they started talking to each other, that was the best part. We worked on how do you discuss a novel, what do you say?" Collette provided students with sticky notes to record the questions they had as they read:

> "What does it mean when they cut Olemaun's hair?" was what Larry wrote. And one of the boys in his group, Timmy, had the answer. I just listened. Timmy figured it out because he is a deep thinker. He's like, "Well it's about power, it's about control, it's about taking away their Indian." He really caught onto that idea of breaking the Indian out of them. It touched him, this story, and he and his father went out to Blue Quills (Albertan Indian Residential School) and looked around. Timmy started to find out that there were residential school survivors in his family.

Following the reading of their novel, the boys chose the issue of residential schooling; Collette explained that "with *Fatty Legs*, it was pretty obvious they'd pick that." In the following excerpt, she describes the process the boys went through once they had identified their issue:

> With residential schooling, they had to research all the background information—the definition, the history, what has been done to this point to resolve or to bring justice to this issue, followed by a plan of what would they do now. They had a mind map where they brain-stormed solutions, and from those, as a group they had to choose what they would do about the issue. What the boys came up with is that you can't do anything about residential schooling; it's done. But how do we repair, how do we heal, what action can we take at this point?

Collette suggested that the group might want to talk with the program coordinator for FNMI (First Nations, Métis and Inuit) Education with the local school district as part of their research. The boys sent her an email invitation, and were excited when she accepted and came to the school to meet with them. The teacher describes the impact the conversation had on the group:

They felt important ... She came for their meeting and we sat down all together in the library and she was fantastic with them. She drew them out and asked them questions. One of their ideas was to turn old residential schools into healing centres and museums and she said well maybe that won't work because people who went there may not want to go back in those buildings; think about the trauma of stepping up those stairs again. So, she made them think again, from all different sides of the issue.

With a topic as complex and contentious as residential schooling, this is extremely important. For young students, it can be hard to understand and appreciate historical events. As an Inuit woman from the Canadian Arctic, the program coordinator was able to provide the students with invaluable background knowledge related to the memoir. Collette explained that she also encouraged them to go beyond the text by doing "something local to reflect their school's diversity."

We're sitting in the library and she says, "Look around. Do you see any books with you on them, because we had a Métis and a Cree in the group. They're like, "No, there are none." And she said that maybe that's a place to start. So, she donated FNMI books to the school and they created a *culture corner*. They put a mirror up which said something like, "See yourself here in these books."

For students who are not used to seeing themselves reflected in the literature, this was powerful. This calls to mind Aldana's (2008) comment that "children need books that are mirrors in which they can see and learn about themselves, and books that are windows open to the rest of the world" (p. 1). Whereas for Timmy, Sheldon, and other students of Indigenous heritage in the school, the culture corner served as mirror, *Fatty Legs* and the other books proved to be a window for other students by introducing them to an aspect of Canadian history with which they were largely unfamiliar. By the time the culture corner was created, the end of the school year was at hand. In some respects, though, this was just the beginning, as can be seen in Collette's explanation as to what happened when the FNMI coordinator extended her challenge beyond representation in the library:

Then she talked about the walls and halls, and about having representations of all different cultures in the hallways, and in the classrooms. She asked them, "After school, when nobody's here, if you walked through the halls, would you know what kind of students go here?" And you wouldn't, because the walls and halls are generic. So that really got them thinking further.

Although these boys moved on to junior high, the school they attended took up the "halls and walls" challenge as a school-wide action. The school was culturally diverse, and the initiative was extended so that students of other backgrounds were represented on the halls and walls of the school as well. Collette speaks to the possibilities that came from the connections Timmy, Sheldon, and Larry made while reading and responding to *Fatty Legs:* "It was really cool, just that whole opening up of what is possible."

Discussion and Implications for Teaching Practice

In this section, we will discuss the ways in which the inquiry group functioned as a community of practice to enable teachers and students to open doors and minds as they read and responded to Canadian literature for social justice. We will highlight our teacher stories, but also incorporate study findings from the inquiry group as a whole.

We begin by returning to Ann's comment that making the selection of *Elijah of Buxton,* and the way she was teaching the text, meant going against the grain at her school. In our view, the choice of *Elijah of Buxton* and using multimodal strategies in her teaching hardly constituted "being fancy"; however, for the other teachers at this traditional school who were not participating in the research project, Ann's choice of text and pedagogy was anything but standard practice. Ann's experience speaks to the community of practice framework, which we introduced earlier in the chapter. In this regard, Philpott and Daganais's (2012) article *Grappling with Social Justice: Exploring New Teachers' Practice and Experiences* is of particular interest. Philpott and Daganais's research, conducted at Simon Fraser University in British Columbia, featured new teachers who had taken a teacher education program focused on issues of social justice; the authors found that the degree to which new teachers were able to incorporate social justice into their own teaching practice depended on the communities of practice in the schools in which they were hired. Drawing on Wang, Odell, and Schwille (2008), Philpott and Dagenais explain that when pedagogy introduced in teacher preparation programs is not supported by the new school cultures, new teachers often abandon what they had come to believe about teaching in their pre-service program. In their study, Philpott and Dagenais found that job assignment, curriculum constraints, and lack of professional support discouraged many of their participants from exploring social justice in their teaching.

Although Ann was an experienced teacher, these study findings resonated with her situation. Due to the community of practice at Dawnbreak School, these factors applied, in varying degrees. We have already mentioned the emphasis on grades at Ann's school; with this came a strong focus on testing. Ann's students took close to six months to complete the novel and follow-up activities, due to competing constraints at her school. For example, during one meeting Ann noted: "I put *Elijah* on the back burner for a bit because we had our exam last week so we were getting ready for that." She was going against the grain, but within limitations—she still had to fit within school expectations. As with the research conducted by Philpott and Dagenais, Ann's experience suggests that "without a collaborative and supportive community, innovative and transformative practice informed by a social justice perspective was not likely to occur" (2012, p. 94). As the support Ann received from the community of practice at her school was minimal, the encouragement, ideas, and feedback of the inquiry group became even more important, as can be seen in the following comment:

> It's great because in my division I teach with teachers who have been teaching for 30 plus years. I am the only teacher who has less than 15 years of experience in that division. So, I work with very traditional teachers who have been at Dawnbreak since the school opened, so it was nice for me. I finally felt comfortable at the school since I have been there. To kind of go against them, but down a different path than maybe what's always been done.

In terms of "what's always been done," we noticed that, over time, Ann's involvement in the inquiry group, along with that of three of her colleagues, begin to shape the community of practice at her school. Lave and Wenger (1991) speak about "oldtimers" and "newcomers" within communities of practice; "oldtimers" are the more experienced members who represent the history of the community, whose role it is to pass on this knowledge to the "newcomers." Referring to the concept of "oldtimers" and "newcomers," Philpott and Dagenais (2012) explain that new members may not share a common path with current members; rather, they may want to present their own views and ways of being as part of the community of practice. This describes well how Ann and her colleagues were introducing change to the established community of practice at their school. The authors go on to say that while these circumstances may offer rich opportunities for combining the experiential knowledge of "oldtimers" and the fresh insights of "newcomers," at the same time, "this negotiation of ideas and knowledge can create tensions resulting in a repositioning of members, or adjustments of the characteristics defining the community of practice" (2012, p. 86). During inquiry group discussions, we saw some evidence that this was occurring at Dawnbreak School. For example, at one of our meetings, Ann was explaining how she wanted her students to "become active, critical, and compassionate heralds for justice … But, at Dawnbreak it's fact-driven—memorize, memorize, memorize. A lot of teachers hate the new curriculum, because it's all inquiry-based thinking, not multiple choice, it's not memorize the facts, which is what we're used to." Ann was trying to disrupt this established community of practice:

> I try to tell my students that, yes, it's important to know knowledge, but it's more important when you leave this school, that you can be a good citizen, and you can have an opinion about something and a conversation with someone. If I asked them something at the beginning of the

year, they just all sat there, like, "What's the right answer?" And I said, "There is no right answer sometimes; if you don't start having an opinion, you're not going to be involved in the world."

At this point in the discussion, one of the other participants, referring to the four teachers from Dawnbreak School, made the following comment: "Well, you guys have been the ones who keep pushing the school that way." To which Ann responded: "I think that sort of thing too. It's a lot of old school, and then it's the new guys that are like, 'Hey, we'll take a risk.'" One of the other teacher participants jumped in: "Well, I'm stereotyping, but these kids that you teach, it's probably the first time anyone told them that what they had to say was valuable and they had their own voice and their own opinions. They didn't just have to toe the line." Ann did not disagree: "Yeah, I can see what you mean ... it is true a lot of the time." But, with four members from the inquiry group, we were cautiously optimistic that the school community of practice could shift, even slightly. And we hoped for such a change, as opening doors for Ann had clearly proven to be good for her students as well.

For Collette, the other teacher participant we profiled in this chapter, the role of the inquiry group was instrumental to her teaching for social justice, but in differing ways to Ann. Rather than feeling she was going against the grain, the community of practice at Collette's school was supportive of teaching for social justice, complementing the community of practice of the inquiry group, which supported her teaching in other ways, as can be seen by the following remark, from the end of the second year of the study:

> Being part of the inquiry group for the last two years has definitely shaped my practice and changed it in a good way. I'm always thinking about how I'm going to integrate social justice messages and learning, and readings into every subject area that I'm teaching now.

The exposure to academic readings and new children's literature, along with the conversations about how to teach social justice, contributed to Collette's "doing it for real."

> And, it's been really exciting to be in this type of academic setting; I haven't been in university for a very long time. I've found a lot of growth personally and professionally from being a part of this group and hearing what other people think, and getting readings I wouldn't have found on my own. Just having my practice informed and opened up to other possibilities has been fantastic.

In turn, informing and opening up her practice played a significant role in Collette's opening her students' minds to "what is justice." However, we noted that her influence in the community of practice at her school went beyond her classroom. Philpott and

Dagenais (2012) maintain that successful mentorship is based on building supportive communities where beginning and experienced teachers work together. We were able to observe the "oldtimers" and "newcomers" concept play out in more productive ways at Steven Powrie School. A case in point is Katelyn, a new teacher at the school who joined our research study in the second year, who explains how Collette mentored her as she tackled the difficult topics of bullying and suicide in the aftermath of the tragic death of Amanda Todd:

> Last year, Collette and I had a discussion about bullying leading to suicide, and I was very apprehensive discussing this issue with my kids, and I didn't know how their parents were going to react. As an experienced teacher, she was fine with the topic and talked me through it almost, like this is what you're going to do. So, I was very scared to do it, but it came down to that mentorship. She was there to say, "You could go this way, you could go this way, but you need to talk about it openly and honestly." And, it was helpful to have that support.

A difficult topic indeed! Katelyn's experience resonates with the notion of a "pedagogy of discomfort" (Boler & Zembylas, 2003), a framework for understanding reluctance to move out of one's comfort zones. While a desire to stay within one's comfort zone may be understandable, teacher avoidance of challenging topics does not serve students well. Over the course of our study, we began to apply Boler and Zembylas's concept to many of our study findings. Collette and her students experienced a pedagogy of discomfort through the readings and conversations that were part of their social justice projects. The topics the students embraced, from the historical injustices of internment camps and residential schooling to the contemporary struggles of AIDS orphans and children living in conflict zones, required challenging dialogue about "difficult knowledge" (Pitt & Britzman, 2006). There were certainly moments when Collette and her students were positioned out of their comfort zones. Boler and Zembylas (2003) explain that this can be discomforting as it means experiencing challenging emotions such as vulnerability. However, the authors explain that, for teachers and students, dwelling in a pedagogy of discomfort "can produce favorable results, including self-discovery, hope, passion and a sense of community" (2003, p. 129). On the day that Shelby and Lynne visited the class for the students' presentation "pitches," this was witnessed tenfold.

Conclusion

The two illustrative teacher stories that we profiled in this chapter were chosen, in part, for the contrast. The inquiry group proved instrumental to both teachers in their teaching for social justice, but in differing ways. However, something that we noticed that these two teachers had in common was the diverse nature of their students. Collette made an observation that called to mind Ann's point that her students, as first-generation Canadians or immigrants themselves, were more readily able to relate to aspects of the novel *Elijah of Buxton*. Similarly, Collette attributed the success of her project, to a degree, to her culturally diverse study body:

> I think that the most important aspect is the multicultural classroom. It's a lot more exciting to study these things when they're sitting there and you can ask questions and the kids can learn about each other and see it in their room. So, if you had a very homogenous room it wouldn't be as tangible to them ... The story is how we're all the same, even though we have all these different experiences. I want them to have empathy, but not sympathy.

Collette's comment speaks, at least in good measure, to the impetus behind our broader national research study. Study findings from our previous project, which explored pre-service teachers' responses to Canadian multicultural picture books, found that the teachers who served as mentors for our student teachers paid little attention to issues of equity and historical marginalizations in their teaching, despite an increasingly diverse population of immigrant and Indigenous students in their schools (see Johnston & Bainbridge, 2013). Study findings from the two teacher stories presented in this chapter emphasize that paying attention to the growing diversity in our Canadian schools is well advised. In closing, we would like to note that not all the teachers in our inquiry group project taught in schools as diverse as where Ann and Collette taught. Their students, too, were engaged in becoming voices for social justice through the reading of Canadian literature. And the inquiry group supported the teachers of both multicultural and homogeneous classrooms in making this happen.

Keywords

- advocacy
- communities of practice
- diversity
- inquiry group
- inquiry learning
- historical marginalizations
- multimodal strategies
- pedagogies of discomfort
- social justice
- thematic instruction

Reflection Questions

1. In what ways could teacher education programs work with schools so that new teachers do not feel the need to abandon what they have come to believe about teaching for social justice during their pre-service programs?
2. How can Canadian children's literature be used as a catalyst to motivate students to action on social justice issues, both historical (e.g., residential schooling) and contemporary (e.g., the refugee crisis)?
3. What types of professional development initiatives could support teachers moving out of comfort zones and into "pedagogies of discomfort" when tackling challenging topics with their students?
4. As Canadian schools become increasingly diverse, how could the concept of "communities of practice" be utilized as a framework for thinking about productive ways to negotiate diverse perspectives?

References

Aldana, P. (2008). Books that are windows, books that are mirrors: How we can make sure that children see themselves in their books [Speech transcript]. Retrieved from http://www.ibby.org/index.php?id=1008

Bainbridge, J., & Hayden, R. (2013). *Constructing meaning: Teaching the language arts K–8* (5th ed.). Toronto, ON: Nelson.

Boler, M., & Zembylas, M. (2003). Discomforting truths: The emotional terrain of understanding difference. In P. P. Trifonas (Ed.), *Pedagogies of difference: Rethinking education for social change* (pp. 110–136). New York, NY: RoutledgeFalmer.

Bender-Slack, D. (2010). Texts, talk and fear? English language arts: Teachers negotiating social justice teaching. *English Education, 42*(2), 181–203.

Cherland, M., & Harper, H. (2007). *Advocacy research in literacy education: Seeking higher ground.* Mahwah, NJ: Lawrence Erlbaum Associates.

Ching, S. H. D. (2005). Multicultural children's literature as an instrument of power. *Language Arts, 83*(2), 128–136.

Cochran-Smith, M. (2004). *Walking the road: Race, diversity, and social justice in teacher education.* New York, NY: Teachers College Press.

Cochran-Smith, M., & Lytle, S. L. (2009). *Inquiry as stance: Practitioner research in the next generation.* New York, NY: Teachers College Press.

Curtis, C. P. (2007). *Elijah of Buxton.* Toronto, ON: Scholastic Canada.

Ellis, D. (2002). *Parvana's journey.* Toronto, ON: Douglas & McIntyre.

Ellis, D. (2004). *The heaven shop.* Markham, ON: Fitzhenry & Whiteside.

Johnston, I., & Bainbridge, J. (Eds.). (2013). *Reading multiculturalism: Preservice teachers explore identity, ideology and pedagogy through Canadian picture books.* Toronto, ON: University of Toronto Press.

Jordan-Fenton, C., & Pokiak-Fenton, M. (2010). *Fatty legs: A true story.* (L. Amini-Holmes, Illus.). Vancouver, BC: Annick Press.

Lave, J., & Wenger, E. (1991). *Situated learning: Legitimate peripheral participation.* Cambridge: Cambridge University Press.

Philpott, R., & Dagenais, D. (2012). Grappling with social justice: Exploring new teachers' practice and experiences. *Education, Citizenship and Social Justice, 7*(1), 85–99.

Pitt, A., & Britzman, D. (2006) Speculations on qualities of difficult knowledge in teaching and learning: An experiment in psychoanalytic research. In K. Tobin & J. Kincheloe (Eds.), *Doing educational research: A handbook* (pp. 379–401). New York, NY: Sense Publishers.

Stroud, B. (2007). *Patchwork path: A quilt map to freedom.* (E. S. Bennett, Illus.). Somerville, MA: Candlewick Press.

Walters, E. (2001). *Caged eagles.* Victoria, BC: Orca Book Publishers.

Wang, J., Odell, S., & Schwille, S. (2008). Effects of teacher induction on beginning teachers' teaching: A critical review of the literature. *Journal of Teacher Education, 59*(2), 132–152.

Wenger, E. (1998). *Communities of practice: Learning, meaning, and identity.* New York, NY: Cambridge University Press.

Wenger, E. (2007). Communities of practice: A brief introduction. *Communities of practice.* Retrieved from http://www.ewenger.com/theory/

Wiltse, L. (2015). Not just "sunny days": Aboriginal students connect out-of-school literacy resources with school literacy practices. *Literacy, 49*(2), 60–68.

Wolk, S. (2009). Reading for a better world: Teaching for social responsibility with young adult literature. *Journal of Adolescent & Adult Literacy, 52*(8), 664–673.

Afterword

Ingrid Johnston

Our book has focused attention on possibilities for teachers from all Grade levels to introduce their students to Canadian literature with potential for raising issues of social justice in the classroom. Canadian literature in English for children and young adults has a relatively short history, increasing slowly over the past century and then with more rapid growth over the past 30 years. Canada's cultural diversity has gradually been reflected more frequently in these Canadian books and, as Saltman (2003) explains, "this reflection has moved from the superficial treatment of multiculturalism as a confined issue in the early books of the 1960s and 1970s to a richer examination of life within a variety of cultures" (p. 25).

Since the 1990s, newer immigrant and second-generation Canadian writers and illustrators have described experiences of diaspora, highlighted stories of acceptance and intolerance in a new culture, and reminded readers of oft-forgotten events in Canadian history; Indigenous authors and illustrators have retold stories from rich oral traditions, engaged readers with the realities of residential schools, and highlighted the lives of Indigenous peoples in contemporary settings. More recently, larger numbers of Canadian authors have taken on the challenges of writing books with characters who are gay, lesbian, bisexual, or transgendered and created stories whose protagonists have physical or mental disabilities.

This increasing wealth and diversity of Canadian literature has not always been reflected in our schools. Teachers have often been reluctant to replace familiar British and American texts with Canadian literature, sometimes because they lack knowledge of these texts or they doubt the literary value of Canadian texts compared to the more canonized literature from elsewhere, and often because their school lacks resources to bring new Canadian books into the library and classrooms.

Our study attempted to address some of these constraints through inquiry groups with practising teachers, in which we selected and read contemporary Canadian texts with relevance for their classrooms and discussed teaching strategies for engaging students with issues of social justice through the literature. As Marilyn Cochran-Smith (2004) explains:

> A commitment to social justice, advocacy for change, and critical
> inquiry requires diverse personal and professional support systems ...
> Transforming teachers into critical inquirers and culturally responsive

pedagogists becomes less demanding and more powerful when teachers build meaningful networks and collaborations that include mentors, supporters, professional colleagues. (p. xii)

Teacher participants in our study had opportunities to share their literary and teaching histories, to hear about new texts and new ways to teach them in collaboration with their peers and with us as researchers. As Cochran-Smith (2004) suggests, "we need more teachers who are actively willing to challenge the taken-for-granted texts, practices and arrangements of schooling through participation in systematic and critical inquiry" (p. 62).

Our funding from the Social Sciences and Humanities Research Council of Canada allowed us to supply our participating teachers with class sets of their selected texts. As the chapters in this book demonstrate, these texts ranged widely from picture books to realistic fiction for children and young adults, historical and fantasy novels, biographies, memoirs, graphic novels, poetry and plays, and selections of adult books suitable for high school readers. The chosen texts addressed a variety of issues related to social justice. These included stories and images of discrimination, historical marginalization, racial and gender intolerance, sexual orientation, and language and cultural issues. The website of annotated Canadian texts we created from the study (http://canlitsocialjustice.wordpress.com/) provides details of this range of texts, and the selected books are also detailed in the Bibliography of Children's Literature at the end of this book.

Chapters from each of our seven research sites highlight the distinctive nature of the provincial inquiry groups, but also present fascinating cross-site similarities. Questions of place and identity resonate throughout, with teachers selecting Canadian texts that offer new understandings of historical events, such as the experiences of Chinese workers who helped to build Canada's railways and the suffering of Japanese-Canadians evacuated from their homes during World War II. Participants did not shy away from bringing books into their classes that were controversial and dealt with difficult issues, such as the abuses and cultural denigration experienced by Indigenous children at residential schools or the racism encountered by immigrants to Canada from Africa, Asia, and the Middle East, or the loneliness and isolation felt by new immigrants whose first language was not English or French. Other teachers focused on Canadian texts that challenged taken-for-granted notions of gender identities, sexual orientation, and disabilities. Following Homi Bhabha's (1994) notions of "third space," we saw how the selected texts offered a relatively safe space within which teacher and students could engage in conversations about ways to address the "difficult knowledge" of difference (Britzman, 1998). For those teachers who encountered student resistance to this difficult knowledge, the inquiry groups provided a welcoming environment to debrief how to address student concerns.

The support of the inquiry groups made it possible for teachers to move out of their comfort zones of teaching familiar texts with previously developed curriculum resources and to develop their own resources and assessment strategies for the new books, allowing for renewed creativity in lesson planning, teaching strategies, and student responses. This creativity extended to teachers embracing more multimodal approaches to literary selection, whether through literature circles with a diverse range of multicultural picture books, teaching a graphic novel or contemporary Canadian play for the first time, or drawing upon social media such as blogs or Facebook to engage with authors and illustrators.

Our study points to the value of teachers introducing students to aspects of critical literacy as they read and respond to newer Canadian multicultural literature and to the need for creating space and safety to explore issues of social justice raised by the books. While teachers in our study were able to address a range of issues related to critical literacy, some aspects of marginalization, such as disabilities, body shape issues, and gender issues were either absent or underrepresented in the selected texts. These could be considered more specifically in a further study. Teacher education programs across Canada can help new teachers develop a deeper understanding of critical literacy by providing opportunities for them to experience how to read and respond critically to a variety of texts. We discovered in an earlier national study (Johnston & Bainbridge, 2013), in which we asked pre-service teachers to respond to a selection of Canadian multicultural picture books, that learning about narrative voice and point of view, about ways to address stereotypes and to probe gaps and absences in a text can help new teachers understand ideologies that underpin the text and enable them to develop criteria for selecting Canadian literature for their own classrooms. As Paul Martin (2013) reminds us, for teachers,

> the decision as to what to teach and write about is never apolitical and never based solely on "excellence." ... Aware of their own agency and that of their colleagues, they cannot overlook the far-reaching effects of their decisions in matters of curriculum, teaching practices, and research. (p. 87)

Our case studies highlight how teachers can envision new strategies for selecting texts that are more inclusive of Canada's diversity and, with the support and collaboration of colleagues, can introduce new strategies and approaches that encourage students to come to deeper understandings about issues of social justice.

References

Bhabha, H. (2004). *The location of culture.* London: Routledge.

Britzman, D. P. (1998) *Lost subjects, contested objects: Toward a psychoanalytic inquiry of learning.* Albany, NY: State University of New York Press.

Cochran-Smith, M. (2004). *Walking the road: Race, diversity, and social justice in teacher education.* New York, NY: Teachers College Press.

Johnston, I., & Bainbridge, J. (Eds.). (2013). *Reading diversity through Canadian picture books: Preservice teachers explore issues of identity, ideology and pedagogy.* Toronto, ON: University of Toronto Press.

Martin, P. (2013). *Sanctioned ignorance: The politics of knowledge production and the teaching of literature in Canada.* Edmonton, AB: University of Alberta Press.

Saltman, J. (2003). Canadian children's literature at the millennium. In A. Hudson & S. A. Cooper (Eds.), *Windows and words: A look at Canadian children's literature in English* (pp. 23–34). Ottawa, ON: University of Ottawa Press.

Bibliography of Children's Literature

The following texts were selected by teacher participants in the SSHRC-funded project "Canadian Literature for Social Justice." Annotations are by Chandra Hildebrand. This bibliography of Canadian texts can also be accessed online at http://canlitsocialjustice.wordpress.com/.

Note on Abbreviations
P – Primary
E – Elementary
J – Junior High
S – Senior High
FNMI – First Nations Métis Inuit

Novels—Primary/Elementary

Daher, A. (2002). *Flight from Big Tangle.* Vancouver, BC: Orca Book Publishers. (E)
[Courage; Nature and wildlife]
Kaylee is afraid to fly since her father and his plane disappeared, but she has no choice if she wants to save herself and her dog from the forest fire that surrounds them.

Daher, A. (2004). *Flight from Bear Canyon.* Vancouver, BC: Orca Book
   Publishers. (E)
[Courage; FNMI; Nature and wildlife]
Kaylee is again forced to fly a plane when she must team up with Jaz to save Jaz's uncle, who is injured in a plane crash on the tundra, and they find themselves in grizzly country.

Daher, A. (2008). *Poachers in the Pingos.* Vancouver, BC: Orca Book Publishers. (E)
[Courage; FNMI, Nature and wildlife; The North]
Set in Tuktoyaktuk, two Junior Rangers investigate the deaths of falcons and find themselves in trouble when Jaz gets trapped on a barge that is sailing out to sea.

Khan, R., & Khosravi, N. (2008). *Coming to Canada*. Toronto, ON: Groundwood
    Books. (Chapter Book) (P)
[Canadian history; Immigration; Non-fiction]
This book provides a comprehensive overview of the history of immigration to Canada
by people from all over the world who now make this land their new home. Beginning
with the "immigration" of the First Peoples across the land bridge during the Stone
Age, the book moves forward through the building of the nation, to the movement
West, to the "new century," and finally to today and the changing face of Canada.
The book also recognizes the difficulties and oppression faced by many immigrants to
Canada. It includes a timeline and further resources, and would be a useful resource
for social studies/humanities.

Khan, R., & Kosravi, N. (2009). *A new life*. Toronto, ON: Groundwood Books. (P/E)
[Family; Immigration; Learning English; Pakistani-Canadians]
Khadija, her brother Hamza, and their parents have just moved from Pakistan to Canada.
Hamza is having an especially difficult time adapting to this strange new land, but
gradually, both he and Khadija find friends, begin to feel more at home, and discover
their new nation on a cross-country road trip with the family. This uplifting book
captures what the experience must be like for many immigrant students starting in a
new classroom, hearing a new language, learning new games and expectations, and
discovering the joy of learning to read in a new language. Both the author and illus-
trator are first-generation Canadian immigrants themselves.

Kogawa, J. (1995). *Naomi's road*. Toronto, ON: Stoddart Publishing. (P/E)
[Discrimination; Historical fiction; Japanese-Canadians; Japanese internment;
    World War II]
As the world is becoming dark with the onset of World War II, times are also uncertain
in Vancouver, where young Naomi is growing up. When her mother and grandmother
leave for Japan to visit a sick relative, Naomi and her older brother Stephen are left in
the care of their *Obasan* (Japanese for "aunt"). The family that is left in Canada must
travel by train on a "vacation" that confuses Naomi. A story of the internment of
Japanese-Canadians during World War II, the reader sees events through the eyes of a
young girl who does not know why her world is changing around her, but is beginning
to understand that war turns friends into enemies, and in Canada, some people think
Japanese-Canadians are enemies.

Perkyns, D. (2003). *Last days in Africville*. Vancouver, BC: Beach Holme
    Publishing. (P/E)
[African-Canadians; Discrimination; Historical fiction; Nova Scotia]
In the 1960s, on the shores of Bedford Basin in Halifax, Nova Scotia, 12-year-old Selina
Palmer is growing up in the community of Africville. Struggling with what it means
to be the only Black student in her Grade 6 class, Selina takes comfort in the fact that

every day she goes home to a loving and vibrant neighbourhood, where friends and family accept her as she is. But ugly rumours are starting to surface about the fate of Africville. Based on the true story of how the city of Halifax relocated the residents of the community and razed it in the name of urban renewal.

Rivers, R. (2008). *Tuk and the whale*. Toronto, ON: Groundwood Books. (E)
[FNMI; Historical fiction; Inuit; The North]
Tuk is a young Inuit boy living on Baffin Island in the early decades of the 1600s. He and the others at his winter camp encounter European whalers, blown far north of their usual route. *Tuk and the Whale* gives readers a glimpse into the history of the Arctic, the collision of two cultures, and a changing way of life.

Walsh, A. (1994). *Shabash!* Toronto, ON: Dundurn Press. (P)
[Discrimination; Identity; Prejudice; Sikhs; Sports]
When Rana joins the local minor league hockey team, he knows he's in for a few stumbles and falls on the ice. But he doesn't expect the cold reception he gets from the other players and their parents. As a Canadian Sikh living in a small BC mill town in 1980, and the first Sikh to join a minor league hockey team, Rana knows he's "different." What starts out as a whim becomes a determined struggle to prove that he is not different—until Rana discovers that, in some ways, he is different, and that he even wants to be.

Watts, I. N. (1998). *Good-bye Marianne: A story of growing up in Nazi Germany*.
    New York, NY: Random House. (late P/E)
[Historical fiction; The Holocaust; *Kindertransport*; World War II]
It's 1938 in Berlin, Germany, and 11-year-old Marianne Kohn's world is crumbling. She is no longer allowed to attend school, her father has been forced to live in hiding, and even day-to-day life is altered as Marianne is now viewed as an enemy. She makes a new friend named Ernest, but soon discovers that he belongs to the Hitler Youth. As the country heads toward war and the Nazis tighten the noose around the Jews, Marianne's mother makes the difficult decision to send her daughter away to what she hopes is safety.

Watts, I. N. (2000). *Remember me*. Toronto, ON: Tundra Books. (P/E)
[Historical fiction; The Holocaust; *Kindertransport*; World War II]
A companion book to *Good-bye Marianne*. In this next installment, Marianne has escaped Germany on one of the first *Kindertransport* trains that were organized to take Jewish children to safety in Britain. At first, Marianne is desperate. She does not speak English, she's not welcome in her sponsors' home, and she misses her mother terribly. As the months pass, she realizes she cannot control the circumstances around her, and she must rely on herself if she is to survive. The *Kindertransport* and the effort to provide homes for refugee children in Britain are based on factual events that took place just as World War II was breaking out.

Watts, I. N. (2008). *Good-bye Marianne: A story of growing up in Nazi Germany*. (K. Shoemaker, Illus.). Toronto, ON: Tundra Books. (graphic novel adaptation) (late P/E)
[Historical fiction; Graphic novel; The Holocaust; *Kindertransport*; World War II]
This is the graphic novel interpretation of the novel of the same name, and the text is accompanied by subdued pencil sketches.

Willett, M. (2008). *The delta is my home*. Markham, ON: Fifth House Publishers.
Willett, M. (2008). *We feel good out here*. Markham, ON: Fifth House Publishers.
Willett, M. (2009). *Living stories*. Markham, ON: Fifth House Publishers.
Willett, M. (2009). *The caribou feed our soul*. Markham, ON: Fifth House Publishers.
Willett, M. (2010). *Come and learn with me*. Markham, ON: Fifth House Publishers.
Willett, M. (2010). *Proud to be Inuvialuit*. Markham, ON: Fifth House Publishers.
Willett, M. (2011). *No borders (The land is our story)*. Markham, ON: Fifth House Publishers.
Willett, M. (2011). *At the heart of it*. Markham, ON: Fifth House Publishers. (E)
[FNMI; Non-fiction; The North; Northwest Territories]
This collaborative book series gives glimpses into the current lives of families in the Northwest Territories. Willett has collaborated with a child or adolescent from various groups in the NWT to tell the stories that are important to the way they live. This excellent series has wonderful photographs of the land and people of the NWT.

Wishinsky, F. (2003). *Just call me Joe*. Victoria, BC: Orca Book Publishers. (P)
[Immigration; Jewish-Americans; Learning English]
Ten-year-old Joseph's parents have sent him and his older sister Anna away from their home in Russia to live with their aunt in America, in hopes of giving them a better life in New York City. But Anna has to work extremely hard at a factory with very few rights, and Joe is stuck in a class of much younger students while he learns English. When Joe's new friend Sam presents him with an "easy" way of making money, Joe must decide what he's willing to do to "look like a real American."

Yee, P. (2007). *Shu-Li and Tamara*. (S. Wang, Illus.). Vancouver, BC: Tradewind Books. (Chapter book) (P)
[Chinese-Canadians; Community; Friendship; Immigration; Multiculturalism; Social action]
Shu-Li's family moved to Canada from China two years ago, and they now run a Chinese deli in Vancouver's multicultural Commercial Drive area. Shu-Li's classmate, Tamara, also recently moved into the neighbourhood. The two girls become good friends, but an ugly rumour threatens their relationship. The story balances immigrant issues and cultural differences with the broader themes of friendship and loyalty. The story is accompanied with recipes for some of the dishes the students in the story prepared for the "Kids Helping Kids" school fair.

Novels—Elementary/Junior High

Aihoshi, S. (2012). *Dear Canada: Torn apart: The internment diary of Mary Kobayashi.* Toronto, ON: Scholastic Canada. (E/J)
[Discrimination; Historical fiction; Japanese-Canadians; Japanese internment; Prejudice; World War II]
It is 1941, and Mary Kobayashi, a Canadian-born Japanese girl, enjoys her life in Vancouver. Although World War II is raging elsewhere, it hasn't really impacted her life in BC. Then, on December 7, 1941, Japan bombs Pearl Harbor and everything changes. Suddenly a war of suspicion and prejudice is waged on the home front, and Japanese-Canadians are stripped of their rights, their jobs, and their homes. Mary's family is torn apart, and she and her two sisters are sent, alone, to a primitive camp in BC's interior. The author draws from the experiences of her family during World War II.

Bastedo, J. (2001). *Tracking triple seven.* Calgary, AB: Red Deer Press. (J)
[Death and grieving; Environment; FNMI; Nature and wildlife; The North]
Still grieving after his mother's death, Benji, a kid from the city, accidentally joins a team of grizzly bear biologists when he is visiting his father's Arctic diamond mine. Frequently switching point of view between bear and boy, Bastedo portrays life and death in the North, and reveals how both technology and traditional knowledge are used to learn about bears and their survival.

Curtis, C. P. (2007). *Elijah of Buxton.* Toronto, ON: Scholastic Canada. (E/J)
[African-Canadians; Courage; Historical fiction; Slavery]
Eleven-year-old Elijah is the first child born into freedom in Buxton, Ontario, a settlement of runaway slaves near the American border. He's best known in his hometown as the boy who made a memorable impression on Frederick Douglass. When someone steals money from Elijah's friend, who has been saving to buy his family out of captivity in the South, Elijah embarks on a dangerous journey to America in pursuit of the thief. There he discovers first-hand the unimaginable horrors of the life his parents fled—a life from which he'll always be free, if he can find the courage to get back home.

Ellis, D. (2002). *Looking for X.* Toronto, ON: Douglas & McIntyre. (E/J)
[Autism; Disability; Homelessness; Mental Health; Poverty]
Khyber is a teenage girl who lives on public assistance in the Regent Park neighbourhood of Toronto with her mother and her five-year-old twin brothers who have autism. Her one friend is X, an elderly homeless woman who often sits with her blue suitcase in the nearby park, convinced she's being pursued by the secret police. Khyber must deal with her mother's decision to send her brothers to a group home, some menacing skinheads, a false accusation of vandalism that gets her expelled, and a search for X, who has gone missing but is the only person who can prove Khyber's innocence.

Ellis, S. (2008). *Dear Canada: Days of toil and tears: The child labour diary of Flora Rutherford.* Toronto, ON: Scholastic Canada. (E/J)
[Child labour; Historical fiction; Poverty]
Flora is happy to leave the orphanage behind and join her aunt and uncle, even though it means working at a textile mill where there is the constant threat of being injured or going deaf. She writes about her feelings in her diary, addressing her father and mother who died when she was five. Then her uncle loses several fingers at the weaving machine leaving him unable to work, and money is very tight. Can Flora help her aunt and uncle survive?

Fullerton, A. (2008). *Libertad.* Markham, ON: Fitzhenry & Whiteside. (E/J)
[Art; Emigration; Guatemala; Immigration; Hope; Latin America; Resilience]
When a freak accident kills their mother, Libertad and his little brother Julio are no longer safe living on their own near the Guatemala City Dump. *Libertad* knows that surviving by their wits alone won't be enough to send his brother to school or give them any hope for the future. So, earning their way as street musicians, they set out on a long and dangerous journey to the Rio Grande, where they will somehow cross into the United States and find their father. Written in free-verse poetry, *Libertad* is based on the journey of a real boy, combined with other children's actual experiences.

Hof, M. (2006). *Against the odds.* (J. Prins, Trans.). Toronto, ON: Groundwood Books. (E/J)
[Family; War]
Life is good for Kiki except for one thing. Her father, a doctor, often goes off on missions to dangerous and faraway war zones. No matter how persuasive her arguments, Kiki cannot convince him to stay home. Kiki's mother explains to her about odds—how it is very unlikely that her father will die. When her father actually does go missing, and as her mother and grandmother get more and more upset, Kiki begins to feel that it's up to her to save him. *Against the Odds* deals with moral issues in a serious way, while still being funny and deeply human.

Kacer, K. (2008). *The diary of Laura's twin.* Toronto, ON: Second Story Press. (E/J)
[The Holocaust; Judaism; Remembrance; Warsaw Ghetto; World War II]
As a special Bat Mitzvah project, Laura has to read the diary of Sara Gittler, a girl who, at Laura's age, was imprisoned by the Nazis in the Warsaw Ghetto. Because Sara never had a chance to celebrate her coming of age, Laura is supposed to share her Bat Mitzvah with Sara by speaking about her "twin" at the ceremony. Reluctant at first, Laura becomes caught up with Sara's struggle to survive and the courage she demonstrates. The book includes photographs, biographies of young heroes of the Warsaw Ghetto uprising, and true accounts of "twinning ceremonies."

Khan, R. (2009). *Wanting Mor*. Toronto, ON: Groundwood Books/House of Anansi Press. (E/J)

[Addiction; Afghanistan; Death and grieving; Education; Girls and women; Orphans; Resilience; War]

Jameela is a girl growing up in post-Taliban Afghanistan. When her mother, Mor, dies, Jameela's unpredictable, opium-addicted father takes her away from the life she knows, and they move to Kabul. Soon her father gets remarried, and because her new stepmother doesn't want her, Jameela is abandoned in the marketplace by her father. First she must adapt to life at an orphanage, and then must learn how to forgive those who have wronged her. *Wanting Mor* is based on the true story of a girl who ended up in an Afghan orphanage supported by the author, Rukhsana Khan, through the royalties of her book *The Roses in My Carpets*.

Kusugak, M. (2006). *The curse of the shaman*. Toronto, ON: Harper Trophy Canada. (E)

[FNMI; Inuit; Legends; The North]

Kusugak uses this novel to tell the story of Marble Island off the coast of Rankin Inlet in Nunavut, which is the place of many Inuit legends. In this novel, the shaman Paaliaq curses a baby wolverine to banishment as a young man. While Paaliaq revokes his curse, the cranky wolverine does not forgive and is now stranded on an island wanting to come home to his family and the girl he loves.

Little, J. (2000). *Willow and Twig*. Toronto, ON: Penguin. (E)

[Family; Homelessness; Poverty]

Willow doesn't know what to do. Her mother has taken off again, leaving Willow to take care of her little brother Twig on the streets of Vancouver, with nowhere to go—that is, until Willow remembers her grandmother, whom she hasn't seen since she was very young. After a couple of urgent phone calls to Ontario, Willow and Twig are on their way across the country. There they discover a household made up of Gram, an eccentric uncle, a hostile aunt, and a motley crew of animals. This is a story about two young people learning to be proud of who they are and having the courage to discover where they truly belong.

Loyie, L. (2002). *As long as the river flows*. (H. D. Holmlund, Illus.). Toronto, ON: Groundwood Books.

[Cree; Elder wisdom; FNMI; Non-fiction; Residential schools; Traditions]

This is the story of Larry Loyie's last summer with his large Cree family in northern Alberta, before entering residential school. It is a time of learning and adventure. He cares for an abandoned baby owl and watches his grandmother make winter moccasins. He helps the family prepare for a hunting and gathering trip, learns patience and discipline, and even faces a grizzly bear. The ending is bleak, however, as at the end of the summer, Larry and the other children are put in the back of a truck and taken away to residential school. The epilogue includes facts about residential schools, more about Loyie's experience, and several photographs.

Loyie, L. (2008). *Goodbye Buffalo Bay.* Penticton, BC: Theytus Books. (E)
[Cree; Cultural heritage; Elder wisdom; FNMI, Friendship; Non-fiction; Residential schools; Resilience]

The sequel to *As Long as the Rivers Flow. Goodbye Buffalo Bay* is set during the author's teenaged years. In his last year in residential school, Lawrence learns the power of friendship and finds the courage to stand up for his beliefs. He returns home to find the traditional First Nations life he loved is over. He feels like a stranger to his family until his grandfather's gentle guidance helps him find his way. New adventures arise, and Lawrence discovers a sense of freedom and self-esteem.

MacLean, J. (2008). *The nine lives of Travis Keating.* Markham, ON: Fitzhenry & Whiteside. (E/J)
[Animal welfare; Bullying; Death and grieving; Social action]

Travis has agreed that, for 365 days, he will go along with his dad's experiment of living in a tiny coastal community in Newfoundland. Here, he has few friends and becomes the target of Hud, the school's meanest bully, who's itching for a fight with the new "townie." When Travis discovers a colony of abandoned cats and attempts to care for them himself, it isn't long before he's in over his head. Who will help him feed the animals and protect them from predators and the harsh elements?

MacLean, J. (2010). *The present tense of Prinny Murphy.* Markham, ON: Fitzhenry & Whiteside. (E/J)
[Alcoholism; Bullying; Community; Education; Learning disabilities]

With an alcoholic mother, a distracted father, and the attention of three relentless schoolyard bullies who get her drunk and blackmail her with embarrassing photos, Prinny Murphy's past, present, and future certainly are "tense." She can't read well enough to escape remedial reading lessons until a kindly substitute teacher introduces her to LaVaughn's inner-city world in the free-verse novel *Make Lemonade.* Longing to read about LaVaughn every day and enlisting the help of others to help her do so, Prinny discovers that life can be full of possibilities—and poetry. A companion book to *The Nine Lives of Travis Keating.*

Maruno, J. (2009). *When the cherry blossoms fell.* Toronto, ON: Napoleon and Co. (E/J)
[Historical fiction; Japanese-Canadians; Japanese internment; Prejudice; World War II]

Nine-year-old Michiko Minagawa bids her father goodbye before her birthday celebration, not knowing the government has ordered all Japanese-born men out of the province. Ten days later, her family joins hundreds of Japanese-Canadians on a train to the interior of British Columbia. Even though her Aunt Sadie jokes about it, they have truly reached the "Land of No." There are no paved roads, no streetlights, and no streetcars. The house in which they are to live is dirty and drafty. At school, Michiko learns the truth of her situation. She must face local prejudice, the worst winter in 40 years, and her first Christmas without her father.

Matas, C. (2013). *Dear Canada: Pieces of the past: The holocaust diary of Rose Rabinowitz.* Toronto, ON: Scholastic Canada. (E/J)
[Historical fiction; The Holocaust; Immigration; Jewish-Canadians; Poland; Refugees; Resistance; World War II]
As Rose begins her diary, she is in her third home since coming to Winnipeg. Traumatized by her experiences in the Holocaust, she struggles to connect with others and to trust again. When her new guardian, Saul, tries to get Rose to deal with what happened to her during the War, she begins writing in her diary about how she survived the murder of the Jews in Poland by going into hiding and, later, by living with a resistance cell deep in the forest. As she delves deeper into her past, she is haunted by the most terrifying memory of all. Will she find the courage to bear witness to her mother's ultimate sacrifice?

McKay, S. E. (2000). *Charlie Wilcox.* Toronto, ON: Stoddart Kids. (E/J)
[Historical fiction; Friendship; Resilience; World War I]
Newfoundland-born Charlie Wilcox wants to go to sea like his father. But never strong to begin with and born with a club foot, Charlie seems destined for quieter pursuits. Determined to prove others wrong, Charlie stows away on what he thinks is a fishing vessel, emerging days later to find himself far out to sea, bound not for the ice but for the battlefields of World War I. While waiting for passage home, he works at a makeshift hospital in France and sees the grisly results of the fighting. When his ticket finally arrives, he gives it to a friend he believes needs it more. Charlie then heads for the front, where he witnesses the horrors of trench warfare during the Battle of the Somme.

McKay, S. E. (2003). *Charlie Wilcox's great war.* Toronto, ON: Penguin Canada. (E/J)
[Community; Historical fiction; World War I]
A follow-up to *Charlie Wilcox*, this book continues the saga of a young boy's experiences on the battlefields of World War I. The Great War has come to an end, and Charlie Wilcox, battle-weary and fatigued, has finally returned home to Brigus, Newfoundland. When he left, he was a boy of 14. Now, at 17, he is a man, his childhood left behind on the battlefields. His homecoming is all he could have hoped for. Yet he is burdened by a terrible secret, one that he fears will inflict more grief on a village that has already suffered so much.

McMurchy-Barber, G. (2010). *Free as a bird.* Toronto, ON: Dundurn Press. (E/J)
[Abuse; Disability; Historical fiction; Resilience]
Born with Down Syndrome, Ruby Jean Sharp comes from a time when being a develop-
mentally disabled person could mean growing up behind locked doors and barred
windows. When Ruby Jean's caregiver and loving grandmother dies, her mother takes
her to Woodlands School in New Westminster, British Columbia, and rarely visits. It's
here, in an institution that opened in 1878 and was originally called the Provincial
Lunatic Asylum, that Ruby Jean learns to survive isolation, boredom, and every kind
of abuse. Just when she can hardly remember if she's ever been happy, she learns a
lesson about patience and perseverance from an old crow.

Nitto, T. (2006). *The red rock: A graphic fable.* Toronto, ON: Groundwood Books. (E)
[Activism; Environmentalism; Nature and wildlife; Social action]
Part picture book, part wordless comic, *The Red Rock: A Graphic Fable* tells the story
of the beautiful valley that is the home of Old Beaver and many other creatures, and
is looked over by a huge, weird, red rock. Developers and planners in the city want
to use the valley for a luxury hotel, dam, and casino. The animals of the valley and a
concerned girl in the city both do their part to try to save the valley. When all seems
lost, in a mysterious dream, Old Beaver and the Red Rock become a magical duo and
show readers that "we need to fight to protect our beautiful world, and we need help
from our friends to do so."

Pearson, K. (1989). *The sky is falling.* Toronto, ON: Penguin Books. (E)
[Family; Historical fiction; War guests; World War II]
This first installment of the Guests of War Trilogy begins in the summer of 1940, when
all of England fears the bombing and possible invasion by Nazi forces. Norah knows
other parents are sending their children to safety overseas, but she is sure her own
would never send her away. Then, despite her protests, Norah is told that she and
her younger brother, Gavin, are being sent to Canada. The voyage across the ocean is
exciting, but as her stay in Canada begins, Norah becomes more and more miserable.
The rich woman who fosters them in Toronto seems to prefer Gavin to her, the children at her new school taunt her, and, as the news from England becomes worse, she
is filled with homesickness. But as Christmas approaches and Norah begins to make
friends, she discovers a surprising responsibility that helps her accept her new country.

Pearson, K. (1991). *Looking at the moon.* Toronto, ON: Penguin Books. (E)
[Family; Historical fiction; War guests; World War II]
The second book in the Guests of War Trilogy, and a sequel to *The Sky Is Falling.* Norah
and Gavin have now lived in Canada for three years with Aunt Florence and Aunt Mary.
Norah is glad to spend August on an island in Muskoka, where she can swim and canoe

and enjoy the company of the many cousins who come to stay. Soon after she arrives, however, she falls in love with Andrew, one of the visiting cousins. Since Andrew is much too old for her and doesn't return her feelings, Norah is plunged into misery. Andrew has his own problems, in that he doesn't want to fight in the war. Both of them have to come to grips with some complex moral questions about war.

Pearson, K. (1993). *The lights go on again.* Toronto, ON: Penguin Books. (E)
[Family; Historical fiction; War guests; World War II]
The third installment of the Guests of War Trilogy, and a sequel to *Looking at the Moon.* For five years, Gavin and his sister, Norah, have lived in Canada as "war guests." But now the war is finally ending, and Gavin and Norah will soon be going back to England. Norah, who's 15, is eager to see her parents again, but 10-year-old Gavin barely remembers them. He doesn't want to leave his Canadian family, his two best friends, and his dog. Then, when their parents are tragically killed in an air raid, Gavin must decide where his heart lies and where his home will be.

Polak, M. (2008). *What world is left.* Victoria, BC: Orca Book Publishers. (E/J)
[Concentration camps; Historical fiction; The Holocaust; Resilience; World War II]
When the Nazis invade Holland in 1942, Anneke and her family are deported to Theresienstadt, a "model" concentration camp in Czechoslovakia—an elaborate hoax meant to convince the world that European Jews are thriving under Nazism. But there is nothing model about the reality: bed bugs, starvation, disease, lice, hard labour, and constant brutality. Despite the conditions, Anneke learns that she is capable of doing whatever it takes to survive, even as she is torn between loyalty to her family and her sense of what's right. Inspired by the experiences of the author's mother, who was imprisoned in Theresienstadt during World War II.

Porter, P. (2005). *The crazy man.* Toronto, ON: Groundwood Books/House of Anansi Press. (E/J)
[Community; Disability; Family; Free-verse poetry; Grieving; Healing; Historical fiction; Mental health; Prejudice]
Twelve-year-old Emaline Bitterman loves her home on the Prairies, even though farming in southern Saskatchewan in the mid-1960s is not easy. One day, Emaline is injured by the tractor her father is driving, leaving her with a permanent disability. In his grief and guilt, her father leaves Emaline and her distraught mother on their own. Emaline's mother then hires Angus, a patient from the local mental hospital, to drive the tractor and sow the fields. Although he is hard working and kind to both people and animals, he continues to endure cruelty from the townspeople, until he performs an ultimate act of heroism that proves to them his worth. Written in a free-verse poetic style.

Richards, D. (1999). *The lady of Batoche*. Saskatoon, SK: Thistledown Press. (J)
[FNMI; Historical fiction; Métis; Northwest Resistance]
This is the story of three young people who are changed by their experiences in the Battle of Batoche. Tom Kerslake, the young bugler, learns that revenge for a dead friend is a hollow victory. Luc, the young Métis warrior, is torn between family pride and a yearning for peace and life with the girl he loves. And Marie, the girl in question, moves between the wounded on both sides and looks for a sign from heaven.

Sherrard, V. (2010). *The glory wind*. Markham, ON: Fitzhenry & Whiteside. (late E/J)
[Community; Discrimination; Friendship; Prejudice]
Set in a small town in rural 1950s Ontario, this story follows Luke. Luke's new neighbour Gracie is unlike anyone he has ever met—fun, charming, imaginative, and full of life. But when the truth about her mother's past challenges local values, Luke finds himself caught up in a whirlwind of confusion and controversy. The townsfolk set out to isolate both mother and daughter, and Luke must decide for himself what is right.

Skrypuch, B. (2006). *Aram's choice*. (M. Wood, Illus.). Markham, ON: Fitzhenry & Whiteside. (E/J)
[Armenian genocide; Immigration; Refugees]
Aram is like all the boys exiled in Greece who have survived the Armenian genocide in Turkey and now live in orphanages, never to return home. One day, Aram learns that he will be 1 of 50 boys who will start a new life in a country called Canada. All he knows about this distant land is there is snow, lots to eat, and no war. But most important of all, Aram has heard that the trees are covered in gold. Will he find a place he can finally call home? Includes a glossary, historical note, and lists of recommended books, films, and websites. Based on the life of an Armenian orphan brought to Canada in 1923, Aram's story is continued with a companion book, *Call Me Aram*.

Skrypuch, M. F. (2010). *Stolen child*. Toronto, ON: Scholastic Canada. (E)
[Historical fiction; World War II]
Nadia arrives in Canada after the end of World War II from the displaced persons' camp where she has spent the last five years. Once she has arrived, however, troubling memories and dreams begin to haunt her. She sees images of another family, Nazi uniforms, Hitler ... but can she believe what her dreams are telling her? Bit by bit she starts to uncover the truth—that the German family she grew up with is not who they say they are. Nadia is a Lebensborn girl—a child kidnapped for her "Aryan looks" by the Nazis in their program to build a master race.

Skuy, D. (2011). *The undergrounders*. Toronto, ON: Scholastic Canada. (E/J)
[Death and grieving; Homelessness; Poverty; Sports]
Ever since his mom died, Jonathan has been on his own, living on the streets. Then he meets Lewis, who leads Jonathan to his new home with a group of kids living in an

abandoned underground shopping mall. Being part of "The Undergrounders" gives him a place to sleep, but it's not like having a real home or being a regular kid. When Jonathan acquires some stolen hockey gear, he starts to play at the community rink, where he befriends kids who welcome him into their game and onto their team. Playing hockey makes Jonathan feel like a "regular" kid again, but keeping his double life a secret proves to be more difficult and dangerous than he ever could have imagined.

Stenhouse, T. (2001). *Across the steel river.* Toronto, ON: Kids Can Press. (late E/J)
[Community; Courage; FNMI; Friendship; Historical fiction; Justice]
It's 1952 in Grayson, a small Prairie town, when best friends Will and Arthur discover a man who has been badly beaten and left for dead near the railroad tracks. The man is Yellowfly, a decorated soldier returned from World War II, who lives on the reserve across the tracks from Grayson. The local police decide the train is the cause of Yellowfly's injuries, and most of the townsfolk tend to agree. But Will and Arthur know better—and realize they'll have to pursue the case on their own. As they discover the truth, Will also starts to recognize the way Arthur and the other Blackfoot people on the reserve are mistreated, and begins to look inside himself at his own racist attitudes.

Sterling, J. (1992). *My name is Seepeetza.* Toronto, ON: Douglas & McIntyre/ Groundwood Books. (E/J)
[Autobiography; Cultural identity; FNMI; Non-fiction; Residential schools; Resilience]
Her name was Seepeetza when she was at home on her ranch. But now that she's living and studying at a residential school, she is called Martha Stone. Everything else about her life has changed as well. Strict and unhappy nuns, arbitrary and unfair rules, and, worst of all, a complete denial of all that being Indigenous means to her govern Seepeetza's new world. At the same time, the other students reject her because she has green eyes and "looks white." Only vacation times at home feed Seepeetza's hunger for the true life she has had to leave behind. Based on the author's own experiences, this autobiographical novel is written in the form of diary entries from her Grade 6 year in the 1950s.

Waldman, D. (2011). *Addy's race.* Victoria, ON: Orca Book Publishers. (E/J)
[Disability; Friendship]
Addy has worn hearing aids for as long as she can remember. Her mother tells her this makes her special, but now that Addy's in Grade 6, she wants to be special for something she's done. When Addy joins the school running club to keep her friend Lucy company, she discovers she is a gifted runner. Lucy isn't, which causes problems. Further troubles surface when Addy gets paired on a school project with Sierra, a smart, self-assured new classmate who wears a cochlear implant. Addy is surprised to discover hearing loss is all they have in common—and a shared disability is not enough of a foundation for a friendship. Through it all, Addy comes to understand that she is defined by more than her hearing loss.

Walters, E. (1998). *War of the eagles*. Victoria, BC: Orca Book Publishers. (E/J)
[FNMI; Friendship; Historical fiction; Japanese internment; World War II;
Tsimshian peoples]
It is World War II, and Jed's English father is serving as a fighter pilot overseas, while
he and his mother have returned to her Tsimshian community on Canada's West Coast.
When the military sets up a naval base near town, Jed is hired to help out. Presented with
a military jacket, Jed finds an allegiance to his country and a pride in his mixed heritage
that he has never felt before. His world is shattered when his best friend, Tadashi, along
with his family and the other members of the nearby Japanese village, are declared
enemy aliens and told to prepare to leave the coast. Now Jed must decide whether his
loyalty belongs to his country's rigid code or to the truth he knows within himself.

Walters, E. (2000). *Caged eagles*. Victoria, BC: Orca Book Publishers. (E/J)
[Friendship; Historical fiction; Japanese-Canadians; Japanese internment;
World War II]
This book is a sequel to *War of the Eagles*, but can stand on its own. After the outbreak of
World War II, 14-year-old Tadashi Fukushima and his family are forced by government
decree to abandon their home. Along with other Japanese-Canadians, they journey to
an internment centre where they await an uncertain fate. His father must live separately from the family, and Tadashi, his mother, sisters, and grandmother now live in
an animal's stall. As he tries to understand the undercurrents of racism and injustice
that have overtaken his life, Tadashi meets a new friend named Sam, with whom he
explores and tests the limits and confines of the camp.

Walters, E. (2011). *Catboy*. Victoria, BC: Orca Book Publishers. (E/J)
[Animal welfare; Community; Multiculturalism; Social action]
Taylor and his mother have moved from a small northern town to the heart of Toronto.
The differences are dramatic as Taylor becomes part of a classroom of kids as diverse
as the city itself. While taking a shortcut across a junkyard with his new best friend,
Simon, Taylor becomes aware of a colony of feral cats that makes the junkyard home.
Assisted by his classmates, his teacher, and the security guard Mr. Singh, Taylor takes
a special interest in caring for the cats. When Taylor discovers the junkyard is being
redeveloped to become condominiums, he worries about the cats' survival, and Taylor
and his new friends work together to save them.

Wilson, J. (2011). *Shannen and the dream for a school*. Toronto, ON: Second Story
Press. (E/J)
[Community; Education; FNMI; Non-fiction; Social action; Youth empowerment]
The true story of how 20 years after a fuel spill forced the closure of the school in
Attawapiskat First Nation in Northern Ontario, students still had nothing but a few
portables to learn in. Shannen Koostachin was one of those students. Every day, she
dealt with the freezing cold air that crept in through the poorly insulated walls; the

small, smelly bathroom; and the long walks between portables. Shannen, her friends, and her community decided to do something about it. They made a YouTube video about the poor conditions, and they travelled to Ottawa, where Shannen made a passionate speech to the politicians, telling them they were failing First Nations children and not just in Attawapiskat. Soon they had captured the attention of children thousands of miles away who supported their cause.

Wiseman, E. (2004). *No one must know.* Toronto, ON: Tundra Books. (E/J)
[Historical fiction; The Holocaust; Hungarian-Canadians; Immigration;
    World War II]
A sequel to *Kanada,* but can stand on its own. It is 1960, and Alex's immigrant family is living the North American dream. Her father is a respected doctor, and she has a warm circle of good friends. Perhaps her mother is a bit nervous—she seems incapable of leaving the house alone, and there is never any talk of the life they left behind in Hungary, but every family has its quirks. Alex's idyllic world is turned upside-down when she discovers that her parents have kept secrets about their past from her: They are Hungarian Holocaust survivors who have hidden their religious identity in an attempt to give Alex a better life.

Wiseman, E. (2006). *Kanada.* Toronto, ON: Tundra Books. (E/J)
[Historical fiction; The Holocaust; Hungarian-Canadians; Immigration; Refugees;
    World War II]
To 14-year-old Jutka, the name "Kanada" means a vast country, free from hatred. This is not the case in her small Hungarian town during World War II. Jutka, her family, and friends are sent to Auschwitz and, in that hellish place, she learns of another Kanada. It is the ironic name given to the storehouse where the belongings taken from those condemned to death are deposited, and where Jutka is put to work. Even when the war ends, her suffering is not over. Famished, diseased, and homeless, she lives in the hopelessness of refugee camps. Jutka then must make the difficult choice between going to Israel with the man she loves or following her own dreams of moving to Canada with her remaining family.

Wong, D. H. T. (2012). *Escape to Gold Mountain: A graphic history of the Chinese in North America.* Vancouver, BC: Arsenal Pulp Press. (E/J)
[Chinese-Canadians; Discrimination; Historical fiction; Immigration; Resilience]
This graphic novel tells the story of how the Chinese came to North America over the course of more than 100 years. It begins with the immigration of Chinese to "Gold Mountain" (what the Chinese called North America) in the 1800s, and progresses through a history filled with discrimination, heartbreak, and separation from loved ones. Despite these obstacles, however, the Chinese persevered, working hard and making sacrifices in order to create a better life for future generations. *Escape to Gold Mountain* is based on historical documents and interviews with elders, but events are

told through the eyes of the Wong family, who exhibit hope and determination as they create an immigrant's legacy in their new home.

Ye, T. (2003). *Throwaway daughter*. Toronto, ON: Doubleday Canada. (late E/J)
[Adoptive families; Chinese-Canadians; Gender; Girls and women)
Grace Dong-mei Parker feels like just a typical Canadian teenager, until the day she witnesses the Tiananmen massacre on television. Horrified, she sets out to explore her Chinese ancestry, only to discover that she was one of the thousands of infant girls abandoned in China since the introduction of the one-child policy, strictly enforced by the Communist government. But Grace was one of the lucky ones, adopted as a baby by a loving Canadian couple. With the encouragement of her adoptive parents, she studies Chinese and travels back to China in search of her birth mother. She manages to locate the village where she was born, but at first no one is willing to help her. However, Grace never gives up and, finally, she is reunited with her birth mother and discovers the truth of what happened to her almost 20 years before.

Novels—Junior High/Secondary

Bastedo, J. (2006). *On thin ice*. Calgary, AB: Red Deer Press. (J)
[Environment; FNMI; Inuit; Spirituality]
Ashley Anowiak is a young Inuk girl trying to understand her spiritual connection to polar bears. Could the changing environment have caused a polar bear to come close to the community and kill a teenager? Ashley is seeking answers to questions about culture, climate, and the environment.

Bastedo, J. (2010). *Sila's revenge*. Calgary, AB: Red Deer Press. (J)
[Environment; FNMI; Spirituality]
In the sequel to *On Thin Ice*, Ashley's drumming group meets a wealthy eccentric during an invited performance at Carnegie Hall in New York. He flies the group to Australia, and there they realize that his plan will endanger the planet.

Britt, F. (2013) *Jane, the fox, & me*. (I. Arsenault, Illus.). Toronto, ON: Groundwood
    Books/House of Anansi Press. (J/S)
[Body image; Bullying; Friendship; Graphic novel]
Originally published in French as *Jane, le rénard et moi*, this book tells the story of Hélène, a young girl who is being bullied by a group of girls at school. She escapes into the story of *Jane Eyre* and is comforted by the novel, using her imagination to over-come her feelings of isolation. Hélène is soon horrified to learn that she will be going with her class on a camping trip at the end of the year, especially because she'll have to wear a bathing suit. While away at the camp, she is placed in a tent along with other girls who are "outcasts." Hélène is miserable until she meets the lively Géraldine, with

whom a friendship blossoms. Hélène gains confidence as she discovers the value of connecting to another, whether they be a friend, a fictional character, or even a fox.

Brooks, M. (1997). *Bone dance.* Toronto, ON: Groundwood Books. (J)
[Cultural identity; Family; FNMI; Heritage]
Alexandra had never even met her alcoholic father, but he nevertheless leaves her his land and cabin on the prairie. That land, which is near a First Nations' burial mound, was purchased from Lonny LaFreniere's stepfather. Lonny, tormented by guilty memories and visions he can't shake, had rejected the land "Pop" always wanted to pass on to him, but now that he knows it's in the hands of a city girl, he's prepared to hate Alex. Alex surprises him, however; she is unlike anyone he has ever met. The novel is narrated from the alternating perspectives of the two characters.

Brown, C. (2003). *Louis Riel: A comic-strip biography.* San Francisco, CA: Drawn & Quarterly. (J)
[Biography; Canadian history; FNMI; Graphic novel; Metis; Non-fiction]
This black-and-white graphic novel tells the true story of the 19th-century Métis leader Louis Riel, whose struggle to win rights for his people led to violent rebellion on the nation's western frontier. It is not a comprehensive biography of Riel's entire life, but rather focuses on Riel's relationship with the Canadian government, from the arrival of Canadian surveyors in what is now Manitoba, to Riel's death on a Regina gallows. Included is a comprehensive notes section with additional information, as well as an index of the names referenced in the book. An ideal resource for social studies or humanities.

Chan, G. (2002). *A foreign field.* Toronto, ON: Kids Can Press. (J/S)
[Historical fiction; World War II]
Life has been tough for 14-year-old Ellen Logan. With her country embroiled in World War II, her brothers in the service, and her parents busily supporting the war effort, Ellen must shoulder many of the family responsibilities. Life is even tougher for Stephen Dearborn, a young British pilot in training at the local airfield. Inexperienced and far from home, Stephen's romantic dreams of being a pilot are shattered by the harsh reality of his training. Ellen and Stephen are forced to grow up before their time, and their friendship begins to deepen just as Stephen must return to England to begin active service.

Desrochers, S. (2011). *Bride of New France.* Toronto, ON: Penguin. (J/S)
[Courage; FNMI; Historical fiction]
Laure Beausejour is an orphan in Paris who dreams of becoming a seamstress and marrying a nobleman. However, she is sent to New France as a *fille de roi* and married to a soldier. She is expected to produce children while living in a forest cabin with a brutish husband who cannot provide. However, her alliance with Deskaheh, an Iroquois, offers new possibilities.

Ellis, D. (2001). *The breadwinner*. Toronto, ON: Douglas & McIntyre. (J)
[Afghanistan; Community; Family; Gender; Girls and women; War]
When her father is arrested by the Taliban, all seems lost for 11-year-old Parvana, her mother, and her siblings. Girls and women are not allowed outside the home without a male escort. Then Parvana's mother and their neighbour Mrs. Weera come up with a plan for Parvana to disguise herself as a boy so that she can move about freely and find work to support the family. Now known as Kazeem, Parvana and her similarly disguised friend Shauzia must navigate Taliban-controlled Kabul on their own and do whatever it takes to provide for their families and neighbours, all while dreaming of brighter futures for both themselves and their nation. Based on the true-life stories of women in Afghan refugee camps.

Fitch, S. (2005). *The gravesavers*. Toronto, ON: Doubleday Canada. (J)
[Community; Courage; Historical fiction]
Minn Hotchkiss is sent to spend the summer with her grandmother on Nova Scotia's Atlantic coast. While there, 12-year-old Minn learns of a shipwreck and a graveyard that is being washed into the sea. Minn, haunted by the ghost of a child who was a passenger on that ship, is determined to preserve the graveyard and ensure that the community knows the story. Through the process, Minn learns about herself and her family.

Ellis, D. (2002). *Parvana's journey*. Toronto, ON: Douglas & McIntyre. (J)
[Afghanistan; Courage; Gender; Girls and women; Perseverance; War]
The second book in The Breadwinner Trilogy, but can also stand alone. After setting off to find the rest of their family in northern Afghanistan, Parvana's father dies, leaving her all alone in the countryside. Still disguised as a boy, she continues on her journey, joining up with other children who, like her, have been left to fend for themselves. Together they face bombs, land mines, and near-starvation as Parvana seeks to reunite with her remaining family.

Ellis, D. (2003). *Mud city*. Toronto, ON: Groundwood Books. (J)
[Gender; Girls and women; Pakistan; Refugees; War]
This third book in The Breadwinner Trilogy (which can also stand alone) follows the travels of Parvana's best friend, Shauzia, who has left Afghanistan. Unhappy at the refugee camp and determined to take control of her own life, Shauzia sets out alone to Peshawar, Pakistan, again in the guise of a boy. With only her dog, Jasper, as a friend, she must scrounge for food, beg for money, and look for a safe place to sleep every night. When a man tries to abduct her, the commotion results in her imprisonment in a Pakistani jail, and Shauzia's fate seems to be sealed. But a couple saves her, and, in their care, she begins to rethink her dreams.

Ellis, D. (2004). *Heaven shop*. Markham, ON: Fitzhenry & Whiteside. (J/S)
[Africa; Death and grieving; Family; HIV/AIDS; Malawi; Resilience]
Binti's father and her mother before him have died of AIDS, even if no one openly says
it. Binti, her sister, and her brother are separated and sent to the home of relatives who
can barely tolerate their presence. Ostracized by their extended family, the orphans
are treated like the lowest servants. With her brother far away and her sister wallowing
in her own sorrow, Binti can hardly contain her rage. She was once a child star of a
popular radio program, and now she is scraping to survive. Binti always believed she
was special; now she is nothing but a common AIDS orphan. But she is not about to
give up. Even as she clings to hope that her former life will be restored, she must face
a greater challenge. If she and her siblings are to be reunited, Binti will have to look
outside herself and find a new way to be special. Inspired by a young radio performer
the author met during her research visit to Malawi.

Ellis, D. (2006). *I am a taxi*. Toronto, ON: Groundwood Books/House of
     Anansi Press. (J)
[Bolivia; Child labour; Drug trade; Family; Justice; Resilience; South America]
Diego and his little sister live with their mother, who has been wrongfully convicted of
drug smuggling, in the San Sebastian Women's Prison in Cochabamba, Bolivia. To help
support his family, he works as a "taxi"—running errands for other prisoners. Then a
stroke of bad luck sets his family back in a major way, and Diego's friend convinces him
they can make easier money working for men who turn out to be involved in cocaine
manufacturing. It is a far different job than Diego ever imagined—one that takes him deep
into the heart of the Bolivian jungle. Diego's story continues in a sequel, *Sacred Leaf*.

Ellis, D., & Walters, E. (2007). *Bifocal*. Markham, ON: Fitzhenry & Whiteside. (J)
[Activism; Community; Immigration; Media; Racism; Religion;
     Responsibility; Rights]
Told in the alternating viewpoints of Jay, a white football player seeking to fit in at his
new school, and Haroon, a quiet, studious member of the Reach for the Top quiz team,
Bifocal takes place in an Ontario high school in the hours, days, and weeks following
a lockdown and the arrest of a student accused of being part of a terrorist plot. Racial
and religious lines are drawn, and tensions erupt. Both boys must decide for themselves
what they believe, where their loyalties lie, and what they will stand up for.

Gilmore, R. (2001). *A group of one*. Markham, ON: Fitzhenry & Whiteside. (J/S)
[Cultural identity; Family; Heritage; Indo-Canadians; Multiculturalism]
Tara Mehta's parents might be from India, but Tara has lived in Ottawa her whole
life—she's as Canadian as everybody else. There are much more important things than
where her family came from. But then Tara meets her grandmother for the first time
and learns about how Naniji fought with Gandhi in the Indian Independence movement. She is a proud and strong woman, and she's horrified that her grandchildren

know very little about their heritage. Shocked and angered by the history that she's never been taught in school, Tara tells Naniji's story to her class. In the wake of the violently mixed reactions that follow, Tara comes to realize that many people need to expand their definition of what it means to be a "regular Canadian"—including herself.

Hawarth-Attard, B. (1999). *Love-lies-bleeding.* Toronto, ON: HarperCollins. (J/S)
[Historical fiction; World War II]
Ambushed by the dreaded "Worm of Jealousy" over her best friend's new diary and fashionable clothes, 13-year-old Bobby announces that she, too, has a diary. Now she is compelled to write every day about the joys and fears of growing up in a world at war. Bobby's beloved eldest brother and uncle are fighting overseas in World War II. Her 16-year-old brother can't wait to enlist, and her worldly sister has her own problems. The narrative is interspersed with authentic letters written by the author's father during World War II.

Horrocks, Anita. (2006). *Almost Eden.* Toronto, ON: Tundra Books. (J)
[Community; Family; Mennonites, Mental Health; Perseverance]
Twelve-year-old Elsie lives in a conservative Mennonite community and thinks her mother's mental illness is her fault. As she tries to make things better, more and more goes wrong, and she loses her sense of place in her close-knit community. However, her perseverance and determination enable her to challenge what doesn't make sense. *Almost Eden* is a sensitive exploration of mental illness and its impact on family.

Huser, G. (2003). *Stitches.* Toronto, ON: Groundwood Books. (J)
[Abuse; Acceptance; Art; Bullying; Disability; Friendship; LGBTQ]
Junior high in small-town Alberta isn't easy for Travis. He lives in a trailer park with his aunt, uncle, and cousins, because his mother is on the road a lot and his father is long gone. At school, Travis is relentlessly bullied. His only support comes from his best friend, Chantelle, who is also a target of bullying because of her scars and physical disability. Travis finds acceptance and an outlet for his creativity in his fashions class, where he designs the costumes for a school-wide puppet production of *A Midsummer Night's Dream.* This increases his persecution, however, and his bully's anger and prejudices erupt in violence.

Kerbel, D. (2008). *Mackenzie, lost and found.* Toronto, ON: Dundurn Press. (J)
[Death and grieving; Israel; The Middle East; Palestine]
Although she is still recovering from the loss of her mother, Mackenzie's eccentric father is forcing her to leave behind the only home she's ever known and move with him to Israel. There, she forges a friendship with an American girl who's also suffered tragic loss, and gets caught up in a forbidden romance with a Palestinian boy. When Mackenzie becomes unwittingly involved in a ring of black-market bandits, she has to find a way to solve the mystery of the stolen artifacts without betraying her first love.

Kositsky, L. (2004). *The thought of high windows.* Toronto, ON: Kids Can
Press. (J/S)
[Historical fiction; The Holocaust; World War II]
Young, Jewish, and on the run from the Nazis, Esther is one of a group of children who
manage to flee Germany for Belgium and then France at the beginning of World War II.
Here, she becomes involved with the Jewish Underground. Since she is from a more
traditionally Jewish family, however, she feels like an outcast amongst the others.
Esther frets over her frumpy looks, is ridiculed by the popular girls, and loves a boy
who only ever treats her like a sister. As the war rages on and Esther bears witness
to its horrors, her pain and isolation grow—until only the highest windows bring the
promise of release.

McPhee, P. (2007/2011). *Newblood.* Toronto, ON: James Lorimer & Company.
(J/S) (Hi-low)
[Bullying; Healing; Immigration; Resilience; Violence]
After a gang beats him up, Callum's parents have had enough of Glasgow's tough streets.
His family moves to Canada to make a fresh start, joining Callum's older brother and
his wife in Winnipeg. But Winnipeg has its share of bullies too. Still healing from his
injuries, Callum also has deep inner scars that will make his new high school, in this
new country, even more of a battleground. Inspired by a true story.

Olsen, S. (2001). *No time to say goodbye: Children's stories of Kuper Island
Residential School.* Winlaw, BC: Sono Nis Press. (J)
[FNMI; Historical fiction; Residential schools]
Although this is a fictional account of five Indigenous children sent to residential school,
the stories are based on the true recollections of a number of Tsartlip First Nations
people. The five characters are isolated on tiny Kuper Island and experience the pain
of homesickness and confusion as their life becomes regimented by the strict school
routine of bells, line-ups, and chores. In spite of the harsh realities of the residential
school, the children find adventure in escape, challenge in competition, and camaraderie with their fellow students. All royalties from the book go toward supporting
Tsartlip First Nation youth programs.

Olsen, S. (2008). *Middle row.* Victoria, BC: Orca Book Publishers. (J/S) (Hi-low)
[Friendship; Racism]
Things have changed since Raedawn and Vince started going out, and the racial bound-
aries in town have slipped a bit. But when Dune, who never took sides, disappears,
Raedawn is determined to find out where he has gone—or what happened to him.
Fighting against ignorance and hate, they track Dune down and find he is in more
trouble than they thought and that nothing is black and white.

Oppel, K. (2010). *Half brother*. Toronto, ON: HarperCollins. (J/S)
[Animal welfare; Ethics; Family]
When Ben Tomlin's mother brings home his new "baby brother," an eight-day-old chimpanzee, Ben is far from thrilled. His father, a renowned behavioural scientist, has uprooted the family and moved them halfway across the country, to Victoria, BC, so he can pursue a high-profile experiment—to determine whether chimpanzees can learn human sign language. The chimp, named Zan, must be raised exactly like a human. Ben is soon smitten. Within months, Zan learns his first signs and becomes a media sensation. But when Project Zan unexpectedly loses its funding, Ben's father is under huge pressure to either make the experiment succeed or abandon it—and Zan. Unable to convince his father that Zan is now part of the family, Ben must risk everything to save his baby brother from an unimaginable fate. Inspired by two actual chimp experiments—Project Nim and Project Washoe—that took place in the 1970s.

Polak, M. (2013). *So much it hurts*. Victoria, BC: Orca Book Publishers. (J/S)
[Abuse; Domestic violence; Elder wisdom]
Iris, an actress, is flattered when Mick, a well-known director, takes an interest in her. He's 14 years older, attractive, funny, charming, and sexy. But when Iris and Mick start a secret relationship, she soon witnesses his dark side and bad temper. Before long, she is the target of his rage and abuse, but keeps making excuses for him. Iris struggles to continue going to school and feels increasingly isolated and in pain. When her family and a new friend—an elderly woman who is Mick's neighbour—realize something is wrong, Iris begins to make the first steps toward self-preservation. *So Much It Hurts* honestly portrays the emotions of a smart young woman who has fallen into an abusive relationship.

Poulsen, D. A. (2004). *Last Sam's cage*. Toronto, ON: Key Porter Books. (J)
[Abuse; Homelessness]
Already labelled a young offender, 15-year-old Eddie runs away from an abusive step-father and takes up residence at the Calgary Zoo. There he meets Jack, a middle-aged man who has been coming to the zoo's playground every day for 32 years to watch the children. Convinced that Jack is either a pervert or just plain weird, Eddie follows him home one day, and eventually breaks into his house to see what he can find. He discovers more than he bargained for—and that discovery changes both Eddie and Jack for good.

Robertson, D. A., & Henderson, S. B. (2012). *Sugar Falls: A residential school story*.
  Winnipeg, MB: Highwater Press. (J/S)
[FNMI; Graphic novel; Residential schools; Resilience]
When Daniel is given a school assignment to interview a residential school survivor, his classmate April takes him to meet her Kokum (grandmother), who tells Daniel her story. Abandoned as a young child, Betsy was soon adopted into a loving family.

A few short years later, at the age of eight, everything changed when Betsy was taken away to a residential school. There she was forced to endure abuse and indignity, but Betsy recalled the words her father spoke to her at Sugar Falls—words that gave her the resilience, strength, and determination to survive. This black-and-white graphic novel is based on the true story of Betty Ross, an Elder from Cross Lake First Nation. A portion of the proceeds from the book support the bursary program for the Helen Betty Osborne Memorial Foundation.

Slipperjack, R. (2008). *Dog tracks*. Calgary, AB: Fifth House. (J/S)
[Anishinaabe; Elder wisdom; Family; FNMI; Traditions]
After having lived most of her life in town with her grandparents, Abby is having trouble fitting in at Bear Creek Reserve. When her grandfather falls ill, Abby must leave her best friends at school and her supportive grandparents, and adjust to living with her mother. But it's not only being back with Mom that is hard—there's a new father, a pesky half-brother, and a schoolroom full of kids who don't know her (and don't seem to want to, either), not to mention a completely different way of life that seems so traditional, so puzzling and complicated. But, with the help of the reserve's chief, a puppy, and her parents' vision of a sled-dog tourist venture, Abby slowly begins to find her rhythm at Bear Creek and rediscover her Anishinaabe culture.

Storm, J. (2007). *Deadly loyalties*. Penticton, BC: Theytus Books. (J)
[Abuse; Homelessness]
Fourteen-year-old Blaise enters the world of street gangs in Winnipeg after she is witness to the murder of a friend at the hands of a rival gang. Blaise must negotiate an intricate maze of enemies and allies, protection and abuse, as she struggles to survive in this new setting.

Stratton, A. (2004). *Chanda's secrets*. Toronto, ON: Annick Press. (J/S)
[Africa; Education; Family; HIV/AIDS; Resilience]
Sixteen-year-old Chanda's family's troubles began after her father was killed in the diamond mines. Her first stepfather abused her, the second died of a stroke, and the third is a drunken philanderer. Although Chanda lives in a world in which illness and death have become commonplace, it is not one in which AIDS can be mentioned. When Mother leaves to visit her family on the cattle post, Chanda is forced to give up her dream of further education to care for her younger sister and brother. Slowly, she comes to realize that her mother has AIDS and that she herself might be infected. Chanda's education serves her well as she faces the disease head-on.

Stratton, A. (2008). *Chanda's wars*. Toronto, ON: HarperCollins. (J/S)
[Africa; Child soldiers; Family; Perseverance; War]
A companion book to *Chanda's Secrets*, but can stand alone. In this continuation, Mother has died, leaving Chanda alone responsible for her young brother and sister.

But, while she is taking them to refuge in their grandparents' village, rebel soldiers brutally attack and kidnap her little brother and sister. Risking their lives, Chanda and a troubled young tracker must pursue the rebels through the unforgiving bush to save her family.

Stratton, A. (2010). *Borderline*. Toronto, ON: HarperCollins. (J)
[Bullying; Family; Islam; Post-9/11]
Fifteen-year-old Sami Sabiri feels like a typical suburban teen, but when his dad sticks him in a private school where he's the only Muslim kid, he begins to be regularly harassed by a group of bullies. He gets no support from the school administration in stopping it. But things get even worse when Sami catches his father in a lie. Sami isn't the only one who gets suspicious, and the FBI descends on their home and arrests his father. Sami's family becomes the centre of an international terrorist investigation, and Sami must fight to keep his world from unravelling.

Tamberg, U. (2012). *The darkest corner of the world*. Toronto, ON: Dancing Cats Books. (J)
[Estonia; Family; Historical fiction; World War II]
Fifteen-year-old Madli is going on her yearly vacation to visit her grandparents for mid-summer celebrations on Hiiumaa Island. But this year is different, because the War has come to Estonia. Her father, along with thousands of others, has been arrested and deported, and Soviet soldiers are everywhere. Not long after, Nazis invade her country. Now, Madli must decide whether she'd rather live under the evil regime she knows, or help another evil regime in hopes her father will be freed and the true story of her nation will be heard.

Trilby, K. (2011). *Stones for my father*. Toronto, ON: Tundra Books. (J/S)
[Colonialism; Death and grieving; Historical fiction; Internment; Resilience; South Africa; War]
Corlie Roux's farm life in South Africa is not easy. When her beloved father dies, she is left with a mother who is devoted to her sons, but cruel to her daughter. Corlie finds solace in her friend Sipho, in South Africa itself, and in the stories she dreams up for her brothers. But when the British invade and begin forcing Boer families like hers from their farms, some escape into the bush to fight the enemy, while the unlucky ones are rounded up and sent to internment camps. Corlie is one of the unlucky ones. Her survival depends on her inner strength and resilience, and perhaps on a soldier from faraway Canada.

Walters, E. (2006). *Shattered*. Toronto, ON: Penguin Books. (J/S)
[Homelessness; Post-traumatic stress disorder; Social action]
Fifteen-year-old Ian has to complete volunteer community service to pass social studies. Choosing to work at "the Club" sounds like fun, until he arrives at what turns out to be a soup kitchen for the homeless. Here he meets Sarge, the pipe-wielding homeless

man who saved Ian from a near-mugging. His real name is Jacques, and he was a soldier in the Canadian Armed Forces, his last tour of duty as a peacekeeper stationed in Rwanda. Ian's view of the world is about to change—and what he learns may just help Jacques, too. With a foreword by Lieutenant-General Romeo Dallaire (Ret'd).

Walters, E. (2008). *Alexandria of Africa.* Toronto, ON: Doubleday Canada. (J/S) [Africa; Community service; Kenya]

As far as Alexandria Hyatt is concerned, being rich and glamorous is simply what she was born to be. When she is arrested for shoplifting, she can't scheme her way out of the consequences. Before she knows it, she is on a plane headed to Kenya, where she has been ordered to work for an international charity. There, 7,000 miles away from home, she will have no hot water, no cell phone reception, and no friends or family. Over the course of her month in Kenya, Alexandria will face a reality she could never have imagined and will have to look inside herself to see if she has what it takes to confront it.

Walters, E. (2009). *Black and white.* Toronto, ON: Penguin Group. (J) [Friendship; Prejudice; Racism; Sports]

Thomas and Denyse share a love of basketball. As they get to know each other, they discover that they have a lot more in common, too. The only major difference is the colour of their skin. When they start hanging out, they are surprised at the cruel glances, name-calling, and hurtful comments that are targeted at them when they are together. Denyse and Thomas can't understand what the big deal is, but the pressure of others' prejudices threatens to break them apart.

Walters, E. (2009). *Wounded.* Toronto, ON: Penguin Group. (J/S) [Family; Post-traumatic stress disorder; War]

Marcus and his sister are counting down the days until their father comes home from Afghanistan. When the big day arrives, the family is overcome by happiness and relief that he is safe, but as the days pass, Marcus begins to feel that there is something different about his father. He barely sleeps, he's obsessed with news from Afghanistan, and while at times he seems almost too happy, at others, he's erratic and aggressive. Marcus knows post-traumatic stress disorder affects many soldiers, but at first he finds it hard to believe his father needs help. When he eventually does realize that counselling is needed, Marcus just can't seem to convince his father.

Walters, E. (2010). *Branded.* Victoria, BC: Orca Book Publishers. (J) (Hi-Low) [Activism; Education; Human rights; Social action]

When the school principal announces a new uniform policy, Ian's best friend, Julia, is determined to get him to protest the policy. The principal is equally determined to convince Ian that uniforms are a good idea. Ian wants nothing to do with the issue—at first. Then, while doing research for a social justice class, he learns that the manufacturer of the uniforms is a known violator of human rights. Now it is impossible for Ian to avoid choosing sides—no matter what the consequences might be.

Walters, E. (2011). *Shaken.* Toronto, ON: Doubleday Canada. (J)
[Haiti; Poverty; Social action]
When Josh accompanies his minister father and his congregation on a mission trip to an orphanage in Haiti, he is forced to confront the poverty and injustice that surrounds him and struggles to find meaning in the world. This becomes even more challenging when Josh finds himself at the centre of the devastating 2010 earthquake. How will he manage to help those around him in the face of almost unimaginable destruction? And how will he ever begin to make sense of a world he finds to be more cruelly uncertain than ever?

Wilson, I. (2003). *Flames of the tiger.* Toronto, ON: Kids Can Press. (J)
[Historical fiction; World War II]
As a boy growing up in Germany during Hitler's rise to power, 13-year-old Dieter has been seduced by the pomp and circumstance of war. But as global hostilities intensify, Dieter is called upon to fight for his country in a conflict that he doesn't fully understand. With most of his family dead, Berlin in ruins, and the Russian army closing in, Dieter can no longer naively cling to his childhood beliefs. The world he is facing is brutal, dirty, and unforgiving, and the most he can hope for is the chance to survive.

Wilson, I. (2005). *Four steps to death.* Toronto, ON: Kids Can Press. (J)
[Historical fiction; Russia; World War II]
A companion book to *Flames of the Tiger*. It is 1942, and the Battle of Stalingrad, one of the bloodiest in history, is underway. Three participants—two soldiers and a boy—are caught in its horrors. Vasily is a patriotic Russian soldier determined to rid his country of the hated Nazi invaders, and Conrad is a German tank officer, expecting a quick victory over Stalin's ill-trained and poorly equipped army. Between them is eight-year-old Sergie, whose home is the maze of rubble that used to be Stalingrad. None of them can know that their fates will be intertwined as the battle and the War engulfs them.

Yee, P. (2008). *Learning to fly.* Victoria, BC: Orca Book Publishers. (J/S) (Hi-low)
[Chinese-Canadians; Friendship; Immigration; Racism]
Jason is an outsider. A recent immigrant from China, he lives in a closed-minded Ontario town with his mother and younger brother. His parents have split up, and Jason must work long hours in his mother's deli to help out. Falling in with the wrong crowd and trying to fit in, Jason takes chances and ends up in trouble with the police. Then he meets "Chief," a First Nations teen who is also an outsider. When Jason is arrested for drug possession and Chief's sister dies from an overdose, the two lean on each other to make it through.

Young, B. (2009). *Charlie: A home child's life in Canada.* Toronto, ON: Key Porter
   Books. (J/S)
[Home Children; Immigration; Non-fiction; Poverty]
The stories of the 90,000 British children who came to Canada as child immigrants
between 1870 and 1938 are not well known. Yet the descendants of these "home children" number more than four million in Canada today. The author is one of them:
Charlie was her father. Charlie was 13 when his shopkeeper father died in 1910. His
mother, Sarah, had no money to care for her seven children, and before long, Charlie
was sent to an orphanage, and then to Canada to live on an Ontario farm. Here he
experienced homesickness, hardship, and great kindness. Eventually, Charlie rose
from a life of poverty to become a member of the RCMP. The book features archival
and personal photographs and informational sidebars.

Novels—Secondary

Badami, A. R. (1996). *Tamarind Mem.* Toronto: Viking. (S)
[Girls and women; Family; Immigration; Indo-Canadians]
This is the story of Kamini and her mother Saroja, nicknamed Tamarind Mem due to
her sour tongue. While in Canada beginning her graduate studies, Kamini receives a
postcard from her mother saying she has sold their home and is travelling through
India. Kamini tries to make sense of her mother's strange messages and the eccentric
family she's left behind, while, in India, her mother travels alone by train across the
country, entertaining fellow passengers with tales from her life. Both women are
forced into the past to confront their dreams and losses, and to explore the love that
binds mothers and daughters everywhere.

Bock, D. (2001). *The ash garden.* Toronto, ON: Harper Flamingo Canada. (S)
[Ethics; Healing; Hiroshima; Reconciliation; World War II]
Emiko Amai is a respected documentary filmmaker who still bears the physical and
emotional scars from the burns that she suffered at the age of six because of the atomic
bomb in Hiroshima. Anton Boll is a professor and refugee German scientist who helped
build the bomb and observed its effects in Japan three weeks after it was dropped.
Though he claims that the bomb was dropped "to save lives," Anton remains acutely
aware of the human cost, both to its victims and himself. He is now caretaker to his
dying wife, Sophie, herself a half-Jewish refugee from Austria who still manages the
strength to support her husband as he struggles with his guilt. When Emiko confronts
Anton in 1995 at a lecture in New York, he surprises himself by agreeing to participate
in a documentary she's filming and invites Emiko to the quiet house he shares with
Sophie in Ontario.

Choy, W. (1995). *The jade peony*. Vancouver, BC: Douglas & McIntyre. (S)
[Chinese-Canadians; Family; Historical fiction; Immigration; World War II]
Set in Chinatown, Vancouver, in the late 1930s and early 1940s, *The Jade Peony* tells the story of three young children of an immigrant family. They each experience a very different childhood, depending on age and sex, as they encounter the complexities of birth and death, love and hate, kinship and otherness. Mingling with the realities of Canada and the horror of war are the magic, ghosts, paper uncles, and the family secrets of Poh-Poh (Grandmother), who is the heart and pillar of the family. Although fictional, the book realistically portrays the difficult lives of early Chinese immigrants in Canada.

Choy, W. (2004). *All that matters*. Toronto, ON: Doubleday Canada. (S)
[Chinese-Canadians; Family; Historical fiction; Immigration; World War II]
A sequel to *The Jade Peony*. Set in the 1930s and 1940s, *All That Matters* continues the story of the Chen family, this time seen through the eyes of First Son, Kiam-Kim. Having left behind the harshness of life in their Toishan village, Kiam-Kim, his father, and his grandmother arrive in Vancouver with dreams of a better future. From his earliest years, Kiam-Kim is deeply conscious of his responsibilities to maintain the family's honour and to set an irreproachable example for his Canadian-born brothers and sister. Kiam-Kim forges a lasting friendship with Jack O'Connor, the Irish boy next door who must struggle with his own inheritance. Both boys approach adulthood against the backdrop of rigid expectations at home and violent war abroad.

Coupland, D. (2011). *Player one*. Toronto: Windmill Books. (S)
[Community; Identity; Religion]
This CBC Massey Lecture takes the form of a real-time, five-hour story set in an air-port cocktail lounge during a global disaster. Five disparate people are trapped inside: Karen, a single mother waiting for her online date; Rick, the down-on-his-luck airport lounge bartender; Luke, a pastor on the run; Rachel, a woman incapable of true human contact; and finally a mysterious voice known as Player One. Slowly, each reveals the truth about themselves while the world as they know it comes to an end.

Fairfield, L. (2009). *Tyranny*. Toronto, ON: Tundra Books. (S)
[Eating disorders; Graphic novel; Mental health]
Pressured by media, friends, fashion trends, her workplace, and personal relationships, Anna starts dieting, but soon descends into an uncontrollable spiral of anorexia and bulimia. Whenever she tries to break the cycle of her disorder, Anna's personal demon, Tyranny, is there to push her back down. In Tyranny, Anna has created a formidable foe, and now, finding the strength to defeat her is a matter of life or death.

Gingras, C. (2005/2009). *Pieces of me*. (S. Ouriou, Trans.). Toronto, ON: Kids Can Press. (S)

[Art; Friendship; Mental health]

Mira is almost 15, and friendless. She watches the world go by from a lonely half-basement apartment that she shares with her mother, plagued with dark thoughts, her only comfort in the company of books. She yearns for love, for friendship, and for her father who ran away. Then free-spirited, confident Catherine steps into Mira's life, and the world explodes in a riot of colour and laughter. Although Cath helps Mira come out of her shell, Mira discovers her new-found confidence can still be easily shattered. First published in French as *La liberte? Connais pas ...*

Hill, L. (2007). *The book of Negroes*. Toronto, ON: HarperCollins. (S)

[African-Canadians; Black Loyalists; Historical fiction; Slavery]

Abducted from her village in West Africa as an 11-year-old child, Aminata is put to work on an indigo plantation on the sea islands of South Carolina. Aminata survives by using midwifery skills learned at her mother's side and drawing on a strength of character inherited from both parents. Aminata learns to read, teaches others to, and befriends anyone who can help her, Black or white. Aminata nevertheless remains trapped, narrowly avoiding the violence that cuts short so many lives around her. Eventually, she has the chance to register her name in the "Book of Negroes," a historic British military ledger allowing 3,000 Black Loyalists passage on ships sailing from Manhattan to Nova Scotia.

Itani, F. (2003). *Deafening*. London, ON: Writes Inc. (S)

[Disability; Education; Healing; Historical fiction; Resilience; World War I]

At the age of five, Grania becomes profoundly deaf after a bout of scarlet fever and is suddenly sealed off from the world that was just beginning to open for her. Her guilt-plagued mother cannot accept her daughter's deafness. Although her grandmother and sister try to teach her to read and speak again, when it becomes clear that she can no longer thrive in the world of the hearing, her family sends her to live at the Ontario School for the Deaf in Belleville. Here, she learns sign language and speech. When Grania's brother-in-law returns from the trenches of Europe severely injured and refusing to speak, it is through her own experiences in coping with disability that she is able to teach him both to speak again and to have hope for a future.

Joe, R. (1996). *Song of Rita Joe: Autobiography of a Mi'kmaq poet*. Charlottetown, PE: Ragweed Press. (S)

[FNMI; Mi'kmaq; Non-fiction; Residential schools; Resilience]

Rita Joe was a poet, an educator, an ambassador, and a Companion of the Order of Canada. But even before those accomplishments, Rita Joe led a remarkable life, from her education in a residential school, to her turbulent marriage, to her daily struggles within her family and community. This is the story of how Joe's battles with racism, sexism, poverty, and personal demons became the catalyst for her first poems and allowed her to reclaim her Indigenous heritage.

Lester, D. (2011). *The listener*. Winnipeg, MB: Arbeiter Ring Publishing. (S)
[Activism; Art; Graphic novel; Social action]
In this graphic novel, two stories collide: the tale of Hitler's rise to power, and that of an artist searching for meaning in the great art of Europe. In 1933, in a small German state, the last democratic election is about to take place before a failed artist named Hitler seizes power. This election is Hitler's last chance to manipulate events that will lead to the death of millions. In the present day, a man falls to his death during a political act inspired by a sculpture. The artist who created it flees to Europe to escape her guilt. Through a chance meeting, she discovers the truth of the 1933 election, and the past becomes pivotal as she decides her future.

Mac, C. (2004). *The beckoners*. Victoria, BC: Orca Book Publishers. (S)
[Bullying; Courage; Taking a stand]
Fifteen-year-old Zoe is new in town, and the first person she meets is Beck, the leader of the Beckoners. Out of fear and curiosity, Zoe is initiated into the group, but then can't escape their intimidation. Help eventually comes from some unlikely sources as she tries to escape without becoming a target herself. Meanwhile, she also tries to save April—or "Dog," as she is called by the Beckoners—from further torment.

Marineau, M. (1992/1995). *The road to Chlifa*. (S. Odriou, Trans.). Calgary, AB: Red Deer Press. (S)
[Discrimination; Friendship; Immigration; War]
Karim has journeyed a long way from his home in war-torn Beirut to his new high school in Quebec, by way of Chlifa. He finds there is contempt and racism here in Montreal, too. After a fight with a classmate, Karim examines what triggered him, going back to his life in Lebanon and his journey out of the country. Karim's diary, letters to his friend, memories, and dreams reveal the harrowing experiences and journey he survived. Thankfully, he soon meets My-Lan, who becomes a friend and source of support in Karim's new and challenging country.

Martel, Y. (2002). *Life of Pi*. Toronto, ON: Alfred A. Knopf Canada. (S)
[Animal welfare; Death and grieving; Immigration; Religion; Resilience]
The son of a zookeeper, Pi Patel, and his family emigrate from India to North America aboard a cargo ship along with their zoo animals, which are also bound for new homes. When the ship sinks, Pi finds himself alone in a lifeboat with a hyena, an orangutan, a wounded zebra, and a 450-pound Bengal tiger named Richard Parker. Before long, only Pi and Richard Parker remain, and the boy must use his knowledge and cunning to

survive. After an incredible 227 days lost at sea, Pi finally reaches shore. The authorities refuse to believe his story and urge him to tell the "truth." Pi then tells a second, more conventional story—but is it more true?

Robinson, E. (2000). *Monkey Beach.* Toronto, ON: Vintage Canada. (S)
[FNMI; Death and grieving; Haisla; Family; Nature and wildlife; Spirituality]
Tragedy strikes a First Nations community when the Hill family's handsome 17-year-old son, Jimmy, mysteriously vanishes at sea. Left behind to cope during the search-and-rescue effort is his sister Lisamarie, a wayward teenager with a dark secret. She sets off alone in search of Jimmy through the Douglas Channel and heads for Monkey Beach. Intertwined with this narrative is a series of flashbacks in which Lisamarie's earlier years are revealed, including her ability to see and hear spirits.

Selvadurai, S. (1994). *Funny boy.* Toronto, ON: McClelland & Stewart. (S)
[Gender; LGBTQ; Immigration; Political turmoil; Sri Lanka]
Arjie Chelvartnam is a Tamil boy growing up in an upper-middle class extended family in Colombo, Sri Lanka. He prefers dressing up in a sari and playing "bride-bride" to playing cricket, and so his father sends him to a strict private academy, hoping it will force Arjie to "be a man." Instead, Arjie develops a romantic relationship with his classmate Shehan. All of this occurs against the backdrop of turmoil and violence, which eventually causes Arjie's family to emigrate to Canada as refugees. Though not autobiographical, Selvadurai draws on his own experience of being gay in Sri Lanka during a time of escalating violence.

Skrypuch, M. F. (1999). *The hunger.* Toronto, ON: Dundurn Press. (S)
[Armenian genocide; Eating disorders; Family; Historical trauma; World War I]
Fifteen-year-old Paula's perfectionism drives every facet of her life, from her marks to her pursuit of a "perfect body." A history project brings her face to face with her grandmother's early life in Armenia, and as she delves deeper, she is disturbed to find eerie parallels between her own struggles and what she learns of the past. As Paula slowly destroys the very body she's trying to perfect, her spirit is torn between settling for her imperfect life or entering the shadowy mystery of her grandmother's past. *The Hunger* is continued in the novel *Nobody's Child.*

Skrypuch, M. F. (2001). *Hope's war.* Toronto, ON: Dundurn Press. (S)
[Art; Family; Historical trauma; World War II]
Kataryna Baliuk, a gifted fine arts student, is hoping to have a fresh start at a new fine arts school after a less-than-successful past. But her hopes are shattered when she comes home from her first day and finds the RCMP interrogating her grandfather. He is accused of being a policeman for the Nazis during World War II in Ukraine, and what's worse, he is suspected of having participated in atrocities against civilians. When the

story is exposed in the local newspaper, Kat and her family become the centre of a media storm and the target of hate crimes. Her only support comes from her family and Ian, a classmate with whom she discovers she has more in common than just artistic promise.

Skrypuch, M. F. (2008). *Daughter of war*. Markham, ON: Fitzhenry & Whiteside. (S/P)
[Armenian genocide; Historical fiction; Resilience; War; World War I]
Set during the Armenian genocide of 1916 in Turkey, *Daughter of War* tells the story of Marta and her sister, two Armenian girls who are rescued by Turks. If it is discovered that the girls are Muslim, however, they will be killed or marched into the desert to die. It is also the story of Kevork, Marta's fiancé, who is rescued by an Arab clan. Separated and hiding their true identities, Marta and Kevork do not even know if the other is alive. All they can do is hope that one day they will be reunited. Based on firsthand accounts of the Armenian genocide in Turkey during World War I.

Small, D. (2011). *Stitches: A memoir*. Toronto, ON: McClelland & Stewart. (S)
[Art; Disability; Healing; Resilience]
One day, David Small awoke from a supposedly harmless operation to discover that he had been transformed into a virtual mute. Now discovering he had a vocal cord removed and his throat slashed and stitched together, the 14-year-old boy had not been told beforehand that he had cancer and was expected to die. Believing that they were keeping him safe by hiding this from him, David's parents did just the reverse. Small tells of his journey from sickly child, to cancer patient, to troubled teen who decides to run away from home at 16 with nothing more than the dream of becoming an artist.

Tamaki, M., & Tamaki, J. (2008). *Skim*. Toronto, ON: Groundwood Books. (S)
[Art; LGBTQ; Death and grieving; Graphic novel; Identity; Mental health]
"Skim" is the nickname of Kimberly Keiko Cameron, a not-slim, aspiring Wiccan goth who goes to a private girls' school. When her classmate Katie Matthews is dumped by her boyfriend, who then kills himself, the entire school goes into mourning overdrive. The popular clique starts a new club (Girls Celebrate Life!) to bolster school spirit, while at the same time, Skim starts to meet in secret with her English teacher, Ms. Archer. When Ms. Archer leaves abruptly, Skim is confused and sinks into an ever-deepening depression. She copes with events through her journal and getting rid of old friendships while developing new ones.

Van Camp, R. (1996). *The lesser blessed*. Vancouver, BC: Douglas & McIntyre. (S)
[Abuse; Addiction; The Dogrib; Friendship; FNMI; The North]
Larry is a young Dogrib man growing up in the small northern town of Fort Simmer. His past holds many terrors: an abusive father, blackouts from sniffing gasoline, and an accident that killed several of his cousins. But now, through his new friendship with Johnny, a Métis boy who just moved to town, he's ready to face his memories—and his future.

Wagamese, R. (1997). *A quality of light*. Toronto, ON: Doubleday Canada. (S)
[Cultural identity; FNMI, Friendship; Ojibway]
Joshua Kane is a young Ojibway boy who has been adopted by white parents. He and his best friend, Johnny Gebhardt, a white boy, become blood brothers and pledge to be loyal and good and kind. A nasty racial incident puts Joshua in the hospital, and Johnny becomes a militaristic advocate of Indigenous rights.

Wagamese, R. (2006). *Keeper 'n me*. Toronto, ON: Anchor Canada/RandomHouse Canada. (J/S)
[Community; FNMI; Homelessness; Ojibway; Redemption; Traditions]
Garnet Raven was taken from his home on an Ojibway Indian reserve and placed in a series of foster homes beginning at the age of three. Having reached his mid-teens, he escapes at the first available opportunity, only to find himself cast adrift on the streets of the big city and eventually thrown in jail. While there, he gets a surprise letter from his long-forgotten family, which spurs him to return to the reserve following his release. Here, his life is changed completely as he comes to discover a sense of place and of self. He is initiated into the ways of the Ojibway—both ancient and modern—by Keeper, a friend of his grandfather and the last fount of history about his people's ways.

Wagamese, R. (2006). *Dream wheels*. Toronto, ON: Doubleday Canada. (S)
[Cultural identity; FNMI, Friendship; Healing]
Aiden Hartley is arrested for his role in an attempted robbery and sent to live with the Wolfchild family at their rodeo stock farm. Joe Willie Wolfchild, aspiring bull rider, has had a career-ending injury and the two young men must find ways to heal themselves.

Wagamese, R. (2012). *Indian Horse*. Toronto, ON: Doubleday Canada. (S)
[Addiction; Cultural identity; FNMI; Healing; Residential schools; Sports]
Saul Indian Horse tells the story of his childhood, his life in a residential school, and his amazing abilities as a hockey player. His professional career is destroyed by racism, and his life becomes one of anger and disillusion. As an old man, he must come to terms with the forces in his life and find out where home is.

Short Stories—Elementary

Khan, R. (1999). *Muslim child: A collection of short stories and poems*. (P. Gallinger, Illus.; I. All, Sidebars). Toronto, ON: Napoleon Publishing. (E) [Islam; Multiculturalism; Religion]
This collection of short stories, poems, illustrations, and activities examines the world through the eyes of Muslim children. Each selection provides insight for all children into everyday Muslim life, revealing aspects of Islam and a way of life practised by millions of Muslims in North America, Europe, and around the world. Sidebars explain Arabic terms referred to in the stories.

Short Stories—Junior High/Secondary

Bates, J. (1997). *China dog and other stories*. Toronto, ON: McClelland & Stewart. (J) [Chinese Canadians; Immigration]
This collection of short stories focuses on the Chinese-Canadian community and the place of home and memory in our lives. Some of the characters find themselves caught between the life left behind and the new realities of their lives in Canada, and others are torn between traditions of the past and the desire to shape their own futures. Mail-order brides, cultural transitions, and finding a place to belong are some of the themes explored.

Berry, M., Chen, Y., Johnson, R. D., Laferriere, D., Manguel, A., Porter, A., ... , & Znaimer, M. (2002). *Passages*. Toronto, ON: Doubleday Canada. (J/S) [Cultural identity; Immigration; Multiculturalism]
In first-hand accounts, celebrated writers explore the excitement and anguish of uprooting to a new country. To leave behind childhood memories, familiar streets, the aromas of local cooking, and long-cherished plans can be traumatic. And yet, to find a haven from oppression and danger, a place to carve out a new identity and put down new roots—this is a thrill only an immigrant can know. *Passages* explores what it means to be a foreigner, what it means to be a writer, and what it means to be a Canadian.

Bissoondath, N. (1990). *On the eve of uncertain tomorrows*. New York, NY: Clarkson Potters/Publishers. (J/S)
[Caribbean-Canadians; Cultural identity; Immigration; Multiculturalism; Refugees]
This collection of ten stories features characters from around the world, at different times in history, who are all waiting to hear word about their refugee status in Canada. All are desperately hoping to find their tomorrows, but only some do.

King, T. (1993). *One good story, that one*. Toronto, ON: HarperCollins. (J/S)
[FNMI; Humour; Legends]
The ten stories in this collection reflect First Nations oral tradition and are full of King's special brand of wit and comic imagination. These stories conjure both Indigenous and Judeo-Christian myths and present-day pop culture and literature, while mixing in just the right amount of perception and experience.

Toten, T. (2010). *Piece by piece*. Toronto, ON: Puffin Canada. (J/S)
[Belonging; Cultural identity; Immigration; Multiculturalism]
The stories in this anthology explore the journeys of 14 Canadian authors who were born in another country, from the shock of their first impressions to the first stirrings of "becoming Canadian" and what that meant to them. This collection provides first-hand accounts of the joyful, mortifying, and sometimes heartbreaking moments of trying to fit in by writers across myriad countries and cultures.

Yee, P. (2002). *Dead man's gold*. (H. Chan, Illus.) Toronto, ON: Douglas & McIntyre/
   Groundwood Books. (J)
[Chinese-Canadians; Folktales; Immigration]
This collection of ten "New World folktales" and ghost stories dramatize the experiences of Chinese immigrants to North America, from the early arrivals who came to "Gold Mountain" to toil in the gold rush, coal-mining, and logging industries, to the new immigrants who arrived from Hong Kong after the Cultural Revolution. These stories describe the resilience and struggles of people who are trying to make new lives, but are always reminded of their home country. Although much like the ones early Chinese immigrants told one another, these stories are all invented by the author in his effort to create a New World mythology where immigrant stories can be told and retold.

Short Stories—Secondary

Baldwin, S. S. (1996). *English lessons and other stories*. Fredericton, NB: Goose
   Lane Editions. (S)
[Gender; Girls and women; Immigration; Indo-Canadians]
Each of the 15 short stories in this collection focuses on the lives of Indian women from 1919 to today, from India to North America, telling stories that happen within the family or outside at the office or university. Some of the women in these stories are imprisoned by silence and choke on their knowledge. Some use knowledge with bloody force against their oppressors, and some harness its power to seize their freedom.

Ghataqe, S. (1997). *Awake when all the world is asleep*. Toronto, ON: House of Anansi Press. (S)

[Community; Death and grieving; Indo-Canadians; Immigration]

It is the mid-1970s, and Shaila has returned to Bombay for her father's 60th birthday party. The linked stories that follow, featuring the varied inhabitants of an apartment complex, reveal a side of India that can only be seen through first leaving and then returning. Stories include that of a young woman who was orphaned in adolescence, who finally comes to recognize and accept what it is to be loved; a mother in search of an acceptable husband for her daughter who rejects one boy because his sister leads her life by the number five; and a man kept from continuing his family line by the hand of fate, when each of the women he marries dies.

Van Camp, R. (2002). *Angel wing splash pattern*. Wiarton, ON: Kegedonce Press. (S)

[FNMI; Healing; The Dogrib; The North]

Honoring his Dogrib ancestry and celebrating life in northern Canada, Richard Van Camp playfully and honestly portrays contemporary Indigenous life. The stories in his collection deal with healing, pain, death, rebirth, hope, friendship, and the search for personal truth.

Van Camp, R. (2009). *The moon of letting go*. Winnipeg, MB: Enfiled and Wizenty. (S)

[FNMI; Healing; The Dogrib; The North]

The stories in *The Moon of Letting Go* celebrate healing through modern-day rituals that honour the author's Dogrib ancestry. Van Camp speaks in a range of powerful voices: A violent First Nations gangster has an astonishing spiritual experience, a single mother is protected from her ex by a dangerous medicine man, and a group of young men pay tribute to a friend by streaking through their northern town. The stories are set in First Nations communities in the Northwest Territories, Vancouver, and rural British Columbia.

Van Camp, R. (2012). *Godless but loyal to heaven*. Winnipeg, MB: Enfiled and Wizenty. (S)

[FNMI; Healing; The Dogrib; The North]

In this collection of stories set in northern Canada, Richard Van Camp mixes tropes from science fiction, horror, Western, and Indigenous traditions. The characters in these stories confront the bleakness of sexual assault, addictions, and violence, but their stories are told with joy and humour.

Poetry and Plays—Elementary

Fitch, S. (1997). *If you could wear my sneakers.* (D. Labrosse, Illus.). Toronto, ON: Doubleday Canada. (P/E/J)
[Empathy; Human Rights; United Nations Convention on the Rights of the Child]
In 15 lively and playfully illustrated poems featuring animals as characters, the formal language of the United Nations Convention on the Rights of the Child is transformed into vibrant images that convey the spirit of the articles in a way everyone can enjoy. The poems communicate a commitment to better lives for children everywhere. The book includes a matching activity with the poems and the Convention Articles from which they are derived.

Poetry and Plays—Junior High/Secondary

Dumont, M. C. (1996). *A really good brown girl.* London, ON: Brick Books. (J/S)
[Cultural identity; FNMI; Métis]
In this collection of poems, Marilyn Dumont writes about the reality of being a Métis in Canadian society and turns the challenges of her Métis heritage into opportunities. She explores the multiple boundaries imposed by society on the self, and she mocks the exploitation of "Indianness," "more-Indian-than-thou one-upmanship," and white condescension and ignorance. She also celebrates the person who defines her own life.

Scofield, G. (1996). *Native Canadiana: Songs from the urban rez.* Vancouver, BC: Polestar Book Publishers. (J/S)
[Cultural identity; FNMI; Sexuality]
The poems in this collection focus on various experiences of Indigenous individuals in the city, or the "urban rez." The poems move through the dark worlds of childhood and manhood while still revealing moments of light and affirmation. Scofield is a Métis activist who divides his time between writing and working with street youth.

Poetry and Plays—Secondary

Clarke, G. E. (2000). *Whylah Falls.* Vancouver, BC: Polestar Book Publishers. (S)
[African-Canadians; Historical fiction; Nova Scotia]
Whylah Falls is a mythic community in the heart of Black Nova Scotia populated with larger-than-life characters: lovers, murderers, and muses. This long narrative poem tells the story of several pairs of Black lovers in southwestern Nova Scotia in the 1930s. The monologues, songs, sermons, sonnets, haiku, and free verse used in *Whylah Falls* sing with the rhythm of blues and gospel, spinning a complex, absorbing tale of unrequited love, earthy wisdom, devouring corruption, and racial injustice.

Iwama, M. (2003). *Skin whispers down*. Saskatoon, SK: Thistledown Press. (S)
[Cultural identity; FNMI; Métis]
This collection of poems tells the story of Iwama's discovery that she is Métis, an identity which has been hidden from her. Presented as a series of emails, the poems are conversations between her new-found cousins and herself.

Mouawad, W. (2009). *Scorched*. (L. Gaboriau, Trans.). Toronto, ON: Playwrights
   Canada Press. (S)
[Family; Historical trauma; Play; War]
Nawal falls into complete silence. Upon her death, her twin children, Janine and Simon, are asked to uproot the source of that silence. They must find the father they never knew and the brother they didn't know they had. Their journey begins in Montreal, but the answers lie in the rubble of a war-torn country. As they dig through the past, they learn (as shown in a series of flashbacks) that their mother, as a young girl, was pregnant out of wedlock and forced to give up her child. The journeys of Simon, Janine, and their mother finally collide in a horrific revelation. *Scorched* follows *Littoral (Tideline)* in Wajdi Mouawad's dramatic quartet, and was adapted into the acclaimed film *Incendies*.

Non-fiction—Elementary

Curtis, A. (2012). *What's for lunch? How school children eat around the world.*
   Markham, ON: Red Deer Press. (Illustrated book) (P/E/J)
[Consumption; Globalization; Inequality; Poverty]
As the world has become more interconnected, what we eat has become part of a huge global system. Unpack a school lunch, and you'll discover that food is connected to issues that matter to everyone and everything, such as climate change, health, and inequality. This book peeks inside lunch trays, bags, mugs, and bowls, revealing the variety found in the food consumed by young people in typical school lunches from 13 countries around the world, including Japan, Kenya, Russia, the United States and Canada, Mexico, Brazil, and Afghanistan. In some countries, the meals are nutritious and well-balanced. In others, they barely satisfy basic nutrition standards. The book includes colour photos of the lunches and informational sidebars that deal with various global food issues. It also provides messages for parents, teachers, and kids about the significance of food, and more importantly, a list of ways in which children can reclaim school lunches for themselves by insisting on healthy, nutritious food.

Hodge, D. (2006). *The kids' book of Canadian immigration*. Toronto, ON: Kids Can
   Press. (P/E)
[History; Immigration; Multiculturalism]
Beginning with Indigenous peoples and moving forward in time, this book charts the migration of immigrants from Britain, Europe, Asia, and around the world, explaining

how Canada became the diverse nation it is today. It features stories of many ethnic groups, mini-profiles, maps, archival documents, first-person accounts, and a glossary of terms. This richly illustrated book is a celebration of multicultural Canada and a comprehensive look at the fascinating history of where Canadians have come from, and why we came.

Jordan-Fenton, C., & Pokiak-Fenton, M. (2010). *Fatty legs: A true story.* Toronto, ON: Annick Press. (E/J) (Available in French)
[FNMI; Inuit; Memoir; The North; Residential schools; Resilience]
Margaret Pokiak's home is in the High Arctic, but she begs her father to let her go to the outsiders' school so that she can learn to read. Before finally relenting, he warns her: As water wears rock smooth, her spirit will be worn down and made small. At the school, Margaret soon encounters the Raven—a nun who immediately disapproves of the strong-willed young girl. To prove her dislike, the Raven passes out grey stockings to all except Margaret, who receives red ones. In an instant, Margaret is the laughingstock of the school, and she becomes determined to face her tormentor. The book is beautifully illustrated and also comes with a "scrapbook" of photographs from residential schools and the author's youth spent in the North.

Jordan-Fenton, C., & Pokiak-Fenton, M. (2011). *Stranger at home: A true story.* Toronto, ON: Annick Press. (E/J)
[Cultural identity; FNMI; Inuit; Memoir; Residential schools]
This sequel to *Fatty Legs: A True Story* finds ten-year-old Margaret Pokiak excited to finally be reunited with her family in the Arctic, after being away for two years at the school run by the dark-cloaked nuns and brothers. The reunion is not what she expects, however. Her mother barely recognizes her, screaming, "Not my girl." Margaret has now become an outsider: She has forgotten the language and stories of her people, and she can't even stomach the food her mother prepares. However, Margaret gradually relearns her language and her family's way of living, discovering how important it is to remain true to the ways of her people—and to herself. The story is highlighted with archival photos and colourful illustrations.

Kacer, K. (2008). *The diary of Laura's twin.* Toronto, ON: Second Story Press. (E/J)
[Historical trauma; The Holocaust; Judaism; Remembrance; Warsaw Ghetto; World War II]
As a special Bat Mitzvah project, Laura has to read the diary of Sara Gittler, a girl who, at Laura's age, was imprisoned by the Nazis in the Warsaw Ghetto. Because Sara never had a chance to celebrate her coming of age, Laura is supposed to share her Bat Mitzvah with Sara by speaking about her "twin" at the ceremony. Reluctant at first, Laura becomes caught up with Sara's struggle to survive and the courage she demonstrates. The book includes photographs, biographies of young heroes of the Warsaw Ghetto uprising, and true accounts of "twinning ceremonies."

Levine, K. (2002). *Hana's suitcase: A true story*. Toronto, ON: Second Story Press.
(late P/E)

[The Holocaust; World War II]

In March 2000, a suitcase arrived at a children's Holocaust education centre in Tokyo, Japan. On the outside were the words "Hana Brady, May 16, 1931" and "*Waisenkind*"—the German word for orphan. The children who saw the suitcase were full of questions and wanted the centre's curator, Fumiko Ishioka, to find the answers. The mystery of the suitcase and her search for clues takes Ishioka back through 70 years, to a young Hana and her family, whose happy life in a small Czech town was turned upside-down by the invasion of the Nazis. The book includes photographs, artwork, and other documents relating to Hana and her family, and Ishioka and her students.

Levine, K. (2004). *Hana's suitcase: A documentary*. Toronto, ON: CBC Audio.
(late P/E)

[Documentary; The Holocaust; World War II]

The documentary adaptation of the story of Hana Brady, a 13-year-old girl killed at Auschwitz in 1944, and the discovery of her story by Fumiko Ishioka, the director of the children's Tokyo Holocaust Education Resource Center. Besides covering the same events as the companion book of the same name, the documentary also portrays Ishioka's mission in Toronto to find Hana's older brother, the only member of her immediate family to survive. Fifty-seven years after Hana Brady's death, George Brady recounts the life of the suitcase's owner—his sister.

Shoveller, H. (2006). *Ryan and Jimmy: And the well in Africa that brought them together*. Toronto, ON: Kids Can Press. (E)

[Africa; Citizenship; Friendship; Social action; Uganda]

Six-year-old Ryan Hreljac kept doing chores around his parents' house, even after he learned it could take him years to earn enough money to build a well to supply safe, clean drinking water in Uganda. Then a friend of the family wrote an article in the local newspaper about Ryan's wish, and people started sending money to help pay for his well. In Agweo, Uganda, villagers were used to walking a long way every day in search of water, which was often contaminated. But when Ryan's well was built, life in the village changed for the better. A boy named Akana Jimmy longed for a chance to thank Ryan in person for the gift of clean water. When they finally met, an unbreakable bond united the two boys from very different backgrounds.

Smith, D. (2011). *This child, every child: A book about the world's children*.
Toronto, ON: Kids Can Press. (E)

[Human rights; Multiculturalism; United Nations Convention on the Rights of the Child]

This book provides a peek inside the lives of children from around the world—their families, homes, health, education, work, play, and more. Some of the world's 2.2 billion children portrayed here are cared for and have enough to eat and a place to call home. Many others are not so fortunate. Each section of the book combines fictional stories and statistics about real children, along with a corresponding Article from the UN Convention on the Rights of the Child. The full Convention in child-friendly language is included at the back of the book.

Walters, E. (2008). *Tell me why*. Toronto, ON: Doubleday Canada. (E/J)
[Activism; Social action; Youth empowerment]
Responding to the questions of a thoughtful 13-year-old, more than 25 influential, inspiring figures—including Canadians Roméo Dallaire, Robert Munsch, Marc Garneau, Lynn Johnston, Rick Hansen, and many others—share their wisdom, their experience, and their convictions about how to counter suffering, cruelty, and darkness. Also profiled are five young people who have already found ways to help, through raising money and awareness for causes such as cancer research, homelessness, the plight of AIDS orphans, and global humanitarian crises.

Non-Fiction—Junior High/Secondary

Bagnell, K. (2001). *The little immigrants: The orphans who came to Canada.*
    Toronto, ON: Dundurn Press. (J/S)
[Home children; Immigration]
In the early years of Canadian Confederation, the emerging nation needed workers that could take advantage of the abundant resources. Because of this, in the decades leading up to the Great Depression, well-meaning philanthropists sent approximately 100,000 impoverished children from Britain to Canada to work as farm labourers. These little immigrants were known as the "home children." This is the story of those lonely and frightened youngsters, to whom a new life in Canada meant only hardship and abuse.

Beah, I. (2007). *A long way gone: A memoir*. New York, NY: Sarah Chricton
    Books. (J/S)
[Autobiography; Child soldiers; Immigration; Resilience; Sierra Leone; War]
Ishamel Beah, now 26 years old, tells his gripping story of how, at the age of 12, he fled attacking rebels and wandered a land rendered unrecognizable by violence. By 13, he'd been picked up by the government army. A gentle boy at heart, Beah nevertheless found that he was capable of truly terrible acts. At 16, he was rehabilitated by UNICEF, learning how to forgive himself, to regain his humanity and, finally, to heal. This book is an unflinching, first-hand look at the realities child soldiers face, and it reveals that hope and rehabilitation is always possible.

Eisenstein, B. (2006). *I was a child of Holocaust survivors*. Toronto, ON:
   McClelland & Stewart. (J/S)
[Family; Historical trauma; Holocaust; Memoir; Non-fiction; World War II]
Bernice Eisenstein's parents met in Auschwitz and married shortly after Liberation, before
coming to Canada. Her memoir begins with recollections and images of her childhood
within a Yiddish-speaking household in Toronto's Kensington Market area in the early
1950s. Her parents' experiences in the War, hardly spoken about, were nevertheless
always present. It was only later, as she gathered the fragments of her parents' harrowing
past and the relatives she would never meet, that Eisenstein began to discover her own
relationship to the Holocaust and how it has shaped who she is. Part of the story is told
in the form of graphic novel panels, with illustrations by the author herself.

Ellis, D. (2005). *Our stories, our songs: African children talk about AIDS*.
   Markham, ON: Fitzhenry & Whiteside. (J/S)
[Africa; First-hand accounts; HIV/AIDS; Malawi; Non-fiction; Resilience; Zambia]
In this collection of first-hand accounts and interviews, Deborah Ellis tells the stories
of children from Malawi and Zambia who have been impacted by the AIDS pandemic.
For some, it has claimed their parents, aunts, or uncles. For others, it has impacted
them even more personally. Here, the reader gets a glimpse at what life is like for these
children, who they care for, and who cares for them. The true stories are interspersed
with facts about AIDS and quotations from authors and public figures.

Ellis, D. (2006). *Three wishes: Palestinian and Israeli children speak*. Toronto, ON:
   Groundwood Books. (J/S)
[First-hand accounts; Israel; Middle East; Palestine; Resilience; War]
In this collection, Deborah Ellis has compiled the true stories told to her by Palestinian
and Israeli children and teens. They tell us about their lives—what makes them happy,
what makes them afraid and angry, how the war has affected them, and their wishes
for the future. Each first-person account is introduced with relevant historical and
political background, clarifying how each child has been affected by past and present
events in the region.

Kamarand, M., & McClelland, S. (2008). *The bite of the mango*. Richmond Hill, ON:
   Annick Press. (J/S)
[Africa; Child soldiers; Memoir; Resilience; Sierra Leone; War]
Mariatu Kamara led a carefree childhood growing up in a small rural village in Sierra
Leone, until the fateful day she was sent to fetch food from a nearby village. When
she arrived there, armed rebels, many no older than 12-year-old Mariatu herself,
attacked. Among other horrors that occurred that day, the young rebels brutally cut
off Mariatu's hands. Miraculously, Mariatu survived to begin an unimaginable journey
that took her from the bush, to begging in the streets of Freetown, and ultimately to
a new life in North America.

Olsen, S. (2001). *No time to say goodbye: Children's stories of Kuper Island Residential School.* Winlaw, BC: Sono Nis Press. (J)
[FNMI; History; Residential schools]
Although this is a fictional account of five children sent to residential school, the stories are based on the recollections of a number of Tsartlip First Nation people. The five characters are isolated on tiny Kuper Island and experience the pain of homesickness and confusion as their lives become regimented by the strict school routine of bells, line-ups, and chores. In spite of the harsh realities of the residential school, the children find adventure in escape, challenge in competition, and camaraderie with their fellow students. All royalties from the book go toward supporting Tsartlip First Nation youth programs.

Robertson, D. A., & Blackstone, M. (2008). *The life of Helen Betty Osborne.* Winnipeg, MB: Highwater Press. (J/S)
[FNMI; Gender; Graphic novel; Injustice; Justice system; Women's rights]
This short graphic novel tells the true story of Helen Betty Osborne, a young Indigenous woman who had dreams of becoming a teacher. Sadly, her dream never came true, because on November 13, 1971, she was abducted and brutally murdered by four young white men. No one would be charged with the crime until 16 years later. An Aboriginal Justice Inquiry concluded that her murder was the result of racism, sexism, and indifference.

Wagamese, R. (2002). *For Joshua: An Ojibway father teaches his son.* Toronto, ON: Doubleday Canada. (S)
[Cultural identity; FNMI; Friendship]
Richard Wagamese writes this book for his young son, telling him the important stories of his people and his own struggles to find his place in these stories.

Yee, P. (2006). *Struggle and hope: The story of Chinese Canadians.* Toronto, ON: Umbrella Press. (J/S)
[Chinese-Canadians; Discrimination; Immigration; Informational]
The first Chinese immigrants came to Canada in 1858. Since then, there have been several waves of Chinese immigration. Throughout Canada's history, people of Chinese descent have contributed significantly to the country's social, economic, and cultural heritage and have played an important part in Canada's history. This book provides an overview of the challenges Chinese-Canadians have faced over the years and expresses the hope that they hold for the future.

Young, B. (2009). *Charlie: A home child's life in Canada.* Toronto, ON: Key Porter
   Books. (J/S)
[History; Immigration; Poverty]
The story of the 90,000 British children who came to Canada as child immigrants
between 1870 and 1938 is not well known. Yet the descendants of these "home children"
number more than four million in Canada today. The author is one of them: Charlie
was her father. Charlie was 13 when his shopkeeper father died in 1910. His mother,
Sarah, had no money to care for her seven children, and before long, Charlie was sent
to an orphanage, and then to Canada to live on an Ontario farm. Here, he experienced
homesickness, hardship, and great kindness. Eventually, Charlie rose from a life of
poverty to become a member of the RCMP. The book features archival and personal
photographs, and informational sidebars.

Picture Books

Bannatyne-Cugnet, J. (2000). *From far and wide: A citizenship scrapbook.* (S. N.
   Zhang, Illus.). Toronto, ON: Tundra Books.
[Art; Citizenship; Immigration]
Xiao Ling Li and her parents are about to take part in the ceremony that will make them
Canadian citizens. To record the day for her soon-to-be-born new sibling, she decides
to keep a scrapbook of every memorable moment. From the recitation of the oath to
the singing of the national anthem and the wonderful welcoming party afterward,
Xiao Ling captures the excitement and the joy of a day that she will always remember.
Xiao Ling's story is full of useful information about the process of becoming a citizen.

Bear, G. (1991). *Two little girls lost in the bush.* (J. Whitehead, Illus.). Saskatoon, SK:
   Fifth House Press.
[Family; FNMI; Nature and wildlife]
Nêhiyaw/Glecia Bear tells about her experience as a little girl when she and her sister
tried to watch over a cow that was about to have a calf. When the cow wandered into
the forest, the girls became lost. Eventually, they followed an owl, who led them back
to safety.

Brière, P. (2008). *The undesirables.* (P. Béha, Illus.). Vancouver, BC: Simply
   Read Books.
[Discrimination; Resistance]
A king and queen, dissatisfied with the "quality" of their subjects, demand that all
"undesirables" be locked up. None of the subjects are spared. Rather than following
through with orders, the king and queen's henchmen devise a way to instead deal

with the "intolerables" — the king and queen themselves. With inventive mixed-media illustrations and clever nonsensical words to describe the many different subjects in the kingdom, this book inspires young readers to think about what it means to be left out.

Brownridge, W. R. (1995). *The moccasin goalie*. (P. Montpellier, Illus.). Victoria, BC: Orca Book Publishers.
[Disability; FNMI; Friendship; Sports]
Danny spends the winters playing hockey with his three best friends. Because of a crippled leg and foot, Danny cannot wear skates, but tends goal in his moccasins. When a "real" uniformed hockey team is established in the community, Danny and his friends are elated at the prospect of becoming members, but their happiness is short lived, as the coach selects only one of them for the team.

Bushey, J. (2004). *Orphans in the sky*. (V. Krykorka, Illus.). Calgary, AB: Red Deer Press.
[FNMI; Inuit; Legends]
Food is scarce in the Inuit community where Brother and Little Sister live with their aunt. While they are out searching for food, the rest of the community breaks camp, leaving the pair stranded. Deciding they cannot live with any of the animals of the North, they decide to live among the stars in the sky instead. Here, Little Sister becomes known as Lightning because of the fire from her flint, and Brother becomes Thunder because of the crash of his sealskin drum.

Butler, G. (1998). *The Hangashore*. Toronto, ON: Tundra Books.
[Disability; Discrimination; Down syndrome; Prejudice]
Set in a tiny fishing village in Newfoundland, World War II has just ended and an important magistrate has arrived to represent the government. The magistrate does not understand John, a boy with Down syndrome, and threatens to have him sent to an institution. It is not until a near-tragedy at sea that the magistrate learns who holds the better set of values.

Button, L. (2010). *Willow's whispers*. (T. Howells, Illus.). Toronto, ON: Kids Can Press.
[Courage; Standing up]
When Willow speaks, her words are soft and shy. Her classmates and teachers do not hear what she has to say. Her father knows one day, Willow's big, strong words will find their way out, though. With the help of her "magic microphone," and later, her own courage, Willow finds a way to make her words heard to all around.

Campbell, N. I. (2005). *Shi-shi-etko.* (K. La Fave, Illus.). Toronto, ON:
　　Groundwood Books.
[Family; FNMI; Indigenous knowledge; Residential schools; Resilience; Traditions]
As Shi-shi-etko counts down her last few days before leaving for residential school, she
tries to memorize everything about her home. She does all in her power to remember
the little things that are familiar to her, and after a family party to say goodbye, her
father takes her out on the lake in a canoe. Her grandmother then gives her a small
bag made of deer hide in which to keep her memories.

Campbell, N. I. (2008). *Shin-chi's canoe.* (K. LaFave, Illus.). Toronto, ON:
　　Groundwood Books.
[Family; FNMI; Indigenous knowledge; Residential schools; Resilience; Traditions]
A companion book to *Shi-shi-etko*. Shi-shi-etko is returning to residential school,
and this time her brother, Shin-chi, is coming with her. On their journey, she helps
him to remember their home—the trees, the mountains, the rivers, and the salmon—
because they will not be able to speak to each other or return home until summer.
Shi-shi-etko then gives her brother a tiny canoe their father has made and tells him
to keep it hidden. Shin-chi is constantly hungry and lonely at the residential school,
but his canoe brings him comfort. When summer arrives, the children are finally
reunited with their family, and Shin-chi is overjoyed to learn he will be making a real
canoe with his father.

Croza, L. (2010). *I know here.* (M. James, Illus.). Toronto, ON: Groundwood Books/
　　House of Anansi Press.
[Art; Community; Nature and wildlife]
A little girl lives with her family in a trailer in northeastern Saskatchewan, where her
father is building a dam. She knows everything about the place—her road, her school,
the forest where she plays hide-and-seek and where the wolf howls at night, and the
hill where she goes tobogganing in winter. But the dam is nearly finished, and when
summer comes, the family will move to Toronto. With her teacher's help, the girl finds
a way to keep everything she loves about home. This book will resonate with anyone
who has had to leave their home for a new place.

Davis, A. (2003). *Bagels from Benny.* (D. Petricic, Illus.). Toronto, ON: Kids
　　Can Press.
[Community; Elder wisdom; Jewish-Canadians; Judaism; Religion]
Benny's Grandpa has a reputation for making wonderful bagels that his customers say
are "made with love." A wise Grandpa explains to Benny that it is God who must be
thanked. Benny wonders how he might also thank God. Inspiration leads him to the
synagogue, where he leaves bagels for God inside the holy Ark.

Delaronde, D. L. (2001). *Flour sack Flora*. (G. Chartrand, Illus.). Winnipeg, MB: Pemmican Publications.
[Community; Co-operation; Elder wisdom; FNMI; Métis]
Going shopping for supplies is a big event for Flora and her family, who live in a Métis community a long way from the nearest town. Flora is disappointed when she can't join her parents, because she doesn't have a dress nice enough to wear. But then her Grandma gets a brilliant idea—to make Flora a dress out of flour sacks. With help from community members, soon Flora and her Grandma have created the perfect dress to be able to wear to town.

Delaronde, D. L. (2003). *Flour sack friends*. (G. Chartrand, Illus.). Winnipeg, MB: Pemmican Publications.
[Community; Co-operation; FNMI; Métis]
A companion book to *Flour Sack Flora*. Flora is thrilled to go on her first visit to town with her parents. What she wants most is to see the dolls for sale there, so she can make one herself with the help of her Grandma. At the store she meets a new friend named Myrtle, who helps Flora find the things she needs to make her own doll. Throughout the day's visits, Flora exchanges goods and odd jobs in return for the various materials and the help she needs.

Delaunois, A. (2011). *The little yellow bottle*. (C. Delezenne, Illus.). Toronto, ON: Second Story Press.
[Friendship; Healing; Hope; Resilience; War]
Marwa and Ahmad live in an unnamed country that could be any one of dozens touched by war. While they know that there is a war being fought, life in their village goes on largely as normal. They are warned that the planes that fly over their village dropped bombs, but after a few days of fright, they forget the danger. Then one day when the two are playing, Ahmad finds a small yellow bottle and picks it up out of curiosity. It explodes—Marwa is cut and scarred, and Ahmad loses a hand and one leg. Both recover and regain hope. Given the serious subject and sophisticated illustrations, this book could be used as a teaching tool for older grades.

Elwin, R. (1990). *Asha's mums*. (D. Lee, Illus.). Toronto, ON: Women's Press.
[Discrimination; Family; LGBTQ]
The story of Asha and her two mums promotes awareness of different kinds of families and different kinds of relationships. When Asha's mums both sign a field trip permission slip for Asha, the teacher requests that the form be re-done "correctly." The story highlights the difficulties children of gay and lesbian families can encounter when teachers are not aware of their family structure.

Eyvindson, P. (1996). *Red parka Mary.* (R. Brynjolson, Illus.). Winnipeg, MB: Pemmican Publications.

[Community; Elder wisdom]

The little boy in this intergenerational Christmas story is afraid of his elderly female neighbour. When his mother reassures him that she is a friendly and kind person, he grows to appreciate and cherish their friendship. Mary has much to teach him, and he has much to give to her.

Flett, J. (2010). *Lii yiiboo nayaapiwak lii swer: L'alfabet di Michif / Owls see clearly at night: A Michif alphabet.* Vancouver, BC: Simply Read Books.

[Alphabet book; Bilingual; FNMI; Métis; Michif; Nature and wildlife]

Michif, the language of the Métis people, combines Cree and French, with a trace of other language elements, into a unified whole. Once spoken by thousands of people across the Prairies of Canada and the northern United States, Michif could potentially disappear within a generation. This alphabet book is part of a resurgence to celebrate and preserve the traditions of the Métis people. Michif and English words combine with images from Métis culture to introduce readers to the unique language. The book also includes an introduction to the language's history, a pronunciation guide, and a list of further resources.

Forler, N. (2009). *Bird child.* (F. Thisdale, Illus.). Toronto, ON: Tundra Books.

[Bullying; Friendship; Speaking up]

Eliza's mother has always taught her to "fly" by looking down to see what is, then looking up to see what can be. When Lainey, a new girl at school, is bullied on the playground, Eliza first does nothing; she just watches as Lainey withdraws into her-self and makes sad drawings. Conflicted, Eliza tells her mother, who encourages her to help Lainey "fly." The next time Lainey is bullied, Eliza speaks up, and her voice is soon joined by others.

Gilmore, R. (2011). *The flute.* (P. Biswas, Illus.). Vancouver, BC: Tradewind Books.

[Folklore; India; Resilience]

When Chandra's parents die in a monsoon, all that she has left of them is the flute her mother used to play for her. Chandra is taken in at first by a cruel aunt and uncle, but they throw her flute into the river. When she then sings her mother's songs on the shores of the river, Chandra incredibly hears the music of the flute. Following that sound and refusing to give up, she is saved more than once by the magic of the flute.

Gregory, N. (1995). *How Smudge came.* (R. Lightburn, Illus.). Red Deer, AB: Red Deer College Press.

[Animal welfare; Community; Determination; Disability; Down syndrome]

Cindy, a woman with Down syndrome, finds a puppy one day as she's walking from work to her group home. Although she initially conceals the puppy and even takes it to her job at the hospice where a patient names him "Smudge," the group home soon finds out and Smudge is sent to the SPCA. Cindy visits Smudge there and, saddened he is living in a cage, is determined to get him back. When she comes back a week later, though, Smudge is gone. All seems lost, until Cindy returns to work at the hospice, where the patients and staff have a special surprise waiting for her.

Gregory, N. (2002). *Amber waiting.* (K. M. D. Denton, Illus.). Calgary, AB: Red Deer Press.
[Family; Imagination; Resilience]
Amber knows there are lots of good things about kindergarten. The one bad thing about it, though, is having to wait for her dad. Sad and lonely as she sits by herself at the end of the day, Amber uses her imagination to dream up a world where her dad has to wait for her—on the moon. That would teach him a lesson, and he and all the late dads and moms would maybe then realize that someone important is waiting for them. Back in the real world, Amber tries to let her father know what it's like to be left alone at school, and he finally seems to get the point.

Handy, F., & Carpenter, C. H. (2010). *Sandy's incredible shrinking footprint.* (A. Steele-Card, Illus.). Toronto, ON: Second Story Press.
[Activism; Community; Ecology; Environmentalism; Social action]
Sandy loves to visit her Grandpa every summer at his home near the beach; it's her favourite place in the world. But on this visit she notices that people are making a mess of her beloved beach with their litter and unrecycled garbage. Then Sandy meets the "Garbage Lady" who is "a little different." The Garbage Lady teaches Sandy to think about her ecological footprint and helps Sandy to be enthusiastic about how she could shrink it.

Harrison, T. (2002). *Courage to fly.* (Z. Huang, Illus.). Red Deer, AB: Red Deer Press.
[Caribbean-Canadians; Chinese-Canadians; Community; Elder wisdom; Immigration; Multiculturalism]
Meg moves from her Caribbean home to a new city where nothing seems familiar. She stays in her room rather than play outside with friends. One day, Meg finds and rescues a sick swallow. Although the swallow quickly recovers, it remains silent and still in the box Meg has provided. An elderly Chinese man, who has become Meg's friend, advises her to release the swallow. This allows both Meg and the bird to find the freedom they need.

Horrocks, A. (2010). *Silas's seven grandparents.* (H. Flook, Illus.). Victoria, BC: Orca Book Publishers.
[Elder wisdom; Family; Multiculturalism]
Silas has seven grandparents. Sometimes this makes him feel especially loved, but sometimes he can't keep up! When Silas's parents leave for the weekend, Silas must

decide which grandparents he will stay with. All of them have something unique and valuable to offer, and the decision seems impossible, until Silas comes up with an especially good idea that makes everyone feel included and happy. This book is a joyful celebration of both the cultural and family diversity of Canada today.

Jordan-Fenton, C., & Pokiak-Fenton, M. (2013). *When I was eight*. Toronto: Annick Press.
[FNMI; Inuit; Memoir; Non-fiction; Residential schools; Resilience; The North]
When I Was Eight is a picture book adaptation of *Fatty Legs*. Olemaun is eight and knows a lot of things. But she does not know how to read, and so she must travel to the outsiders' school to learn. The nuns at the school take her Inuit name and call her Margaret, and they cut off her long hair and force her to do chores. When one of the nuns tries to break her spirit, Margaret only becomes more determined to read and to stand up to her tyrant.

Ka, O. (2009). *My great big Mama*. Toronto, ON: Groundwood Books / House of Anansi Press.
[Body image; Family; Self-esteem]
The young protagonist of *My Great Big Mama* loves how large his mother is; she is comfortable, cuddly, and soft. But because of what others think, Mama goes on a diet. Unhappy with how unhappy it makes her, the son tries out a diet himself, almost as a protest. He finally makes it clear to his mother that he loves her, and she's perfect just the way she is.

Khan, R. (1988/2004). *The roses in my carpets*. (R. Himler, Illus.). Markham, ON: Fitzhenry & Whiteside.
[Afghanistan; Art; Family; Refugees; War; Youth empowerment]
This is the story of a young refugee who is haunted by nightmares and fears resulting from the war he experienced. He cares for his mother and younger sister, but is left with only memories of his father. Though he goes to school, it is in weaving carpets that he escapes the jets and the nightmares, and creates a world that war cannot touch, where every colour has a meaning. It is in his skill at his craft that his hopes for a better future rest. *The Roses in My Carpets* was inspired by the author's meeting with one unforgettable boy and his family.

King, T. (1992). *A Coyote Columbus story*. (W. K. Monkman, Illus.). Toronto, ON: Groundwood Books.
[Colonialism; FNMI; Trickster]
A trickster named Coyote rules the world, and all she wants is someone to play ball with her. Things go awry when Columbus arrives and changes plans. Unimpressed by the wealth of moose, turtles, and beavers in Coyote's land, he'd rather figure out

how to hunt human beings and sell them back in Spain. In this retelling of Columbus's "discovery" of the Americas, the author overturns many myths about colonization, telling the story instead from the First Nations' perspective.

Kusugak, M. (1993). *Northern lights: The soccer trails.* (V. Krykorka, Illus.).
    Toronto, ON: Annick Press.
[Death and grieving; Family; FNMI; Inuit; Legends]
Soccer is a traditional game of the Inuit, and it is their belief that the northern lights are the souls of the dead, running all over the sky chasing a walrus head they use for a soccer ball. Kataujaq learns about her Arctic home from her mother, travelling with her across the sea ice, picking flowers during the summer, and gathering berries in the autumn. When tuberculosis strikes, her mother is flown to a hospital in the south. Kataujaq never sees her again and is deeply saddened by her loss. Grandmother tells Kataujaq the story of the northern lights, and it helps Kataujaq accept her mother's death.

Littlechild, G. (1993). *This land is my land.* San Francisco, CA: Children's
    Book Press.
[Art; Autobiography; FNMI; Non-fiction]
This is an autobiographical account of the struggles George Littlechild's family endured through many generations. The author offers poignant stories of delight, humour, and healing as he tells of his family, his childhood, and his work as an artist. The book heightens awareness of the history and experiences of Indigenous people in Canada.

Loewen, I. (1993). *My kokum called today.* (G. Miller, Illus.). Winnipeg, MB:
    Pemmican Publications.
[Community; FNMI; Girls and women]
Whenever her kokum (grandmother) phones from the reserve, a young Indigenous girl living in the city knows she can expect a special experience. This time it's a dance on the reserve. She learns that women, especially grandmothers, are the ties that hold together the many Indigenous families dispersed in rural and urban communities.

Maclear, K. (2010). *Spork.* (I. Arsenault, Illus.). Toronto, ON: Kids Can Press.
[Cultural identity; Multiculturalism]
Spork is neither a fork nor a spoon, but is a little bit of both. Mixing of cutlery is uncommon, and so Spork doesn't fit in anywhere and doesn't feel like he has a place. But then the "messy thing" arrives and knows nothing of cutlery customs or table manners. Spork proves to be "just right"—just what this messy thing needs. Spork is a whimsical, allegorical celebration of hybrid identities, for all those who have ever felt like a misfit or wondered about their place in the world.

Manson, A. (1996). *Just like new*. (K. Reczuch, Illus.). Toronto, ON: Groundwood Books. (J/S)

[Community; Historical fiction; Social action; World War II]

One morning at church, Sally learns that, because of the War, children in England will have no Christmas presents that year. Sally and her classmates are encouraged to bring a gift for one of these children for White Gift Sunday—a gift that is not purchased, but one they already have that is meaningful and loved and "just like new." Sally generously chooses her best doll, Ann Marie. After worrying about Ann Marie for weeks, Sally finally receives a letter from England. It comes from a girl named Deborah, who promises to look after the doll and asks Sally to be pen pals.

McGugan, J. (1994). *Josepha: A prairie boy's story*. (M. Kimber, Illus.). Red Deer, AB: Red Deer College Press.

[Immigration; Historical fiction; Learning English]

The story, narrated by a young boy, tells of the difficulties encountered by his friend, Josepha, an immigrant from Eastern Europe in 1900. Josepha is adjusting to a new home and a new language. Since he doesn't speak English, Josepha is seated with the very young children in school. Eventually Josepha makes some precious friends among the primary grade children, and when he has to leave school to work on the farm, the children are sad to see him go.

Munsch, R., & Ascar, S. (1995). *From far away*. (M. Martchenko, Illus.). Toronto, ON: Annick Press.

[Immigration; Lebanese-Canadians]

Robert Munsch co-authors the heartwarming story of Saoussan, who came to North America from Beirut when she was five years old. Saoussan tells her own story, one that grew out of a series of letters she wrote to Munsch, capturing the emotions and frustrations of being a newcomer to Canada.

Nielsen-Fernlund, S. (2007). *The magic beads*. (G. Côté, Illus.). Vancouver, BC: Simply Read Books.

[Abuse; Domestic violence; Homelessness; Imagination; Poverty]

Seven-year-old Lily has just moved into a shelter with her mother, away from her abusive father and his often violent temper. When she starts at her new school, her teacher asks her to bring something for show-and-tell at the end of the week. Worried she doesn't have anything to bring, and anxiously watching her classmates show off their toys, Lily gets more and more troubled by the butterflies in her stomach. Finally, she uses her imagination to make an ordinary string of beads seem magical.

Pendziwol, J. (2005). *The red sash.* (N. Debon, Illus.) Toronto, ON:
    Groundwood Books.
[Community; FNMI; Historical fiction; Métis]
The story is set in the early years of the 19th century and is told through the eyes of a young Métis boy living just outside Fort William. One day, the boy helps rescue a white trader whose canoe is destroyed in a storm on the lake. The clear mixed-media illustrations capture the people and the place, contrasting the harsh storm in the wilderness with the final rendezvous at the fort, where the voyageurs (including the boy's father), the traders, and the local community dance and celebrate together.

Quinlan, P. (1994). *Tiger flowers.* (J. Wilson, Illus.). Toronto, ON: Lester Publishing.
[Death and grieving; Family; HIV/AIDS]
When Joel's uncle dies of AIDS, Joel does not know how to deal with his grief. He is reassured when he talks to his mother, and she tells him that she also feels sad and lonely. When he goes to the tree house that he and his uncle had built, Joel picks a tiger lily (his uncle's favourite flower) to give to his sister Tara, who is also grieving the loss.

Sanderson, E. (1990). *Two pairs of shoes.* (D. Beyer, Illus.). Winnipeg, MB:
    Pemmican Publications.
[Elder wisdom; FNMI]
Maggie receives a pair of dress shoes from her mother for her birthday. They were shoes she had wanted for a long time. When she goes to show them to her grandmother, who is blind, grandmother tells her to open a special box. In the box is a pair of beautiful, hand-made beaded moccasins. Maggie is told that she now has two pairs of shoes and that she must learn when and how to wear each pair.

Setterington, K. (2004). *Mom and Mum are getting married.* (A. Priestley, Illus.).
    Toronto, ON: Second Story Press.
[Family; LGBTQ]
The up-coming wedding of Rosie's two mothers, Mom and Mum, is seen through the eyes of an excited eight-year-old. Perhaps she can get to be a bridesmaid or at the very least flower girl. Disappointed when these two suggestions are nixed, Rosie is ready to take on her role when the wedding day rolls around. All goes famously, with rings exchanged, petals scattered, and celebratory bubbles floating around the happy couple.

Skrypuch, M. F. (1996). *Silver threads.* (M. Martchenko, Illus.). Toronto, ON:
    Penguin Books Canada.
[Historical fiction; Immigration; Internment; Poverty; Prejudice; Resilience;
    Ukrainian-Canadians; World War I]
Based on historical events and the author's grandparents' experiences, this is the story of a couple who escape poverty and hardship in Ukraine to move to the Canadian frontier. Tragedy strikes when Ivan is imprisoned as an "enemy alien" when World

War I breaks out. Anna struggles alone to keep their property and valuables, but hope comes from an unexpected source.

Smith, D. (2011). *This child, every child: A book about the world's children.* Toronto, ON: Kids Can Press.
[Human rights; Multiculturalism; Non-fiction; United Nations Convention on the Rights of the Child]
This book provides a peek inside the lives of children from around the world—their families, homes, health, education, work, play, and more. Some of the world's 2.2 billion children portrayed here are cared for and have enough to eat and a place to call home. Many others are not so fortunate. Each section of the book combines fictional stories and statistics about real children, along with a corresponding Article from the UN Convention on the Rights of the Child. The full Convention in child-friendly language is included at the back of the book.

Steffen, C. (2003). *A new home for Malik.* (J. Stopper, Illus.). Calgary, AB: Calgary Immigrant Woman's Association.
[Immigration; Learning English; Sudanese-Canadians]
This is the story of a five-year-old boy who has just moved to Calgary from Sudan. Everything is new and different for him. Readers follow Malik as he meets new friends, learns a new language, and experiences Canada's four seasons for the first time.

Steiner, C. C. (2001). *Shoes for Amelie.* (D. Rodier, Illus.). Montreal, QC: Lobster Press.
[France; French Resistance; Friendship; Historical fiction; The Holocaust; World War II]
In France during World War II, Lucien feels left out; his brother Abel carries messages, and his father is away on secret, dangerous business. Strangers, who Lucien knows to be Jews, come to stay briefly, and then leave. Finally, Lucien gets his own job, helping a new arrival named Amelie. *Shoes for Amelie* is based on true events that occurred during the French Occupation, when descendants of Huguenots, who remembered their own persecution, opened their homes to those escaping danger.

Thien, M. (2001). *The Chinese violin.* (J. Chang, Illus.). Vancouver, BC: Whitecap Books.
[Art; Chinese-Canadians; Family; Immigration]
In this immigration story, a young girl and her father leave everything familiar behind when they move to Canada from China. The only memento they bring with them is a Chinese violin. As they face the challenges of starting new lives in a new place, the music of the violin connects them to the life they left behind—and guides the girl to a musical future.

Trottier, M. (1999). *Flags.* (P. Morin, Illus.). Toronto, ON: Stoddart Kids.
[Community; Friendship; Japanese internment; Historical fiction; World War II]
This is a story of innocence and friendship between Mary, a child visiting her grandmother for the summer during World War II, and Mr. Hiroshi, a Japanese man living next door. When Mr. Hiroshi is taken away from his home to a camp, Mary tries to keep her promise to look after his garden until he returns. Although Mary doesn't fully understand the War in far-off places, she soon realizes Mr. Hiroshi will not be coming home. Still, she keeps her word to care for his garden, and when new people come to live there, she knows just what to do.

Trottier, M., & Arsenault, I. (2011). *Migrant.* Toronto, ON: Groundwood Books.
[Immigration; Migrant workers; Mennonites]
Anna sometimes feels like a bird, flying north in the spring and south in the fall. That's because she and her family are Low German-speaking Mennonites from Mexico, who travel north to Canada every year to work as migrant labourers. She feels like many other things—a bee, a jackrabbit, or a kitten—but wonders what it would be like to be a tree with roots sunk deeply into the earth. This story is filled with beautiful figurative language.

Ulmer, M. (2001). *M is for maple: A Canadian alphabet.* (M. Rose, Illus.). Chelsea, MI: Sleeping Bear Press.
[Alphabet book]
From British Columbia to Newfoundland, this alphabet book shares some of Canada's symbols, history, people, and culture. In rhymes and informative text, details of Canada's past and present are described, from the northern lights, to Mounties, to the cities of Toronto, Victoria, and Quebec.

Umpherville, T. (1997). *Jack Pine fish camp.* (C. Rice, Illus.). Winnipeg, MB: Pemmican Publications.
[Cree; Family; FNMI; Nature and wildlife]
A young girl named Iskotwe (Cree for "little fire") explains what it is like to travel by boat to the fish camp where her family spends their summers. She describes their camp and how her father and older brother go out on the lake to check the fish nets, how the fish is processed, how the families spend their Saturdays at a movie, and how the families live on credit from a local store. The text is illustrated with black-and-white and pastel drawings that show what life is like at a contemporary fish camp.

Upjohn, R. (2007). *Lily and the paper man.* (R. Benoit, Illus.). Toronto, ON: Second Story Press.
[Empathy; Homelessness; Poverty; Social action]
Walking home with her mother one day, Lily encounters a tall man in a raggedy coat selling newspapers. At first she is scared of him. The next time she sees him, she notices

he is cold and doesn't have socks, good boots, or a hat. As she lies warm in bed, she comes up with a plan for how she can help the Paper Man. Lily's story shows readers the joy that can come from helping others in need.

Wang, R., & Yu, H. (2008). *Grandpa Joe*. Toronto, ON: Kevin & Robin Books.
[Community; Elder wisdom; Multiculturalism]
Like many elderly people, Grandpa Joe lives alone. Since he is lonely, Grandpa Joe always tries to start up conversations with people in the neighbourhood, but everyone is tired of listening to him and what they see as repeated, meaningless talk. There is one little boy who does not speak, however, who loves listening to Grandpa Joe. When Grandpa Joe breaks his leg and is taken away, the little boy finally finds his voice.

Warner, J. (2010). *Viola Desmond just won't budge*. (R. Rudnicki, Illus.) Toronto, ON: Groundwood Books.
[African-Canadians; History; Non-fiction; Nova Scotia]
In Nova Scotia in 1946, an usher in a movie theatre told Viola Desmond to move from her main floor seat up to the balcony. She refused to budge. Desmond knew she was being asked to move because she was Black. In no time at all, the police arrived and took her to jail. The next day she was charged and fined, but she vowed to continue her struggle against such unfair rules. She refused to accept that being Black meant she couldn't sit where she wanted to. Desmond's act of refusal awakened people to the unacceptable nature of racism and began the process of bringing an end to racial segregation in Canada. An afterword provides a glimpse of African-Canadian history.

Author Biographies

Geraldine Balzer is an Assistant Professor of Curriculum Studies in the College of Education at the University of Saskatchewan. Her experiences teaching Inuit students led to her interest in decolonizing pedagogies and transformative education. Her teaching focuses on ways of disrupting the hegemony of Standard English and embracing the diversity of Englishes within our world, incorporating Indigenous and postcolonial literature into secondary classrooms, and preparing teachers to be advocates of social justice. Her research focuses on decolonization and social justice. She works with teachers to explore the use of diverse literary texts and literary theory in order to engage students in critical thinking about societal issues. She also studies International Service Learning and its impact on Canadian participants and host communities in Central America.

Anne Burke is an Associate Professor in Literacy Education and Early Learning at Memorial University of Newfoundland, where she teaches undergraduate and graduate courses in children's literature and New Literacies and digital media. She maintains strong community connections in Canadian schools as a classroom- and community-based researcher. She researches and writes about children's literature, digital media and children's play lives, teacher education, and social justice. She has published peer-reviewed articles, chapters, and books, and has presented nationally and internationally as an invited speaker. Book titles include *Children's Play Worlds: Culture, Learning and Participation* with Jackie Marsh (Peter Lang, 2012), *Ready to Learn* (Pembroke, 2010), *Digital Principal* with Janette Hughes (Stenhouse, 2014), and *Assessing New Literacies: Perspectives from the Classroom* with Roberta Hammett (Peter Lang, 2009).

Laura Butland is currently the Vice Principal of a large inner-city elementary school in Newfoundland. She has a passion for social justice and includes children's literature as a vehicle in her exploration of Canadian society, school, and community issues. She holds an M.Ed. in Literacy and Language Studies with a social justice focus.

Shawnee Hardware is a Ph.D. candidate at York University whose research interests include English learning, culturally responsive pedagogy, student engagement, and youth community engagement. She holds an M.Ed. in Curriculum, Teaching and Learning Studies, specializing in Language and Literacies Studies, from Memorial University of Newfoundland. She also has varied English-language teaching experiences in Jamaica, Japan, and Canada.

Bill Howe has worked primarily as a secondary English teacher in the province of Alberta for over 25 years. He currently holds the position of consultant for research and innovation for student learning in Edmonton public schools, and has worked in various capacities for the province in both curriculum development and assessment. In his spare time, he keeps busy volunteering for various local and international non-profit organizations, and working with student social justice groups. In addition, he is trying to complete his Ph.D. studies in curriculum in the Faculty of Education at the University of Alberta.

Karen Jacobsen is currently Department Head of English and Languages Other Than English at a large, multicultural high school in Edmonton. She has been a secondary teacher since 1981, during which time she has also fulfilled the roles of Language Arts and Literacy Consultant for Edmonton Public School Board and Field Experience Associate in the University of Alberta Faculty of Education, supervising and instructing student teachers. Her M.Ed. in Secondary Education explores mindfulness and contemplative practices in secondary English language arts. She is a contributing author to *Beyond Five Paragraphs: Advanced Essay Writing Skills* (McGraw-Hill, 2015), a publication for high school students preparing for university study.

Ingrid Johnston is a Professor Emerita of English Education and Curriculum Studies in the Department of Secondary Education at the University of Alberta. She received her first degrees at the University of Kwa-Zulu Natal in South Africa and an M.Ed. and Ph.D. from the University of Alberta. Her research and teaching interests focus on postcolonial literary theories and pedagogies, Canadian literature, young adult literature, multimodal texts, and teacher education for diversity. She has published numerous refereed articles and chapters on her research and has authored and edited four books. She has been an invited speaker at universities in South Africa, Australia, Austria, Scotland, Northern Ireland, Taiwan, and China.

Shelby LaFramboise-Helgeson is a teacher with Elk Island Catholic Schools where she teaches part-time. She completed her M.Ed. in the Department of Elementary Education at the University of Alberta in the area of language and literacy. Her Master's thesis was titled *Fatty Legs: Teachers Helping Students Explore FNMI Perspectives in Literature.* Previously, she taught with Saskatoon Catholic Schools and Edmonton Catholic Schools. Her research interests include social justice perspectives and FNMI perspectives in Canadian curriculum and how Canadian teachers delve into these practices. She is passionate about writing, such as re-storying Canadian history through her own familial stories. It is her hope to share these stories in current and contemporary ways.

Theresa Powell is a Master of Arts candidate in the Department of English at Memorial University of Newfoundland. Throughout her academic career, her research has focused on media studies, Renaissance literature, colonialism and postcolonialism, power structures, and critical theory. Of pertinent interest is her Honours dissertation, titled *"Fite dem Back": The Lived British-Caribbean Experience in the Dub Poetry of Linton Kwesi Johnson.* She is currently completing her M.A. thesis, the working title of which is *Jacobean "Social" Media: The Royal Entry Pamphlets of King James I.* In April 2015, she was awarded the SSHRC Joseph-Armand Bombardier Canada Graduate Scholarship for this project.

Teresa Strong-Wilson is an Associate Professor in the Faculty of Education at McGill University and Editor-in-Chief of the *McGill Journal of Education.* She is interested in memory, literacy/ies, stories, teachers, and early childhood and social justice education. She has published extensively in peer-reviewed journals, such as *Changing English, Educational Theory,* and *Journal of Curriculum Studies,* and has authored or co-edited several books including *Bringing Memory Forward: Storied Remembrance in Social Justice Education with Teachers* (Peter Lang, 2008) and *Productive Remembering and Social Agency* (with Mitchell, Allnutt, & Pithouse-Morgan; Sense Publishers, 2013).

Angela Ward is a Professor Emerita at the University of Saskatchewan, where she served as Assistant Dean of Education and Associate Dean for Research in Education. She was also Vice-Provost for Teaching and Learning for the University of Saskatchewan. Her research and professional interests in language and literacy have always foregrounded the context of social justice, especially with students and teachers from Indigenous backgrounds. She is currently involved in an early literacy project with Maasai teacher leaders in Kenya. Her recent publications highlight the voices of students from five countries as they describe their engagement in language arts classrooms. Co-authored and edited books include *Classroom Conversations* (Nelson, 1997), *Resting Lightly on Mother Earth* (Nelson, 2001), and *Valuing Literacy: Rhetoric or Reality* (Detselig Enterprises, 2006). She is a contributing author to *Reading Diversity through Canadian Picture Books* (University of Toronto Press, 2013) and has written numerous articles on critical literacy.

Lynne Wiltse is an Associate Professor in the Department of Elementary Education at the University of Alberta, where she teaches courses in the areas of language and literacy and children's literature. She holds a Ph.D. from the University of Alberta. Previously, she taught at Thompson Rivers University and in First Nations communities in British Columbia. Her research interests include multicultural children's literature, teaching for social justice, minority language education, sociocultural theory, teacher education, and qualitative methodologies. She has published on various topics, including pedagogy for English language learners, Aboriginal English, Canadian children's literature, and text selection and cultural diversity. Her research study "Drawing on

Students' Funds of Knowledge to Improve School Literacies for Aboriginal Youth" won the Alberta Teachers' Association Educational Research Award in 2012. Currently, she is conducting research with a group of Edmonton-area teachers for the national study "Developing a Pedagogy of Social Justice through Postcolonial Literature."

Amarou Yoder is a doctoral candidate in the Department of Integrated Studies in Education at McGill University in Montreal. Her doctoral work focuses on questions around narratives, violence, and language arts curricula. She was a language arts teacher at an urban high school in the United States before undertaking her current graduate studies. She recently co-authored the chapter "And Yet: Storying Complexity in Teacher Narratives" in *Provoking Curriculum Studies* (Routledge, 2015).

Aedon Young is a doctoral student in Education at Memorial University of Newfoundland. Her research interests are identity and postcolonialism, landscape and language, and children's literature criticism. Her Master's thesis was entitled *The Quest for Identity in Children's High and Wainscots Fantasy*. She is also an actor and author and has written a novel for young adults, *Mara Roams* (Eloquent Books, 2010), as well as numerous works for theatre, film, and television. She works as a teacher in secondary classrooms.

Index